Coming into Contact

Coming into Contact

EXPLORATIONS IN
ECOCRITICAL THEORY
AND PRACTICE

Edited by Annie Merrill Ingram, Ian Marshall,

Daniel J. Philippon, and Adam W. Sweeting

The University of Georgia Press   *Athens & London*

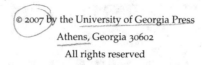© 2007 by the University of Georgia Press
Athens, Georgia 30602

All rights reserved

Set in Palatino by Bookcomp
Printed and bound by Thomson-Shore
The paper in this book meets the guidelines for
permanence and durability of the Committee on
Production Guidelines for Book Longevity of the
Council on Library Resources.

Printed in the United States of America

07 08 09 10 11 C 5 4 3 2 1

07 08 09 10 11 P 5 4 3 2 1

Library of Congress Cataloging-in-Publication Data

Coming into contact : explorations in ecocritical
theory and practice / edited by Annie Merrill
Ingram . . . [et al.].

p. cm.

Includes bibliographical references and index.

ISBN-13: 978-0-8203-2885-0 (alk. paper)

ISBN-10: 0-8203-2885-5 (alk. paper)

ISBN-13: 978-0-8203-2886-7 (pbk. : alk. paper)

ISBN-10: 0-8203-2886-3 (pbk. : alk. paper)

1. Ecology in literature.   2. American
literature—History and criticism.
3. Environmental literature—History and
criticism—Theory, etc.   4. Human ecology
in literature.   5. Environmental protection in
literature.   6. Nature in literature.
7. Ecocriticism.   I. Ingram, Annie Merrill, 1961–

PS169.E25C66 2007

810.9'355—dc22   2006026041

British Library Cataloging-in-Publication Data available

To our friends and colleagues in ASLE,
the Association for the Study of Literature and Environment

Contents

Part 3. Contact! Contact!
Interdisciplinary Connections

Acknowledgments

FIRST AND FOREMOST, we would like to thank the authors of the essays in this collection for their patience and good humor as we have brought this volume to fruition. All of our contributors have been a pleasure to work with, and they have inspired us with their creativity, intelligence, insight, and passion. The two anonymous reviewers who read (and reread) the entire manuscript offered both incisive criticism and generous praise, and the book you are holding is the better for their detailed scrutiny and helpful suggestions. We have also been fortunate to work with a team of dedicated professionals at the University of Georgia Press—including Christa Frangiamore, Nancy Grayson, Jennifer Reichlin, and Christina Cotter—whose editorial, design, and marketing skills have helped the book read well, look good, and (we hope) get noticed. Finally, our greatest thanks must go to our families, whose generous combination of enthusiastic support and selfless sacrifice have helped to make this, and all of our work, possible. All errors, of course, are our own.

ANNIE MERRILL INGRAM, IAN MARSHALL,
DANIEL J. PHILIPPON, AND ADAM W. SWEETING

Introduction

Thinking of Our Life in Nature

ONE OF THE many paradoxes confronting students of literature and the environment is the fact that "environments" are both places and processes. On the one hand, deserts, mountains, prairies, watersheds, and other familiar environments are clearly places; they "take place" in particular locations and inspire legions of devoted citizens to work for their protection. On the other hand, environments are never stable; they change all the time, shaped not only by the biogeochemical cycles of carbon, water, and nitrogen but also by the anthropogenic changes that accompany population growth and technological innovation. What may not be as obvious is that the term most often used to describe the study of literature and the environment— *ecocriticism*—is equally paradoxical, signaling at once the physical products of this lively form of critical theory and practice and also the ongoing process of scholarly conversation, the boundaries of which are as fluid as the sea itself.

The title of this collection—*Coming into Contact*—aims to acknowledge these paradoxes both in use of the progressive verb tense and in the allusion to Henry David Thoreau's well-known passage from "Ktaadn": "Talk of mysteries! Think of our life in nature—daily to be shown matter, to come in contact with it—rocks, trees, wind on our cheeks! the *solid* earth! the *actual* world! the *common sense! Contact! Contact! Who* are we? *where* are we?"

We allude to Thoreau not because we view him as an "environmental saint" (see Lawrence Buell's *The Environmental Imagination*) but because his gradual awakening while descending Mount Katahdin in 1846 so clearly illustrates the significance of the first of these paradoxes to ecocritical theory and practice. Upon observing in "Ktaadn" that the land through which he was passing was not merely a place but also a process—"untamed, and forever untameable *Nature*"—Thoreau became filled with awe, first at the ground on which he was walking, then at his own wild body, and finally at

1

the interaction of the two. Coming into contact with the physical world, in other words, challenged Thoreau to reflect not only on the world as it appeared to him but also on the relationship he had to that world, and on the ways in which a full understanding of the relationship of *nature* and *culture* inevitably calls both of those terms into question. Thoreau's observation, therefore, is more than that our life in nature is a mystery—significant as such an observation is. It is also that "thinking of our life in nature" necessarily causes us to consider the very ground of our being and, eventually, to recognize that—like nature itself—we are all simultaneously both in place and in process.

Our title attempts to build on this observation by adopting a progressive verb tense to describe the ongoing process of "coming into contact" in which ecocritics, in particular, are engaged. Just as it is easy to fall into established patterns of thinking about the location of Thoreau's musings and see Katahdin as a place but not a process, so too is it easy to lapse into thinking that ecocriticism is a static or monolithic "school" of criticism instead of a continuing process of critical inquiry in which a wide variety of differently minded individuals are now engaged.

With two book-length introductions to ecocriticism now available (Greg Garrard's *Ecocriticism* and Lawrence Buell's *The Future of Environmental Criticism*), our aim in this collection is not to offer a definition or overview of this scholarly process but rather to provide a snapshot of it in action—and, in so doing, to encourage this process to continue.

Coming into Contact is not the first volume of its kind, of course, nor is it likely to be the last, which is as it should be. If the study of literature and environment is to retain its critical vibrancy, its subjects and methods will require constant scrutiny and revision, with scholars exploring an ever-expanding diversity of literary and cultural texts and practices while also refining our critical methods—and creating new ones as appropriate. The sixteen new essays collected here contribute to this process of ecocritical engagement by coming into contact with the physical environment, with the wide range of texts and cultural practices that concern it, and with the expanding scholarly conversation that surrounds this concern.

While any attempt to organize such an endeavor is admittedly artificial, we have chosen three broad themes that we believe reflect some of the most promising new directions in the study of literature and environment. The five essays in part one all explore the boundaries of ecocriticism, in that they address previously unexamined or underexamined aspects of literature's relationship to the environment—including swamps, internment camps, Asian American environments, the urbanized Northeast, and lynch-ing sites—all the while asking, as Thoreau did, how *who* we are is related to *where* we are. In part two we have gathered six essays that similarly ask how our ways of speaking and writing about the environment relate to our *actions* in it, with each essay engaging some form of environmental praxis—from the teaching of green design in the composition classroom to the restoration of damaged landscapes, from the choice of discursive strate-gies by environmental activists to the practice of urban architecture and the impact of human technologies on nature. Finally, in part three, we have chosen five essays that put ecocriticism into greater contact with the natural sciences, including elements of evolutionary biology, biological taxonomy, and geology.

Some of these essays could, of course, be placed in other sections, and some could be reclassified altogether, but our goal is not to defend a partic-ular organizational structure so much as to identify some of the principal concerns of ecocritics working today, which we believe these three thematic categories represent. Previous collections have explored the boundaries of ecocriticism (see, most recently, Armbruster and Wallace's *Beyond Nature Writing*), but *Coming into Contact* is unique in acknowledging the continu-ing importance of this work while also building on the growing interest in environmental discourse and practice (see, for example, Adamson, Evans, and Stein's *Environmental Justice Reader*) and the relationship of ecocriticism to the environmental sciences (see Glen Love's *Practical Ecocriticism*). While these three categories certainly do not exhaust ecocritical concerns, they do represent some of the most prominent directions that the field has taken in the last few years—and that we believe it will continue to take.

Part 1: Who Are We? Where Are We? Exploring the Boundaries of Ecocriticism

The title of this section begins with two seemingly different questions: Who are we? Where are we? Neither question, of course, can be easily answered. If we have learned anything from the ecocritical scholarship of the last fifteen years, we should know that issues of identity and location are in-timately related and cannot be teased apart. Perhaps a more meaningful question would be *how* is who we are related to where we are? But as we might expect, there is no simple answer to this question, either. For as the five essays in this section reveal, the questions "who are we?" and "where are we?" have been posed—and answered—in multiple ways. The best approach may therefore be to set out and explore, to wander across the terrain and have a look; hence the second half of our section heading, "Exploring the Boundaries of Ecocriticism."

Students of the field will recognize that our chosen verb *explore* differs from the verb that more commonly appears in discussions of literature and the environment. For several years now, ecocritics have rightly been called upon to *expand* our horizons beyond the canonical nonfictional nature writings of figures such as Henry David Thoreau, John Muir, and Aldo Leopold. These calls have not gone unanswered, as a review of any recent issue of *ISLE (Interdisciplinary Studies in Literature and Environment)*, the field's flagship journal, attests. Important collections such as Michael Bennett and David Teague's *The Nature of Cities: Ecocriticism and Urban Environments* have brought critical attention to traditions and spaces that had previously been underrepresented in ecocritical publications and conferences. Similarly, Patrick Murphy's monograph *Farther Afield in the Study of Nature-Oriented Literature* has provided a much-needed critical vocabulary to discuss the increasingly transnational range of environmentally inflected writing. Environmental justice activists and scholars have also insisted that we expand our literary, critical, and political concerns to consider how and why environmental pollutants and toxins remain concentrated in areas occupied by marginalized groups. To be sure, ecocritics have more to do before we can collectively pat ourselves on the back for successfully responding to these challenges, a point made by several contributors to this volume. Yet, without question, the field has changed, in no small part because of the deserved criticisms leveled by both ecocritics and scholars and activists outside the field.

In many ways the essays in this section continue this work of expansion. Together they bring ecocritical theory and practice to places and texts that are often ignored by scholars and students active in the field. They include such subjects as the landscapes of megalopolis, haiku in Japanese American internment camps, and songs about lynching in the segregated South. But these essays do not simply aim to add places to the ecocritical map, valuable as that project is. Certainly, some of them explicitly call attention to previously overlooked literary traditions (see, for example, Robert Hayashi on recent Asian American literature and Lee Schweninger on Native American poetry written in the eastern United States). But in so doing, they also begin the important work of opening up previously ignored texts to ecocritical analysis. Others assume the case for expansion has been made and simply set out to explore writers and communities that need to be brought to our attention. What all these essays do is draw upon cultural theory and criticism to explore how contact with nature leads to new understandings of our sense of nations, communities, identities, and bodies. To borrow a term used by historians of early America, these structures function as contact zones. They help us partially answer the questions "who are we?" and "where are we?" The essays in this section do the same for ecocriticism: by no means exhausting the possible terrains open to exploration, they allow critics to take stock and see where we stand as a field.

In the opening essay, "Of Swamp Dragons: Mud, Megalopolis, and a Future for Ecocriticism," Anthony Lioi urges ecocritics to become more firmly rooted in the body of the world, offering "the figure of the swamp dragon as a new model for ecocritical activity that does not shun compromised places and the politics of poison." Long feared for their associations with confusion, illness, and death, swamps have also provided refuge for renegades and runaways such as escaped slaves. And in Lioi's native New Jersey, they have also been the dumping grounds for the toxic effluvia of the eastern megalopolis. Yet Lioi avoids the easy cliché of condemning such landscapes out of hand. Rather, he looks to works such as Susan Griffin's *Woman and Nature: The Roaring Inside Her* (1979) and Robert Sullivan's recent *Meadowlands: Wilderness Adventures at the Edge of a City* (1998) to suggest a starting point for a "swampy" ecocritical practice that can help us learn "how to love the land that has been poisoned, and may be poisoning you." To that end, he offers the swamp dragon—a legendary literary figure that has served as an emblem of violence and greed but also of wisdom and guile—as the ideal icon of this new muddy and swampy approach.

The other essays in this section explore a range of places where we can encounter the varieties of embodied contact with the world. Not all such places are pristine or ideal. Angela Waldie and Daniel Martin, for example, examine the imaginary possibilities that inhere in landscapes people did not wish to inhabit. In "Challenging the Confines: Haiku from the Prison Camps," Waldie examines haiku written by Japanese Americans confined to internment camps during World War II. Despite the challenges of facing a hostile and unfamiliar landscape, the imprisoned writers of haiku turned to a familiar form of creative expression and adapted it to their peculiar circumstances; at the same time, they managed to honor many of the form's classical themes and concerns. Interned haiku writers such as Yajin Nakao and Shiho Okamoto turned to the natural world, and especially the seasons, for solace, wisdom, and hope, finding glimpses of the familiar in an alien land. On one level, the history of internment haiku supplies a bracing affirmation of human will, for from the midst of imprisoned despair emerged a body of deeply moving haiku. But as Waldie's essay suggests, the existence of internment haiku also raises tantalizing new possibilities for ecocritical practice. As she notes at the start, she "once considered environmental literature to be a series of tributes to landscapes known and loved." What would happen, she asks, if we turn our attention to writers "exiled in a foreign environment, not by choice but by force?" In many ways her essay challenges us all to explore such places.

Certainly, locations where African Americans were lynched must be understood as places that people were forced into against their will. But as Daniel Martin shows in "Lynching Sites: Where Trauma and Pastoral Collide," the sadistic violence associated with lynching was often employed in the service of a distorted pastoral ideal that celebrated southern customs and rites. Indeed, the settings for such acts were often themselves quite pastoral. As Martin sees it, the collision of pastoral imagery and racially motivated lynching gave rise to an important antipastoral strand in African American culture, a strand he explores through close readings of Richard Wright's poem "Between the World and Me" and sections of Wright's autobiography, *Black Boy*. Martin also turns his attention to one of the definitive songs of the twentieth century, Billie Holiday's haunting rendition of "Strange Fruit," the second stanza of which directly evokes the hideous fusion of lynching and pastoral:

> Pastoral scene of the gallant south,
> The bulging eyes and the twisted mouth,
> Scent of magnolias, sweet and fresh,
> Then the sudden smell of burning flesh.

For Martin, "Strange Fruit" and other works that link these motifs convey antilynching sentiment by "alluding to the cultural values that should, but do not, prohibit brutalities such as lynching." We understand that protest, he suggests, when we understand how the pastoral has functioned in African American culture.

The other essays in this section highlight works by contemporary authors for whom matters of ethnicity or sexual orientation are closely connected to their sense of the natural world. In "Beyond Walden Pond: Asian American Literature and the Limits of Ecocriticism," for example, Robert Hayashi notes "the absence of Asian American authors from the field," a statement that unfortunately has proved true for several other groups as well. One place we might expect to find greater attention to works by Asian Americans is the environmental justice movement. But here, too, Hayashi finds a conspicuous silence. "Although Asian Americans are by no means free of such problems," he notes, "their literature less directly addresses obvious examples of environmental racism or inequity, and so these texts may be easily overlooked by the ecocritic." In response to this situation, Hayashi offers careful readings of recently published works by authors such as Agha Shahid Ali, Maxine Hong Kingston, and David Mas Masumoto, all of whom provide suggestive reworkings of ecocritical concerns. Kingston's "The Grandfather of the Sierra Nevada Mountains," for example, recounts the stories of Chinese immigrants working for the Union Pacific Railroad in the 1880s. Ecocritics know these mountains as the landscape of John Muir, the place where, as Hayashi notes, Muir "scrambled over dangerous passes testing his manhood." But in Kingston, this same landscape is the site of dangerous, humiliating, and poorly paid work carried out by Chinese immigrants who, because of official policy, were denied the right to move freely through their new homeland—a freedom that the Scottish immigrant Muir exercised with relish.

In "To Name Is to Claim, or Remembering Place: Native American Writers Reclaim the Northeast," Lee Schweninger similarly examines contemporary works that explore the environmental and landscape histories conceived by a group that has been largely overlooked by the ecocritical community. To be sure, there exists an extensive bibliography of ecocritical inquiries devoted to works by Native Americans living in the western United States. The same cannot be said for those living in the East. But it is not just ecocritics who have apparently written off the history of eastern Native Americans. As Schweninger notes, several white historians, novelists, and poets have done so as well. Histories, however, can never be completely erased, as Schweninger's examination of contemporary eastern Native American poetry demonstrates. As he shows, the pasts claimed by poets such as Peter Blue Cloud, Beth Brant, and Joseph Bruchac are embedded with a sense of place; they are tales of inhabitation, verses sung to honor the long-standing and ongoing creative presence of Native Americans in the East. Schweninger's essay, then, does double work. On the one hand, he introduces ecocritics to a group of poets whose work deserves further attention. But beyond simply expanding our own levels of awareness, his essay reminds us that our understanding of the past is enriched when we step outside the conventional narratives to embrace mythical, poetic, and ceremonial contemplations of those who came before us.

As these essays suggest, life at the boundaries of ecocriticism is alive and well. Like forest edges, this field of discourse is bursting with activity as new approaches and literatures enter the contact zone. Ecocriticism may have even reached a point where it no longer makes sense to talk of boundaries. After all, they can continue to divide the field even as they expand. At this point in history, there really is no place where ecocritics cannot or should not tread. Indeed, looming environmental crises obligate ecocritics to remain alert to any opportunity where their unique blend of environmental imagination, criticism, and activism can be of help. Yet boundaries also serve a useful purpose. They keep the field on its critical toes and alert it to the enriching possibilities of difference. When we cross the edges with respect, we return the better for having made the trek. And that is what these essays do. They explore the range of ecocriticism, showing what is out there while pointing out work that still needs to be done. Like the other essays in this collection, they can help ecocritics answer the questions "who are we as a group?" and "where are we going?"

Part 2: The Solid Earth! The Actual World!
Environmental Discourse and Practice

In comparison to the solid earth and the actual world, literary criticism can seem to be a rather ephemeral endeavor, subject not only to frequent shifts in aesthetics and ideology but also to the impermanence of its material constructions in books and journals. As the essays in part two show, however, environmental discourse and practice are decidedly solid and actual, and ecocriticism is an effective means of inscribing the materiality of the natural world onto the materiality of the printed page. By considering the wide range of environmental discourse and the many implications of environmental practice, the authors of this section critique the current limits of ecocriticism and suggest ways both to broaden its scope and to ground its concerns in real world applications.

When Thoreau wrote the "Ktaadn" passage in *The Maine Woods* from which we take our section titles, he was not only meditating on the place of humans in nature; he was also questioning the human presence in nature altogether, noting how "it is difficult to conceive of a region uninhabited by man. We habitually assume his presence and influence everywhere." By emphatically foregrounding "the *solid* earth!" and "the *actual* world!" Thoreau made the then radical move from an anthropocentric to a more biocentric or ecocentric view. As the writers in part two note, however, the time has come for ecocriticism to make another shift: to consider how our inherently anthropocentric discourses and practices can redirect their focus to environments other than traditionally conceived "nature." In keeping with the emphasis in this volume on the interdisciplinary quality of ecocriticism, these essays reveal in their critical genealogies the influences of activism and social justice, ecological architecture and design, and philosophy and theology. Complementing the disciplinary variety is a diversity of historical periods, from the ancient Middle Eastern society of the biblical Job to the futuristic visions of utopian and apocalyptic narratives. Similarly, rural North American settings no longer dominate as the subjects of ecocriticism; instead, our reading practices travel from London and Grasmere to Japan, India, and beyond. We are a long way from Thoreau's America here, and as these essays assert, the future efficacy of ecocriticism depends on exploring those distances in both time and space.

In the first essay in this section, "Composition and the Rhetoric of Eco-Effective Design," Tim Lindgren draws inspiration from the concepts outlined in William McDonough and Michael Braungart's *Cradle to Cradle: Remaking the Way We Make Things*, a work that emphasizes infinite recycling and reuse over cradle-to-grave built-in obsolescence. In a provocative application of McDonough and Braungart's concept, Lindgren posits a cradle-to-cradle approach to the composition classroom. Rather than create assignments and courses with a fifteen-week lifespan, Lindgren challenges us to design our students' papers "to be used and reused, to be circulated among students and other classes, and to serve as an ongoing resource in the lives of the authors themselves, providing ideas and inspiration through their college education and beyond." In another interdisciplinary excursion, Jim Barilla connects ecocriticism to indigenous studies by reconsidering narratives of ecological restoration. Barilla notes the limitations of texts that ignore the equal importance of cultural restoration, such as Leopold's *Sand County Almanac*. In redressing those limitations, he analyzes J. M. Coetzee's novel *Life and Times of Michael K* and Leslie Marmon Silko's novel *Gardens in the Dunes* as narratives that "suggest the need to consider the ecological restoration of landscapes in light of their indigenous cultural history, not just their ecological past."

In choosing several works of nonfiction as the focus of her argument, Amy Patrick locates environmental discourse in one of its more immediate and widely accessed genres. Rachel Carson's classic work of precautionary environmentalism, *Silent Spring*, yields as its literary progeny works such as E. O. Wilson's *The Future of Life* and Sandra Steingraber's *Living Down-stream*. While each of these texts could be considered part of a tradition of "apocalyptic" narrative, Patrick argues that such a label inspires fear and reinforces a basis in irrationality rather than objective scientific information. By preferring the term *precautionary* to *apocalyptic*, she asserts an approach that is more informed, accountable, effective, and ultimately hopeful. Bruce Allen's discussion of two Asian writers of precautionary narratives dovetails with Patrick's call for ecocritics to pay more attention to this genre. Allen chooses two contemporary writer-activists, Japan's Ishimure Michiko and India's Arundhati Roy, and discusses how their fiction and nonfiction foreground environmental issues particular to a region of the world often overlooked by North American ecocritics. Ishimure's and Roy's concerns with the effects of dam construction provide an interesting parallel to the arguments posed by Jim Barilla about restoration narratives—for in considering the consequences of dam building on cultural as well as natural landscapes, both these writers provide a kind of prospective rather than retrospective restoration narrative.

Such visionary possibilities similarly inform the essay by Onno Oerlemans, which builds on the work of contemporary ecocritics who expand the idea of "environment" to include urban as well as rural and wilderness spaces. He takes a new look at the anti-urbanism of Romanticism by investigating the period's growing attention to urban spaces as an incipient form of "green architecture," one where the human interactions with the built environment receive emphasis. Oerlemans finds "deeply problematic in environmental terms" Wordsworth's "categorical antipathy to the city"—a stance that productively destabilizes our traditional sense of Wordsworth as one of the premier environmental poets in the English language. David Mazel's essay closes this section by considering the elements of a "postnatural ecocriticism," one shaped by present-day "techniques for rendering nature increasingly transparent," such as global biosurveillance. As one aspect of postmodern ecology's radical revision and problematizing of our understanding of "nature," Mazel's postnatural ecocriticism is part of the ongoing process of the "changing material relations to nature." Taking as his primary texts of analysis Annie Dillard's *Pilgrim at Tinker Creek* and the biblical book of Job, Mazel investigates how intersections of theology and nature come to be read by their respective audiences, and how those audiences are informed by their own historical and subject positions. Arguing that Dillard's perspective is one already informed by global biosurveillance, Mazel argues that reading Dillard's "spiritual quest in a fundamentally changed world" as such is "to read *Pilgrim* much as alert readers have long read *Job*"—that is, as one where "irony complicates the book's interpretation."

As these brief summaries suggest, one common concern of all the essays in this section is the complication and critique of the commonly held definitions, frequently analyzed texts, and complacently applied approaches of ecocriticism to date. One could liken this critique to the controlled burning of wilderness areas, in which natural processes have been so long disrupted that carefully monitored human intervention becomes one form of positive recourse. If such a critique from within is ecocriticism's necessary controlled burn, then what emerges from the landscape of charred timber and ash is a subsequent generation of new growth, where precarious monocultures give way to greater diversity.

Yet these essays also sensitize us to the possibility that this image of controlled burn is too apocalyptic and too metaphorical, that its focus on a wilderness environment devoid of human inhabitants dangerously ignores the crucial significance of other kinds of environments. As Lindgren notes toward the close of his essay, ultimately, it is about "designing hope." As these authors so rightly articulate, hope comes in many forms: for example, in making ephemeral theory more concrete, in restoring cultural as well as natural ecologies, and in reaching beyond the boundaries of literary criticism to embrace the contributions of design, philosophy, and theology. Our discourses *are* our practice, and discourses have consequences. Fortunately, as informed and responsible ecocritics, we have the power to determine whether those consequences are positive or negative.

Part 3: Contact! Contact! Interdisciplinary Connections

"When we try to pick out anything by itself," said John Muir, "we find it hitched to everything else in the universe." Muir's insight gets at the foundational principle of ecological thought, and perhaps it is close to a foundational principle of literary ecocriticism as well. Or, to cite an author less associated with the literature of arboreal embrace, ecocritics seeking to justify their prefix seem to be heeding the advice of E. M. Forster: "Only connect."

In a sense, and without too much of a conceptual stretch, perhaps every essay in this collection can be seen as connecting to other disciplines. The foray by Onno Oerlemans from romantic poetry to green architecture could certainly qualify, as could essays that concern themselves with the business of policy making or with questions of environmental justice, or Tim Lindgren's application of eco-effective design principles to composition. What is different in this final section of *Coming into Contact* is that these contributions foreground their interdisciplinary nature in making connections between literature and the natural sciences. That impulse is not new to ecocritical scholarship. Since the founding of the Association for the Study of Literature and Environment (ASLE), ecocritics have sought ways to practice a brand of literary scholarship informed not just by an awareness of the policy implications of literature but by ecological awareness as well. Over a dozen years, Glen Love has made repeated calls for the greening of literary criticism via the incorporation of biological principles, and his own *Practical Ecocriticism: Literature, Biology, and Environment* puts into practice what he envisioned for a scientifically informed ecocriticism.

But there seems to be something new at work in these essays. The brand of ecocriticism practiced here does not simply import ideas from the natural sciences and put those ideas and principles to work in the service of literary analysis. Rather, there is some give as well as take, a kind of intellectual nutrient cycle at work. We see, on the one hand, an interest in writers who made imaginative use of the most recent scientific understanding of their day (see, for example, Jeff Walker on John Burroughs or Tina Gianquitto on Mary Treat) and, on the other hand, a new concern with what ecocriticism has to offer to our understanding of science. Knowledge of another discipline can be seen as enriching ecocritical endeavor, but ecocritics are now exploring further how the insights of ecocriticism can be of some use in the practice of other disciplines. In either case, there is a principle of reciprocity at work, and ecocriticism seems to have reached a stage where it is not just absorbing information from other disciplines but giving something back.

The essays by Laura Dassow Walls, Jennifer Wheat, and Michael P. Cohen, for example, while informed by biological science, all offer, to varying degrees, a critique of science and ask not so much what science can do for literature but what literature can do for science. In "Seeking Common Ground: Integrating the Sciences and the Humanities" Walls challenges Edward O. Wilson's idea of consilience for privileging the reductionism of science and relegating literature to a merely expressive art (the essay was originally presented as part of a plenary session with Wilson). Literature, Walls says, is a way of knowing, one that reminds us of our subjective position in the world. In place of Wilson's consilience, she recommends that science and the humanities find common ground in Humboldt's notion of

Cosmos, a view of the creation as an ordered and beautiful whole built on the integration of subject and object, mind and nature.

Jennifer Wheat's "Mindless Fools and Leaves That Run: Subjectivity, Politics, and Myth in Scientific Nomenclature" explores the subjective dimension of scientific naming, a process that invariably reflects the agenda of the namer. One thing that literature can offer science, then, one thing it can show us, is that sensitivity to language and an awareness of its power to enhance or erode or shape understanding can alert us to the prejudices, worldviews, and stories implicit in Linnaean nomenclature.

Michael P. Cohen's "Reading after Darwin: A Prospectus" calls for ecocriticism (or, as he suggests it might be called, "*evo*criticism") to find ways to integrate the methodology of evolutionary biology—but he also suggests that it might be productive for those skilled in understanding narrative to examine how evolutionary narratives might be "treatable as texts," how "evolutionary narratives intersect evolutionary theory," and how we can "profitably apply literary methods to . . . evolutionary theory and scientific critique"—all in the name of finding ways for scientists and humanists to work together.

Even when not necessarily offering a critique of science, the essays in this section suggest that ecocriticism has something to offer to science as well as something to learn from it. In "Of Spiders, Ants, and Carnivorous Plants: Domesticity and Darwin in Mary Treat's *Home Studies in Nature*," Tina Gianquitto shows that Treat, a nineteenth-century naturalist who lived in and wrote about the New Jersey pine barrens, was influenced by Darwin in her dedicated and systematic study of adaptive behavior of the plants and animals in her home environment. But her role as naturalist was balanced by her role as defined by the cult of domesticity, which required women to attend to affairs of the home. Within those constraints Treat found her subject, exploring the idea of home in the lives of the species she studied. Again, we are reminded that all views of the world are situated in some way, and that our position matters, inevitably affecting our view of reality.

In "The Great, Shaggy Barbaric Earth: Geological Writings of John Burroughs," Jeff Walker examines essays by Burroughs that explored geological concepts, or where he relied on "geology to help set the scene," where he contemplates "scientific mysteries" implied by recent geological discoveries or engages in speculations in which geology serves as backdrop. The essays show Burroughs's fascination with the emerging science of geology and his "ability to distill scientific concepts into plain language." Walker shows us that the same curiosity that underlies science motivates writers like Burroughs, and that both essayist and scientist follow the same pattern in satisfying their behavior—from "interest in a phenomenon . . . to careful observation" and understanding. Here is part of the common ground that Walls and other ecocritics have been seeking.

In all this we see a change in the interdisciplinary nature of ecocritical endeavor. Ecocritics continue to explore connections to the sciences as well as other disciplines. But now the tactic of bringing in ideas from the outside in order to figure out just what sort of ground ecocritics can stand on, or how ecological understanding can be incorporated into our work, is just half of it. Ecocriticism seems a little surer of itself these days, and these essays suggest that other disciplines can, at least in part, be informed by ecocriticism. We are tempted to say that ecocriticism is becoming less marginalized. But the truth is, perhaps the margin is not such a bad place to be. As Bakhtin said, "The most productive work of a culture takes place on the margins." Ecologists know that an ecotone, the edge where two habitats meet, is a precarious place, where predators can approach from either side. But it is also a rich and diverse and productive space. How refreshing it can be, and satisfying, to walk from the meadow to the forest and back, lingering at the edge, coming into contact.

PART 1

Who Are We? Where Are We?

Exploring the Boundaries of Ecocriticism

ANTHONY LIOI

Of Swamp Dragons

Mud, Megalopolis, and a Future for Ecocriticism

IN HER CLASSIC *Purity and Danger*, anthropologist Mary Douglas defines ritual pollution as "matter out of place" and concludes that such pollution can be a door to whole cosmologies: "Where there is dirt, there is a system" (44). Accordingly, she distinguishes between "dirt-affirming" and "dirt-rejecting" cultures based on their reaction to ritual pollution (202). To affirm dirt is to recognize that impurity is inevitable, and to offer it a carefully defined place that recognizes and contains its power. To reject dirt is to imagine that it can be separated from what is sacred, and to finalize that separation by annihilating pollution from the cosmic order itself. I want to suggest that despite its desire to affirm Earth, much of ecocritical culture has been dirt-rejecting. In our quest to promote wildness and nonanthropocentric cosmologies, ecocritics have shunned texts and places compromised by matter-out-of-place, the ritual uncleanness of cities, suburbs, and other defiled ecosystems. Though I am not the first to notice this problem, the pattern of dirt-denying has continued. Therefore, we must consciously construct a symbolic place in ecocriticism for dirt and pollution, an alias or icon that allows us to give dirt its due. I suggest that American ecocritics consider the figure of the swamp dragon—embodying elemental mixture, ethical impurity, and serpentine wisdom—as an alternative to the posture of prophet and judge, the arbiters of purity and righteousness.[1] The critic need not always stand on a mountaintop, declaiming. Before I explain further, however, we need to take a short trip into the slippery terrain of disciplinary flux.

A glance at recent publications reveals that ecocriticism is entering a moment of transfiguration. Though ecocritics have been asking ourselves what methods and canons constitute the field for as long as the field has existed, the last five years offer signs that this questioning has entered a peculiarly intense phase. As ecocriticism moves out of the margins of literary studies, as the founders of the field acquire tenure, departmental chairs, and emeritus positions, it becomes possible to transform as well as defend the field. Evidence of this change can be seen even in a brief list of works that seek to expand the domain of ecocriticism and to question its founding assumptions: Karla Armbruster and Kathleen R. Wallace structured *Beyond Nature Writing: Expanding the Boundaries of Ecocriticism* (2001) to encompass nations, genres, traditions, and periods beyond American nature writing of the past two centuries, as did Patrick Murphy in *Farther Afield in the Study of Nature-Oriented Literature* (2000). Lawrence Coupe's *The Green Studies Reader* (2000) attempted with great success to reverse-engineer the theoretical foundations of the field to include British and Continental philosophy and more recent work in Cultural Studies. Steven Rosendale, in *The Greening of Literary Scholarship: Literature, Theory, and Environment* (2002), mixed old and new texts and approaches, balancing our traditional strengths with original directions. In the first *summa* since Cheryll Glotfelty's *Ecocriticism Reader*, Michael P. Branch and Scott Slovic edited *The ISLE Reader: Ecocriticism, 1993–2003* (2003), representing a more assured critical center culled from our flagship journal. More radical challenges appeared as well. Joni Adamson, Mei Mei Evans, and Rachel Stein edited *The Environmental Justice Reader* (2003) to recenter the discipline on activism and non-Anglo, non-middle-class texts and cultures, while Dana Phillips's *The Truth of Ecology: Nature, Culture, and Literature in America* (2003) issued a challenge to rethink what we know about ecology as a science and its relationship to literary-critical method. Finally, Lawrence Buell, long the defender of the Thoreauvian center of green letters, moved decisively toward the literature of environmental crisis in *Writing for an Endangered World* (2001). In the midst of these magisterial contributions, I offer a more modest rubric for critical transfiguration at the beginning of a new century.

My investigation of the swamp dragon as a figure for ecocritical work begins in the swamps of home. Growing up in New Jersey, I always wondered what "purple mountains' majesty" of "America the Beautiful" was: my mountains, in the Kittatinny Range, are green and not exactly majestic. As many friends from the West have said, "Those aren't really mountains," meaning that the Appalachians lack the grandeur of the Rockies and the Cascades.[2] They are not the summit of a sublime landscape. They are not the mountains from which the law is given to the people, not the setting for a Mosaic environmentalism.[3]

Thus I became slowly aware that my allegiances to the land are different than the ecocritical norm and that my land is often a wetland: Burnt Fly

Bog, the Superfund site two miles from my childhood home; the Raritan River, just recovering from centuries of industrial use; and the cedar-water streams of the Pine Barrens that stain white clothes wood-brown.[4] These places are damaged and unspectacular, even ugly, when your standards of loveliness are Mount Hood and the Sierra Madres. They have nonetheless provoked a blaze of environmentalist work, as in the late 1960s, when the core of the Barrens was preserved against plans for a second international airport for Philadelphia, and more recently when Raritan Riverkeeper became an integral part of the national Waterkeeper Alliance. But if sublime beauty is not the heart of such efforts, what is? I suggest that a swamp dragon moves through these regions, that the unlovely worlds where water and land meet spawned a spirit to which ecocritics must pay attention, if we are to sway the millions of people who live in the East, where very little is pure and high, and the distant hope of repristination cannot be the foundation of environmentalist devotion.

The East and its landforms have fared about as well in the annals of ecocriticism—Walden Pond and Tinker Creek are the exceptions that prove the rule. Michael Bennett's analysis of the "cultural geography" of ecocriticism in "From Wide Open Spaces to Metropolitan Places: The Urban Challenge to Ecocriticism" still holds true: though the encounter with urban nature has begun, most ecocritics still identify with wilderness and the West (Bennett 302–12).[5] Conversely, the East is categorized in the ASLE Bibliography as a regional subtopic while there is no corresponding category for "West," because the West is everywhere.[6] The presence of Bennett's article in the ISLE *Reader* demonstrates an awareness of this problem, and the proliferation of ecocritics in the East is a hopeful sign. However, more will need to be done, and at a deeper level, if the cultural geography of the discipline is to include the Norport Megalopolis, as the Maine-to-Virginia sprawl has been called, not to mention the rest of the East. We can see the need for deeper thought in the name of ASLE's first conference east of the Mississippi in June 1999: "What to Make of a Diminished Thing."[7] Thomas Bailey, the organizer of the conference, explained the meaning of the name:

"We have seen a real ecological crisis come upon us in the last 35 years. The East doesn't have the natural world it once did, hence the 'diminished thing,'" Bailey explains, noting this is the first time the ASLE conference has been held east of the Mississippi. "When it comes to nature, there's a big difference between East and West. Natural descriptions of the East are less rhetorical than

those of the West as well. We have hills, not grand mountains; woods, not
forests. But our nature is just as complex and worthy of study." ("Nature Writers Come to Kalamazoo," n.p.)

Let me be clear that one would easily understand from the conference's
promotional materials in the *ASLE Newsletter* and from the conference website that its name was meant to evoke the practice of ecological restoration
("'The Third Biennial ASLE Conference' Update"). Nonetheless, even as
apologia, Bailey's explanation expresses a number of attitudes that need to
be overcome: the sense that the East is ruined; that it is "diminished," like a
musical chord, by minor materials at its core; and that even before ecological
crisis it was literally diminutive, suggesting lesser value or interest.

There is, however, some comfort in this discourse: it explains why I shud
dered when I first heard the name of the conference, which confirmed the
attitudes I felt were implicit in American ecocriticism in the 1990s. This com-
pensatory sense that the East is not as good as the West is, perhaps, understandable, given that ecocriticism braced itself against an urban hegemony
in literary studies.[8] It is understandable, but unsustainable: one cannot decide how to care for a place while calling it diminished, because condescen-
sion cannot be the basis for love or respect.

In many ways, the swamp is the exemplary figure in the American semiotics of place for chaos, desecration, and diminishment, and these associations began long before ecocriticism. As David C. Miller points out in *Dark
Eden: The Swamp in Nineteenth-Century American Culture*, love and respect
were not the traditional European sentiments attached to the swamp: "Its
associations had been traditionally tied to theological and folkloric contexts: It was the domain of sin, death, and decay; the stage for witchcraft;
the habitat of weird and ferocious creatures" (Miller 3). Swamps were both
the land of death and a traditional image of Hell (47). This attitude began
to change in 1850s America, however, and the swamp began also to represent a "matrix of transformation" (23) that sheltered a variety of rebels,
including slaves, Native Americans, and white southerners (8), coming to
symbolize, as Victorianism progressed into Modernism, unconscious mental processes, repressed matriarchy, and anarchism (8). In *Postmodern Wetlands: Culture, History, Ecology* the Australian critic Rod Giblett points to
several non-American parallels to this tradition of the swamp as site of
political resistance and repressed psychic materials: the English Fens, the
Mekong Delta of Vietnam, and the wetlands of Perth, Australia, which were
cartographically erased as part of the symbolic progress of white settle-

ment (Giblett 205–27). In a memorable sentence, Ingrid Bartsch, Carolyn Di-Palma, and Laura Sells describe how this historical set of wetland dynamics iterated into a contemporary bureaucratic context: "Wetlands are literally and figuratively a terrain of struggle for government agencies, developers, environmentalists, scientists, and ducks, all of whom have competing interests in questions of definition, jurisdiction, regulation, and control" (Bartsch et al. 187). As ecologist Ralph W. Tiner demonstrates exhaustively with *In Search of Swampland: A Wetland Resource and Field Guide*, the commonsense definition of a wetland as land-covered-in-water-some-of-the-time is complicated by the needs of farmers, for whom swamps and other wetlands were obstacles to agriculture; by the taxonomy of ecology, which makes fine distinctions among swamps, marshes, bogs, and vernal pools; and by state and federal agencies engaged in a rearguard effort to protect remaining American wetlands from corporate development (Tiner 3–13).

These historical, symbolic, and political tangles return us to the swamps of home. The Great Swamp National Wildlife Refuge, located in Basking Ridge, New Jersey, about twenty-five miles west of Manhattan, is a remnant of Lake Passaic, which formed after the Wisconsin glaciation retreated ten thousand years ago and left much of northeastern New Jersey covered in fresh water (Great Swamp National Wildlife Refuge website). Lake Passaic finally drained into Newark and Raritan bays, leaving the marshes and swamps that would become, among other things, the Meadowlands, where the New Jersey Nets basketball team plays. In the mid-1990s, just as ecocriticism was getting off the ground, the Nets did an unexpected thing: they considered changing their name to the New Jersey Swamp Dragons, in a bid, I think, to seem more local, much as New Jersey's professional hockey team had done by employing the folklore of the Jersey Devil. The Nets never did change their name, perhaps because the native swamp dragon was already taken, but I found the possibility of such a thing intriguing.[9] As I walked through the Great Swamp one bright day in fall not too long ago, I thought about what it might mean to know or become a swamp dragon.

Drakon and *draco* mean "serpent" in Greek and Latin; the root of these words means "to watch" or "to guard with a sharp eye," a hopeful etymology, environmentally.[10] The winged serpent appears across classical world cultures, often in the shape of messenger or wisdom divinities such as Isis, Hermes, and Quetzalcoatl. In the Hippocratic tradition of medicine, the serpent is a power of healing, and in Indian yogic disciplines, *shakti* coils up and around the spine as the force of enlightenment. In many Greek and Hebrew texts, however, the serpent is demonized in narratives of patriarchal defeat of chaos. Zeus, for instance, must fight Typhon, a chaos-dragon, before he can ascend to the throne of the gods, and the hero Perseus must rescue the princess Andromeda from Cetus as it prepares to devour her at the ocean's edge. Likewise Leviathan, the great sea-monster of Hebrew scripture, is portrayed, in Job and the Psalms, as a power of watery chaos that God has subdued. Leviathan is related to the waters God divides in Genesis 1:6–7, and these waters, *tehom* or the Deep, according to strong scholarly consensus, are a memory of the water-dragon Tiamat, the mother goddess who is killed by her grandson Marduk in the Babylonian creation story, the *Enuma Elish*.[11] In *Face of the Deep*, feminist theologian Catherine Keller demonstrates an enduring "tehomophobia," or fear of the sea as a power of chaos, pervading Hebrew and Christian scripture, finally manifesting in the book of Revelation as the defeat of Satan-as-dragon and the drying up of the sea (27–28). In Christian legend both Saint Michael and Saint George slay dragons; this conflict is feminized in Catholic iconography in the figure of Mary, Queen of Heaven, who crushes the serpent underfoot and tames the waters as Our Lady, Star of the Sea. My attempt to rehabilitate the swamp dragon as a positive figure must admit openly to this phobic history. I see it as an advantage, however; truly to accord a proper place to pollution, ecocritics must retain a sense of pollution's danger, and our own connection to it, rather than reduce its power through domestication.

The danger of the dragon of waters is more than symbolic: it has manifested in the history of the Great Swamp as a Superfund site. The dumping of industrial pollutants into a wetland suggests the dragon of unrestrained corporate capitalism guarding its filthy horde amidst the suffering of others. This is the dragon out of European folk tradition, typified in contemporary Anglophone literature by Smaug, the central monster in J.R.R. Tolkien's *The Hobbit*. To a native New Jerseyan, such a dragon poses an important problem: how to love the land that has been poisoned, and may be poisoning you. Here, the other dragon comes in: the dragon of wisdom, once native to Asia but now part of New Jersey through the influence of Taiwanese, Cantonese, and other East Asian immigrants. The *long*-dragon, whose snakelike body and crested head are familiar throughout the Chinese diaspora, is a hydrological power of oceans, clouds, and rivers (Bates 14). This dragon is culturally impure in diaspora: most people would know it from Chinatown New Year's celebrations, through its appropriation in *Dungeons & Dragons*, from album covers in the era of progressive rock, and in Ursula Le Guin's Taoist-influenced *Tehanu* and *The Other Wind*.[12] Nonetheless, the dragon of wisdom has not been absent from the Great Swamp. Getting into the

Halloween spirit, the staff at the visitor center once mounted a display, at once poignant and farcical, of the tombstones of extinct and endangered species. Approaching the center entrance, one could not avoid the names *Passenger Pigeon*, *Bog Turtle*, *Right Whale*, and many others. Surrounded by the brilliant gold and scarlet of fall foliage, the viewer could not remain innocent of the swamp's function as refuge or the environmental crisis that created the need for refuge in the first place. While many people come to the Great Swamp for its spectacular birding, the permanent park apparatus—constructed paths across the water, signage, bird blinds—forces visitors to see that the swamp has to be protected from us as much as we have to be guided through it. This apparatus, along with the more ephemeral tombstones, suggested the workings of ecological wisdom, of dragons moving through clouded waters.

I want to hold out the figure of the swamp dragon as a new model for ecocritical activity that does not shun compromised places and the politics of poison but encompasses the ironies of diminishment under the aegis of critical affection. The dragon can be an alias insofar as we assume its role in critical practice; it can be an icon insofar as it provides an ideal image for contemplation of these new values. [13] A swampy, draconian criticism will require a new practice of reading, a new attitude toward canon formation, and the consideration of compromised texts as well as compromised environments. As a beginning, I turn toward two contemporary books, Susan Griffin's *Woman and Nature: The Roaring inside Her* (1979), and Robert Sullivan's *The Meadowlands: Wilderness Adventures on the Edge of a City* (1998), in an attempt to discern a swampy hermeneutics, a heuristic for swamp dragons, under the surface of the text.

The Lyric Swamp: The Undoing
of Dualism in Woman and Nature

The lyric swamp—the wetland figured as the fusion of intelligence and passion, body and mind, matter and spirit—is the alternative offered by Susan Griffin in *Woman and Nature* to the tradition of swamp-as-disease-and-damnation. Griffin is a poet, essayist, playwright, and activist who has been publishing since the late 1960s. Though her work has continued to win literary prizes and is widely anthologized, *Woman and Nature* is her most famous and influential book. It was published in 1979, when the idea of ecofeminism had already arisen in Western Europe and the United States, but it was widely hailed by radical feminists as a theoretical and artistic breakthrough.[14] It is a beautiful and difficult work. Though there is a plot, the book is also hypertextual: it can be read by jumping in nonlinear fashion from any section to any other section. Because every section of the book is a comment on, addition to, or explanation of what happens in the others, because the sections depend on one another but do not require one way of reading, it can be characterized as an *ecological hypertext,* a form of writing that tries to mimic the physics of biological communities as the metaphysics of discourse. This is one reason, I think, for the confusion that so characterizes the interpretation of *Woman and Nature*: more than most essayistic prose, it requires the reader to move through it as a process and to hold seemingly contradictory positions without immediate resolution. Her method is not accidental: as many critics have pointed out, the aim of *Woman and Nature* is to undo the hierarchical dualisms of Western thought, which Griffin believes to be the origin of the political oppression of women and nature.[15] This principle, that a world gendered into master-slave opposites must be remade, may fairly be said to be the central tenet of contemporary Anglophone ecofeminism.

It is equally fair to say that ecofeminism is having a hard time undoing dualism in the intellectual and political realms. Why should this be the case? A clue appears in Myra Jehlen's 1981 essay "Archimedes and the Paradox of Feminist Criticism," where Jehlen points out the difficulty of establishing a new ground for the lever of feminist criticism:

> Reconsideration of the relation between female and male can be a way to reconsider that between intuition and reason and ultimately between the whole set of such associated dichotomies: heart and head, nature and history. But it also creates unusual difficulties. Somewhat like Archimedes, who to lift the earth with his lever required someplace else on which to locate himself and his fulcrum, feminists questioning the presumptive order of both nature and history—and thus proposing to remove the ground from under their own feet—would appear to need an alternative base. For as Archimedes had to stand somewhere, one has to assume something in order to reason at all. So if the very axioms of Western thought already incorporate the sexual teleology in question, it seems that, like the Greek philosopher, we have to find a standpoint off this world altogether. (Jehlen 192)

What seems to be required is a discourse that would allow us to be in several worlds at once, such that the history of culture and nature is not ignored, as if we were not ourselves a product of it, even as we stand in the place of a new fulcrum, intent upon moving the world we still inhabit. I believe that *Woman and Nature* is designed, in structure and content, to further this project of walking in many worlds, to provide for the lever of feminist cosmology a ground that is simultaneously inside and outside the old world of dualism. Griffin is a keen observer who wants a feminist empiricism, a contemplative who wants to change the world, a seeker after ecstatic union with otherkind who seeks to preserve its autonomy. *Woman and Nature* is built, therefore, on strategies of critique and reconstruction, separation and reunion, dialectical movements through previously polarized ideas and events. The goal of this movement is not an absolute holism in which Many become One forever; instead, it is a dynamic interrelationship among the elements of a cosmos, neither unchanging order nor random chaos. It should come as no surprise that Griffin embodies this idea in the figure of the swamp, a local manifestation of the cosmic music that only the spheres used to sing, a swamp that shines with the light of the stars.

It is ironic, then, that Dante's *Comedy* is a crucial intertext to *Woman and Nature*, because Dante casts many parts of Hell as wetland. The central pattern of the *Comedy*—a pilgrimage through suffering, purgation, and redemption—is also the pattern of Griffin's book, with the delusions of patriarchy standing in for the Wood of Error. *Woman and Nature* does not, however, follow the plot of vertical ascent of the *Comedy*, which is governed by a Neoplatonic logic of the Great Chain of Being and identifies the lowest part of the universe, Hell, with absolute matter, and the highest part, Heaven, with absolute Spirit. Instead, Griffin begins and ends with sections called "Matter," but these sections are not equivalent, so the book's structure is not quite circular. While the first "Matter" section is a critique and rejection of materialism and its obverse, idealism, the final section, "Matter: How We Know," is an intensely lyrical account of a nondualistic cosmos as experienced from the inside, or, perhaps, from a place where inside and outside are no longer halves of a dualism.

The beginning of "Matter: How We Know" is a kind of manifesto and an interpretive key for the rest of the section. It does not appear, at first, to be a manifesto; rather, it appears to be a poetic meditation on the continuity of the human and the natural. Because it is poetic, it appears to be unphilosophical, because poetry and philosophy are opposed in Anglophone cultures. But in accordance with her nondualistic agenda, Griffin brings poetry and philosophy together, resulting in a sensual and imagistic prose that resembles the work of Loren Eiseley and Annie Dillard in particular.[16] Here is the beginning:

Because we know ourselves to be made from this earth. See this grass. The patches of silvers and brown. Worn by the wind. The grass reflecting all that lives in the soil. The light. The grass needing the soil. With roots deep in the earth. And patches of silver. Like the patches of silver in our hair. Worn by time. This bird flying low over the grass. Over the tules. The cattails, sedges, rushes, reeds, over the marsh. Because we know ourselves to be made from this earth. Temporary as this grass. Wet as this mud. Our cells filled with water. Like the mud of this swamp. Heather growing here because of the damp. Sphagnum moss floating on the surface, on the water standing in these pools. Places where the river washes out. Where the earth was shaped by the flow of lava. Or by the slow movements of glaciers. Because we know ourselves to be made from this earth, and shaped like the earth, by what has gone before. (223; italics in original)*

This passage is lyric in the most direct way: it is structured like a song; it could be separated into stanzas and a refrain. The refrain "because we know ourselves to be made from this earth" is perhaps the most famous line of ecofeminist literature and certainly one of the most famous lines in contemporary nature writing. But why should that be? Griffin seems to have gone out of her way to avoid the sublime here, identifying earth with a quotidian marsh scene: grass, mud, water, birds. It seems we are not made of very elevated stuff at all, and that is exactly the point. This opening is the start of a manifesto because Griffin's strange singing about marshes and mud and birds is pointed right at the heart of dualism in Western culture. It is pointed at Plato's Allegory of the Cave, which teaches suspicion of the senses, and the seeking of a light that comes from outside of material existence; at Descartes' *Discourse on Method*, which posits a fundamental ontological split between living mind and dead matter; and at every version of Christianity that identifies the Kingdom of God with a disembodied realm.[17] (This is why Griffin allies herself with Dante, who understood that a Neoplatonic heaven that lasted forever was a contradiction of a final resurrection of the faithful in their bodies.) So instead of seeking the light from a changeless world, Griffin has returned to matter to write an account of it as the source of the light itself. This is signaled by the continuity of the section title with the refrain: the question of "how we know" is answered by "because we are made from this earth." This is both a metaphysical and an epistemological argument with the idealist tradition. If the light of the Divine Mind flows into the object-world of matter as its motive force and principle of consciousness, the light is fundamentally unlike matter, and consciousness points outside of the created universe to a space of the Absolute that is finally self-sufficient and self-justifying. But in Griffin's account, the light is part of the grass's reflection of everything that lives in the soil. The light is not opposed to the soil or the grass but implies and is implied by them. Griffin does not use the technical term *photosynthesis* to ground her claim in science itself, but she could: it is literally true that the chloroplasts of plants use the light of the sun to drive metabolism. This is what the "cattails, sedges, rushes, [and] reeds" are all doing. Griffin indicates that she understands the connections of her claims to cellular biology by drawing the analogy between "Our cells full of water" and the muddy swamp: the cell is a swamp, the swamp is a cell, we are made of cells and thus made of swamps. This celebration of our connection to wetlands that move and change and age and die is a transvaluation of values, a shifting of loyalties from the old order that valued transcendence, changelessness, and control to a new order that finds the transcendence of light inside the material world, eternity in the flux of matter, and distance as a sign of respect for the autonomy of otherkind. The last phrase of the book, "and I long to tell you, you who are earth too, and listen *as we speak to each other of what we know: the light is in us*," signifies this transformation (emphasis in original). The light, which at the beginning of the book was said to be outside of the world entirely, is now in the narrator and the entire cosmos. The knowledge of light-in-the-world is no longer a special possession of the narrator but dwells in the reader as well. This is Griffin's new order, the world for the fulcrum of ecofeminism: a swamp that sings.

The Comedic Swamp: The Irony of Urban Wilderness in *The Meadowlands*

In his classic analysis of American pastoral literature and ideology, *The Machine in the Garden*, Leo Marx describes the intrusion of industrial technology as "noise clashing through harmony" (Marx 17), and nothing in *Woman and Nature* would disrupt that idea. Indeed, Griffin's organic cosmology drove Donna Haraway to declare, "I would rather be a cyborg than a goddess" (Haraway 181). It may be, as Haraway argues, that a model of nondualism that does not address the dualism of human and machine is not nondualistic enough: the next step would be to accept the machine into the garden.[18] This problem is implicit in what Michael Bennett has called "Deep ecocriticism," after Deep Ecology: the claim that only pristine wilderness is enough to unite humanity and nature (Bennett 297–302). In *The Meadow-*

lands: Wilderness Adventure on the Edge of a City, Robert Sullivan addresses this problem directly by writing a parodic adventure narrative about exploring the New Jersey Meadowlands, perhaps the most thoroughly polluted wetland on the planet, which I first mentioned as the direct inspiration for the idea of the swamp dragon. That Sullivan knows he is engaged in a parody of adventure narrative—specifically, a parody of pioneering in the West—becomes clear almost immediately, when he describes people in Newark Airport

> with travel books or maybe brand-new water-repellent hiking clothes or Powerbars and polypropylene underwear [who are] heading West to travel and explore. But I am creeping slowly back East, back to America's *first* West—making a reverse commute to the already explored land that has become, through negligence, through exploitation, and through its own chaotic persistence, explorable again. (14–15)

There are multiple levels of parody here: a sarcastic lighting out for the territories, which diminishes into a "reverse commute," but also a parody of contemporary eco-adventuring, known well to Sullivan in his work for *Outside* magazine. Even deeper is the practice of self-parody, repeated throughout the book, in which Sullivan himself appears most ridiculous for embarking on a "wilderness adventure" in New Jersey when he is coming from Portland, Oregon, one of the jewels of Ecotopia. But all of this perversity leads to something impossible in the diminished-thing paradigm, namely, an assertion of the agency of the Meadowlands themselves, which become "explorable again" in part through their own stubbornness. This is where many supportive reviewers have it wrong: *The Meadowlands* is not merely an entertainment but a postmodern *Walden* for a toxic age.[19] Sullivan is not just a raconteur—though his wit illuminates even the most frightening details—but an advocate and philosopher. His humor is not gratuitous but a studied response to the hopelessness that polluted landscapes inspire. His writing is "postnatural" nonfiction in Cynthia Deitering's sense, inscribing an awareness of toxicity as environmental norm, and akin to Don DeLillo's *White Noise* and John Updike's *Rabbit at Rest* in the realm of the novel (Deitering 196–97).

Sullivan's attachment to Thoreau is especially strong; he refers to Thoreau directly many times, especially in the chapter called "Walden Swamp," which contains a parody of *Walden*'s supply list, including a compass, insect repellent, beef jerky, the ubiquitous Powerbars, water filtration kits, and an appropriately named "Mad River" canoe (77). The visual joke is funny—

Sullivan has gone to some lengths to reproduce the appearance of Thoreau's list—but the underlying message is clear: the Meadowlands are, through no fault of their own, far more deadly than a Concord pond and could kill the narrator just through skin-to-water contact. This setting is even deadlier in its own way than the typical western river-with-rapids that populates so many eco-adventure stories, in that rapids can be shot with the proper level of skill, whereas no one is sure whether Sullivan's detoxification and antimicrobial kits will allow him to drink the swamp water safely. In fact, pollution and microbial activity surface again and again, indicating not only the writer's careful research into the ecology of garbage but also his awareness of the conventions of American nature writing. Here, for instance, Sullivan presents a set piece on anaerobic decomposition, with sinister results:

> The big difference between the garbage hills and the real hills in the Meadowlands is that the garbage hills are alive. In some completely peopleless areas of the swamp, there are billions of microscopic organisms thriving underground in dark, oxygen-free communities. They multiply and even evolve so that they can more readily digest the trash at their disposal. It can take a team of three organisms to finish off a dump-buried piece of cellulose in a bit of newspaper too small to even see. Eventually, there are whole suites of organisms in each hill, as if each hill were a bacterial high-rise. After having ingested the tiniest portion of New Jersey or New York, these cells then exhale huge underground plumes of carbon dioxide and of warm moist methane, giant stillborn tropical winds that seep through the ground to feed the Meadowlands fires, or creep up into the atmosphere, where they eat away at the Earth-protecting layer of ozone. (96)

This passage turns the lyricism of Griffin's swamp-song on its head, even as it participates in a related rhetoric. There is a kind of Morlock appeal to Sullivan's account of the garbage hill ecosystem; it is, as he points out, more alive than the blasted wrecks of the original hills. However, no sooner do we admire the virtuosity of microbial teamwork and the conviviality of the anaerobic world than we see the hellish results: garbage decomposition feeds swamp fires and the destruction of the ozone layer (not to mention contributing to global warming, not quite the issue in 1998 that it would soon become). Suddenly, the swamp is demonic again, though its malignity is domestic rather than alien. After Griffin's triumphant revision of Dante's *Comedy*, this vision is more sobering. Though the Meadowlands were once a fine cedar swamp, human abuse has turned them into an engine of Hell, complete with wildfires from Central Casting.

It is fascinating to note, however, that passages like this one made *The Meadowlands* an immensely popular text in a course on nature writing I taught at Rutgers University, New Brunswick, New Jersey, in 2001—far more popular than its Thoreauvian ur-text. Mostly from Cook College, the agricultural-biotechnical wing of Rutgers, and highly literate environmentally, my students found Thoreau prissy and moralistic, but in Sullivan they found a kindred spirit (Puck rather than Ariel) who approached environmental disaster with something like our native attitude. Had Sullivan simply made fun of the swamp, or of New Jersey as a stinking pit, he would have joined the chorus of disdain my students had heard since childhood and would have been ignored. Instead, by finding a way into the Meadowlands physically, Sullivan found a way into local culture rhetorically. Like the people of North Jersey he encounters throughout his travels, Sullivan manifests disgust and awe at the presence of the swamps, which are friend and enemy, refuge and prison, victim and perpetrator. In his own way, he enacts an undoing of dualism that makes such undoing a realistic project for the people of the Meadowlands: the possibility of a Manichean destruction of the "bad side" of swamps is disavowed. If Griffin creates an ideal landscape to contain matter's own light, Sullivan shows how light and darkness, survival and destruction, coinhere in a postindustrial swamp. For this reason, my students embraced *The Meadowlands* as a model of nature writing that did not alienate them from their native place.

One student, a fan of *Walden* who despaired of writing like Thoreau because, as he put it, "Jersey isn't like that," found a way to talk about his East Brunswick pond and its waterfowl by using Sullivan's tone as a model. East Brunswick, a Central Jersey suburb bisected by the Turnpike, is less compromised than the Meadowlands but nothing like the western ideal of text-worthy land. The student was trying to describe an experience of love and loyalty inspired by "a crappy little pond and some ducks," and though *Walden* fueled a desire to write, it failed to provide a rhetoric that could encompass affection and disdain, attachment and revulsion, at the same time. Ironically, Sullivan's smart-ass routine allowed this student to narrate the very mystical oneness that his neighbor in Princeton, Joyce Carol Oates, decried in "Against Nature," which the class also read. In that essay, Oates substitutes an attack of tachycardia for an Emersonian eyeball-experience, taking nature writers to task for their limited set of responses to a morally ambiguous world. My students thoroughly agreed with her—they too were tired of reverence as the only option—but Oates failed to produce an alternative to cynicism, which they already had in abundance. Sullivan, on the other hand, revealed irony as a vehicle of love, when the object of love, like Socrates in Plato's *Symposium*, is a pug-nosed thing that shines with divine light from within.

It is appropriate, then, when Sullivan, after a book full of muckraking, allows himself an indulgence: a fantasy of resurrection for the crucified land at the start of a chapter called "Digging":

> If, by magic or the assistance of angels or with the help of a grant awarded through the Federal Enterprise Zone program, I could turn the bottom of the Meadowlands to the top and restore what was thrown into the muck to its pristine predumped condition, the place would be instantly de-wasteland-ized. I'd sit on Snake Hill and watch as Swartwout's old muskrat-chewed dikes restored themselves and his farm returned and prospered and he danced in his fields with his family. I'd watch demolished buildings reassembled in the pristine marsh. I'd see barrels of toxic waste rise from the no-longer-polluted water and levitate harmlessly above the ground. Among the most enthusiastic of reanimated items would be the small bands of executionees, roaming together—their hands patting their chests, pinching their cheeks in wonderment—each clumsy step rousing a pheasant or a wild turkey. (141–42)

With all the moxie of Donne's "Holy Sonnets," this passage imagines what Eliot's "The Waste Land" tithes to caution: the Final Trumpet blowing, and the swamp with all its lost denizens arising in their proper forms in a New Jerusalem. There is in this passage a Catholic-boyishness—Gerard Manley Hopkins's "God's Grandeur" is one of the book's epigraphs—that infuses much charm into otherwise disturbing stories. Unfortunately, the larger function of this vision, in a chapter devoted to finding Jimmy Hoffa's body, is to insist on its own impossibility: no power, human or angelic, will ever separate all the toxic waste from the swamp bottom, and the other miracles are likewise impossible.

Sullivan thereby demands that the Meadowlands be taken as they are, or not at all. This, too, bespeaks a kind of sacramental consciousness: the world is flawed but good and must be loved as a broken embodiment of the grandeur of God. It is not permissible to despair of it permanently, and not even the Meadowlands may be abandoned. This consciousness is the center of the tough talk, the sweetness at the core of Sullivan's humor. Literary criticism calls it "cosmic irony" when the universe turns out to be hiding the opposite of its surface contents, though critics are more used to the Thomas Hardy version, in which defeat is snatched from the jaws of ambiguity. Hardy may not know why his "Darkling Thrush" sings through the bitter cold, but Sullivan does, and therein lies his value for aspiring swamp dragons. Though he is disgusted by the Meadowlands, he does not turn away; though his fear is justified, it does not drive him out. Persisting until it finds a hidden loveliness, Sullivan's parody turns in on itself to become a real adventure and revelation. Having chosen one of the most abused places for his experiment, Sullivan overcomes the logic of diminishment and finds his way past Snake Hill to a serpentine wisdom.

Horror of Horrors, or Becoming a Swamp Dragon

In his indispensable guide to the semiotics of swamps, *Postmodern Wetlands*, Rod Giblett points out that just as the swamp has been a locus of death and decay in traditional Western cultures, so it has been the lair of something even worse: "As the marsh or swamp itself is often represented as a place of horror, the swamp serpent is doubly horrific, the horror of horrors" (Giblett 179).

So now I must admit that the swamp dragon is not just an atavism of nerdy childhood, a piece of folklore, or even a mild bit of Orientalism, but the advocacy of our own nightmares. By asking ecocritics to consider the swamp dragon as a new identity or an icon for further work, I am asking us to do something terrifying: to become the monster under the bed, the thing we dare not touch, the evil bent upon the destruction of civilization.[20] I do so in part because Susan Griffin and Robert Sullivan traveled into the nightmares of philosophy and the ruins of industry and returned with a stronger way to love the world we actually live in. Learning to love a postlapsarian world is not just a countermove to pastoral retreat but an anodyne for injury we did not prevent.[21] As the environmental justice movement reminds us, white, middle-class environmentalism in the United States has often been guilty of protecting wilderness and its charismatic megafauna while ignoring the suffering of urban ecologies. The logic of the swamp dragon is a way out of this dilemma. Impure and defiled, both literally and figuratively, the swamp dragon is uncharismatic but still alive, an ecstatic identification with a beleaguered cosmos. It prevents the idealization of nature *or* culture and thereby avoids traditional dualism *and* its reversal, which Karla Armbruster and Kathleen Wallace have warned us against (Armbruster and Wallace 4). In a political landscape ruled by the sublime, by the "enchantment of distance," as Rick van Noy has said (van Noy 182–83), the swamp dragon offers the enchantment of proximity and proximity's curse: a view of the damage to the world that cannot be completely undone.

What would the rubric of the swamp dragon do for ecocriticism as a literary discipline? First, it would focus our attention on the stakes of our game. In his moving foreword to *The Greening of Literary Scholarship*, Scott Slovic tells the story of his lost dog, Sally, hit by a truck one day while he was at work. Sally's tragedy, he thinks, is that she did not see the truck coming and never knew what hit her (Slovic vii–xi). A swampy, dragonlike ecocriticism would keep its hundred eyes of Argus on the monsters around us to understand better the dangers we face; it would also admit that we are partially monstrous ourselves, not quite separable from the oncoming truck, transforming the guilt of complicity into an appreciation of finitude and impurity. At the same time, the swamp dragon is a figure of resistance from a land of refuge. If Griffin's swamp exudes a cosmic music, so might we; if the Meadowlands survived its own destruction with stubbornness and humor, the ends of comedy might be our ends, too. As arbiters of the canon, ecocritics might choose, then, to counter the matter of environmental crisis with the matter of restoration, as Bill McKibben has already done in his own work, balancing *The Ends of Nature* with *Hope, Human and Wild*. We might, like Sue Hubbell in *Waiting for Aphrodite*, encourage our students to become experts on some part of the nonhuman world—even to make their own homes speakable, as in the case of my students at Rutgers—knowing that amateurs are sometimes the best, and the only, naturalists where certain places and creatures are concerned. Finally, the swamp dragon is a figure of guile and nonlinear connection, which ecocritics might apply to ourselves and our institutional alliances. ASLE has been very good at creating structures where no structures existed before, such as mentoring programs for graduate students and communal bibliographies. What if we extended that work to combine the powers of institutions that do not normally talk to each other—community colleges and state schools with elite, private universities, technical schools with environmental liberal arts colleges—in bioregional consortiums and networks of networks? Serpentine alliances like these might stand a chance of countering the logic of academic competition and harnessing the swamps of bureaucracy for our own ends. By thinking of ourselves in collective terms and working toward collective goals, by becoming a swamp dragon en masse, ecocritics might wield the influence we all hope for in the name of conservation and restoration, survival and flourishing.[22]

NOTES

1. Prophet, judge, serpent: those who see a biblical typology here are not mistaken. It would be surprising if American ecocritics, as heirs to a tradition of sermon and jeremiad, never took up rhetorical postures with biblical roots. I leave it to ecocritics from other national/rhetorical traditions—and American ecocritics of nonbiblical backgrounds—to ponder their own rhetorical archetypes.

2. This is ironic, given that the name Kittatinny means "Biggest Mountain," according to local accounts of Lenape/Delaware place names. The highest point in the New Jersey Kittatinnies is about eighteen hundred feet above sea level.

3. This problem is related to American ecocriticism's largely uncritical appropriation of an Anglo-Protestant righteousness, of which it should become more aware, particularly in the Muirish heritage of nineteenth-century conservationism. How different would American ecocriticism be if it transcended the logic of purity versus pollution in the valuation of environments? That question, however, is the project of another essay.

4. The Superfund is a program administered by the federal government to clean up toxic waste sites. The official EPA home page for Burnt Fly Bog is located at http://www.epa.gov/superfund/sites/npl/mar72.htm. More information about the Raritan's recovery is available through Raritan Riverkeeper, http://www.nynjbaykeeper.org/riverkeeper/riverkeeper%20open.htm. The New Jersey Pinelands Commission Home Page is located at http://www.state.nj.us/pinelands.

5. Michael Bennett, "From Wide Open Spaces to Metropolitan Places: The Urban Challenge to Ecocriticism," in *The ISLE Reader 1993–2003*, ed. Michael P. Branch and Scott Slovic (Athens: University of Georgia Press, 2003), 296–317. Two helpful volumes in this regard are Michael Bennett and David W. Teague, eds., *The Nature of Cities: Ecocriticism and Urban Environments* (Tucson: University of Arizona Press, 1999), and William Cronon, ed., *Uncommon Ground: Toward Reinventing Nature* (New York: W. W. Norton, 1995). For an explanation of urban nature that traces the connections between polis and region, see William Cronon, *Nature's Metropolis: Chicago and the Great West* (New York: W. W. Norton, 1991).

6. It is sometimes difficult to say exactly where the East is, however. For my purposes, the East excludes the Midwest and the South, which might be considered eastern by westerners, because they are both culturally and geographically distinct from what most people mean by "East" in the pejorative sense: the area bounded by Maryland in the south, Pennsylvania in the west, and Maine in the north. I therefore make no attempt here to account for the lakes of Minnesota or the Florida Everglades, though these places might be eastern in other accounts. This problem of regional boundaries is explored from the other direction in Michael E. McGerr, "Is There a Twentieth-Century West?" in *Under an Open Sky: Rethinking America's Western Past*, ed. William Cronon, George Miles, and Jay Gitlin (New York: W. W. Norton, 1992), 239–56.

7. The title of the conference is a quotation from Robert Frost's sonnet "The Oven Bird," which itself presents a curious theory of summer as the diminishment of spring: "He says the leaves are old and that for flowers / Mid-summer is to spring as one to ten." Frost anticipates the ironic posture of Robert Sullivan's *The Meadowlands*, examined later in this essay, toward lyric pastoralism, because the bird's sense of diminishment is directly connected to its unbirdlike suspicion of singing: "The bird would cease and be as other birds / But that he knows in singing not to sing. / The question that he frames in all but words / Is what to make of a diminished thing." The fact that the bird is singing near a highway, of course, is directly related to the East's diminished condition in the early twentieth century.

8. This hegemony is by no means overthrown; however, megalopolitan ecocritics should not be assumed to support or accommodate it. For a brief but revealing account of the history of the West's resentment against eastern capitalism and cultural elitism, see Clyde A. Milner II, "The View from Wisdom: Four Layers of History and Regional Identity," in *Under an Open Sky: Rethinking America's Western Past*, ed. William Cronon, George Miles, and Jay Gitlin (New York: W. W. Norton, 1992), 203–22.

9. The Jersey Devil has certain draconian characteristics, such as bat wings, a pointy tail, claws, and an elongated, reptilian face. For a summary of the relevant folklore, see http://njfolkfest.rutgers.edu/devil.htm.

10. The Online Etymology Dictionary (www.etymonline.com) derives the word from the Greek "*drak-*, the strong aorist stem of *derkesthai*, 'to see clearly.' " The *American Heritage Dictionary*, 4th edition, notes its relationship to *derk-*, the Indo-European root for "to see." Both sources suggest that the intended meaning is something like "beast with the sharp glance" or "creature with the evil eye."

11. The rewriting of the Babylonian creation story by the priestly writer of the Torah is now so conventional an idea that it is included prominently in the notes to many popular Bible editions in English. See, for instance, *The HarperCollins Study Bible: New Revised Standard Version*, ed. Wayne Meeks (New York: HarperCollins, 1993), 6–8, notes on Genesis 1.1–2.7.

12. This diasporic figure has manifested recently on television in the Disney Channel's show *Jake Long: American Dragon*. Here the grandson of Chinese immigrants, and later his little sister, inherit the power of the *long*-dragon to fight magical evil and to assert a continued, if transformed, ethnic identity inside American culture.

13. Here I am drawing upon the tradition of Greek Orthodox Christianity, in which icons of Christ, Mary, and the saints are gazed upon as gateways to the spiritual realm.

14. The most important critic to analyze *Woman and Nature* is Alicia Ostriker, who in *Stealing the Language: The Emergence of Women's Poetry in America* (London: Women's Press, 1986) characterizes Griffin's logic as separatist, at least in certain

passages (231). Ostriker offers the most convincing argument for the book as an artifact of a moment in Second Wave feminism that imagined men as too violent to be trusted.

15. Karla Armbruster offers the most convincing argument about Griffin's anti-dualism, in which she claims that *Woman and Nature* works strongly against dualism while not entirely escaping it. See Karla Armbruster, "'Buffalo Gals Won't You Come Out Tonight': A Call for Boundary-Crossing in Ecofeminist Literary Criticism," in *Ecofeminist Literary Criticism: Theory, Interpretation, Pedagogy*, ed. Greta Gaard and Patrick Murphy (Urbana: University of Illinois Press, 1998), 97–122.

16. Griffin thanks Dillard in the acknowledgments, and Eiseley was one of Dillard's own models as an essayist.

17. In this sense, Griffin is allied with Latin American liberation theology and North American feminist theology, which see the Kingdom of God as a this-worldly phenomenon.

18. By this I do not mean that it should be impossible to ban snowmobiles in a national park but rather that the exclusion of postindustrial technology from the traditional cosmos of pastoralism forces people to choose between modernity and cosmic harmony, excluding the possibility that the machine might participate in such harmony.

19. Here I have in mind the reviewers on the back of the original hardcover edition, who, with the exception of Frank McCourt, emphasize the book's value as a good read.

20. David E. Jones, in *An Instinct for Dragons* (London: Routledge, 2000), theorizes that the universality of the dragon image across cultures may be the result of an atavistic conflation of the raptor, the big cat, and the serpent, enemies of our primate relatives and our anthropoid ancestors (25–38).

21. I have no quarrel with a dialectical mode of retreat, such as Thoreau practiced at Walden, in which one moves away from society for a time as one step in a synthesis of contemplation and action. However, a model of pastoralism in which the goal is to escape, as permanently as possible, all involvement with the human world in the name of ethical purity is elitist at best and delusional at worst. It fosters a fall-of-Rome mentality in which the spiritual elite flee to the desert to await the collapse of the corrupt empire. It could never be practiced even by a significant minority of megalopolitan citizens without enormous destruction of local environments. The suspicion that such exclusion may be precisely the point of radical green praxis leads to the fear that ecocriticism is not merely ecocentric but misanthropic.

22. I would like to thank my ecocritical colleagues, and two anonymous readers, for the opportunity to present and discuss earlier drafts of this material. I would also like to thank Kristen Abbey, Aryana Bates, Lauren Butcher, John Fitzgerald, Marc Manganaro, Leo Marx, Mary Ellen O'Driscoll, Jim Paradis, Jun Ho Son, Mary Beth Son, Adam W. Sweeting, and the Woonasquatucket River Watershed Council of Providence, Rhode Island, for their help, interest, and encouragement. Finally, I

dedicate this essay to Itzam Ka, a green iguana I once knew—a very good dragon indeed.

WORKS CITED

Adamson, Joni, Mei Mei Evans, and Rachel Stein. *The Environmental Justice Reader: Politics, Poetics and Pedagogy.* Tucson: University of Arizona Press, 2003.

Association for the Study of Literature and Environment website. http://www.asle.umn.edu.

Bartsch, Ingrid, Carolyn DiPalma, and Laura Sells. "The Jeremiad's Promise: Cyborg Wetlands and Vampire Practices." *Intertexts* 3, no. 2 (1999): 180–91.

Bates, Roy. *Chinese Dragons.* New York: Oxford University Press, 2002.

Bennett, Michael. "From Wide Open Spaces to Metropolitan Places: The Urban Challenge to Ecocriticism." In *The ISLE Reader 1993–2003*, ed. Michael P. Branch and Scott Slovic. Athens: University of Georgia Press, 2003. 296–317.

Bennett, Michael, and David W. Teague, eds. *The Nature of Cities: Ecocriticism and Urban Environments.* Tucson: University of Arizona Press, 1999.

Branch, Michael P., and Scott Slovic, eds. *The ISLE Reader: Ecocriticism, 1993–2003.* Athens: University of Georgia Press, 2003.

Buell, Lawrence. *Writing for an Endangered World: Literature, Culture, and Environment in the US and Beyond.* Cambridge: Harvard University Press, 2001.

Coupe, Lawrence, ed. *The Green Studies Reader: From Romanticism to Ecocriticism.* London: Routledge, 2000.

Deitering, Cynthia. "The Postnatural Novel: Toxic Consciousness in the Fiction of the 1980s." In *The Ecocriticism Reader: Landmarks in Literary Ecology*, ed. Cheryll Glotfelty. Athens: University of Georgia Press, 1996. 197–203.

Douglas, Mary. *Purity and Danger: An Analysis of the Concepts of Pollution and Taboo.* New York: Taylor and Francis, 2003.

Giblett, Rod. *Postmodern Wetlands: Culture, History, Ecology.* Edinburgh: Edinburgh University Press, 1996.

Glotfelty, Cheryll, ed. *The Ecocriticism Reader: Landmarks in Literary Ecology.* Athens: University of Georgia Press, 1996.

Great Swamp National Wildlife Refuge website. http://greatswamp.fws.gov.

Griffin, Susan. *Woman and Nature: The Roaring Inside Her.* San Francisco: Sierra Club Books, 2000.

Haraway, Donna J. *Simians, Cyborgs, and Women: The Reinvention of Nature.* New York: Routledge, 1991.

Howarth, William. "Imagined Territory: The Writing of Wetlands." *New Literary History* 30, no. 3 (1999): 509–39.

Jehlen, Myra. "Archimedes and the Paradox of Feminist Criticism." In *Feminisms: An Anthology of Literary Theory and Criticism*, ed. Robyn Warhol and Diana Price Herndl, revised edition. New Brunswick: Rutgers University Press, 1997. 191–212.

Keller, Catherine. *Face of the Deep: A Theology of Becoming.* New York: Routledge, 2003.

Marx, Leo. *The Machine in the Garden: Technology and the Pastoral Ideal.* New York: Oxford University Press, 1967.

Miller, David C. *Dark Eden: The Swamp in Nineteenth-Century American Culture.* Cambridge: Cambridge University Press, 1989.

Murphy, Patrick D. *Farther Afield in the Study of Nature-Oriented Literature.* Charlottesville: University of Virginia Press, 2000.

"Nature Writers Come to Kalamazoo to Discuss 'Diminished Thing.' " *WMU News*, http://www.wmich.edu/wmu/news/1999/9905/9899–273.html (accessed October 31, 2003).

Phillips, Dana. *The Truth of Ecology: Nature, Culture, and Literature in America.* Oxford: Oxford University Press, 2003.

Rosendale, Steven, ed. *The Greening of Literary Scholarship: Literature, Theory, and Environment.* Iowa City: University of Iowa Press, 2002.

Slovic, Scott. Foreword. In *The Greening of Literary Scholarship*, ed. Steven Rosendale. Iowa City: University of Iowa Press, 2002. vii–xi.

Sullivan, Robert. *The Meadowlands: Wilderness Adventure on the Edge of a City.* New York: Scribner, 1998.

"The Third Biennial ASLE Conference" Update. *ASLE News: A Biannual Publication of the Association for the Study of Literature and Environment* 11, no. 1 (Spring 1999): 3.

Tiner, Ralph W. *In Search of Wetlands: A Wetland Resource and Field Guide.* New Brunswick: Rutgers University Press, 1999.

van Noy, Rick. "Surveying the Sublime: Literary Cartographers and the Spirit of Place." In *The Greening of Literary Scholarship*, ed. Steven Rosendale. Iowa City: University of Iowa Press, 2002. 181–206.

Wallace, Kathleen R., and Karla Armbruster. "Introduction: Why Go Beyond Nature Writing, and Where To?" In *Beyond Nature Writing: Expanding the Boundaries of Ecocriticism*, ed. Karla Armbruster and Kathleen R. Wallace. Charlottesville: University of Virginia Press, 2001. 1–25.

ANGELA WALDIE

Challenging the Confines

Haiku from the Prison Camps

ON A SMALL scrap of paper lying on a plywood table in a cramped room that was once a horse stable, in a form restricted to seventeen syllables—as unyielding as the barbed wire fence that traps the cold night—with a pen that is almost out of ink, imagine writing freedom. Imagine finding the words that move against one another and against your loneliness and frustration in such a way that they create, if only for a moment, a place of peace. And imagine that in these few words, intrinsic to your language and cultural heritage, you can convey the essence of a historical atrocity to future generations, communicating your experiences through a profound attentiveness to the nuances of the natural world.

Reading from within the confines of canonized environmental writing, such as that of Thoreau, Muir, and Leopold, I once considered environmental literature to be a series of tributes to landscapes known and loved. In the experience of these celebrated nature writers, residence in remote places is often portrayed as a welcome escape from civilization; harsh and secluded landscapes are regarded as places of refuge and rejuvenation; new environments are to be explored and this exploration is recorded for the benefit of future generations. But what if this experience were to change? What if a group of writers were exiled in a foreign environment, not by choice but by force?

Japanese Americans imprisoned in internment camps during World War II were exiled, within their own nation, in landscapes unfamiliar to them. While confined to the camps, many of the internees practiced traditional art forms. Watercolor paintings revealed the camps juxtaposed against the often vast and uninhabited landscapes that surrounded them. Japanese gardens arose from deserts and swampy lowlands, as plants known and unknown were cultivated side by side in familiar patterns. Similarly, haiku provided a form through which internees could orient themselves to the nuances of their harsh, yet often beautiful, environments.

The haiku of the internment camps provide a unique perspective on various American landscapes. Written by internees who were struggling to exist in unfamiliar places and who, rather than being free to explore these new environments, experienced them from within the confines of fenced enclosures, these haiku reflect the observations of a group of poets who gained an intimate understanding of places previously unknown to them. Often with little activity to fill their days, the internees had ample time to reflect on the surrounding landscape: to learn the qualities of dawn and dusk; to consider the character of the passing seasons; and to wonder at the names of the plants, birds, deserts, or mountains that inhabited their new surroundings. Internment haiku, which convey such precise attentiveness to the natural environment, deserve recognition in the canon of environmental literature. Although the internees did not seek out the environments of which they wrote, their haiku convey a mindfulness to details of the places in which they found themselves as well as poignant recollections of the places they had left behind.

ON FEBRUARY 19, 1942, just over two months after the bombing of Pearl Harbor, President Franklin D. Roosevelt signed Executive Order 9066, allowing for the designation of "military areas . . . from which any or all persons may be excluded" ("Executive Order 9066," reprinted in Girdner and Loftis 521). In March 1942, all people of Japanese descent living in the western half of the West Coast states and Arizona were ordered to move from this "militarily sensitive area" (Gesensway and Roseman 41). Of the approximately 113,000 West Coast residents of Japanese ancestry, 80,000 were Nisei, American citizens, most under the age of twenty-five. The rest were Issei, who had been born in Japan and subsequently immigrated to the United States. A federal statute prevented the Issei from becoming American citizens.[1]

The Tolan Committee, established to conduct a survey of intermountain states searching for possible voluntary resettlement sites, found that "all the governors except Ralph Carr of Colorado refused to permit the West Coast Japanese into their states except under armed guard and behind barbed wire" (Gesensway and Roseman 42). The committee then recommended that the federal government oversee the removal of the Japanese Americans to internment camps, also referred to as "concentration camps." During the internment period, which lasted from the spring of 1942 until 1945, many internees turned to creative pursuits in an attempt to combat the frustration, boredom, and monotony of camp life. Artists, such as Chiura Obata, captured the surrounding landscape in stunning watercolor paintings, and poets evoked the landscape in words. Poetry societies were established in many of the camps, and members practiced time-honored forms of Japanese verse, including haiku.

Haiku clubs, such as the Delta Ginsha Haiku Kai and Valley Ginsha Haiku Kai of California, had existed in the United States prior to World War II. Unfortunately, most of the poetry from the prewar haiku clubs was destroyed following the bombing of Pearl Harbor, as "fearing reprisals, the majority of Japanese Americans, including Central California haiku poets, destroyed most of their collections, including all forms of Japanese literature" (de Cristoforo 24). Many of the Delta Ginsha and Valley Ginsha members, however, continued to write haiku from their various internment camps. Violet Kazue de Cristoforo, the last surviving member of the Delta Ginsha and Valley Ginsha haiku clubs, compiled and translated a selection of haiku written in the internment camps, which were published in 1997, in the anthology entitled *May Sky: There Is Always Tomorrow*.

Born in Hawaii in 1917, de Cristoforo moved to Japan with her family at the age of seven. When she reached her mid teens, her parents felt she should be receiving an American education, so she moved to Fresno, California, where she lived with friends of her family and attended high school. After graduation she married Shigeru Matsuda, a charter member of the Valley Ginsha Haiku Kai, and she subsequently joined this enthusiastic group of haiku poets. Although few of the prewar haiku written by de Cristoforo's contemporaries have been retained, she recalls a sense of "peacefulness and tranquility" that inhabited these poems, "as well as hope for [the poets'] future[s] in America" (29).

In my experience of reading haiku, I find that peacefulness and tranquility aptly characterize many of the poems written in this genre, in addition to a sense of belonging within the cyclical flow of time. As Robert Hass notes in *The Essential Haiku* (1994), the haiku "traditional themes—deep autumn, a sudden summer shower, the images of rice seedlings and plum blossoms, of spring and summer migrants like the mountain cuckoo and the bush warbler, of the cormorant-fishermen in summer, and the apprentices on holiday in the spring—gave a powerful sense of a human place in the ritual and cyclical movement of the world" (xiii). The very essence of haiku seems contrary to the unfamiliarity and uncertainty of life in the internment camps. Yet despite this apparent disparity, many internees found solace in writing haiku. When reading the poems they produced, questions inevitably arise: To what extent do these poems diverge from the characteristic tranquility of haiku? Are there unique patterns of words and images that appear in the haiku of internment poets? And how did these poets find ways, in so few words, to convey the immensity of their situations? By comparing haiku written in the internment camps to classical haiku written in Japan, I hope to gauge the effects of barbed wire on a genre that is simultaneously confining and freeing.

TRADITIONAL HAIKU masters, such as Matsuo Bashō, Yosa Buson, and Kobayashi Issa, are renowned for their ability to express thoughts of boundless depth and beauty in only seventeen syllables. Although haiku are often printed in three lines, in *Haikai and Haiku* (1958), a committee of Japanese scholars explains: "*haiku* is always treated as a one-line poem, having three parts of 5, 7 and 5 syllables each. This springs from the conception that each emotion is a single, indivisible, perfect whole, the momentary essence of which can only be expressed by a few significant words" (Ichikawa ix). As Kenneth Yasuda notes in *The Japanese Haiku* (1957), seventeen syllables are "the average number . . . that can be uttered in one breath" (32). Therefore, at the juncture of these two descriptions, a haiku becomes the essence of emotion that can be uttered in a single breath. Traditionally connected to Zen Buddhism, haiku strive to capture the significance of a moment and the emotion contained within that moment. This emotion is generally revealed obliquely, rather than explicitly, as the poet conveys a sensory experience. While the brevity of haiku would seem to limit a poet's ability to communicate details such as time and place, the haiku form allows its writer to capture nuanced immensity in few words.

   In *The Essential Haiku*, Hass notes that "insistence on time and place" is an intrinsic feature of traditional haiku (xii). The place in haiku is almost invariably a place within nature. The time is located primarily within the cycle of seasons and is indicated by a *kigo* or "seasonal reference." This reference may name a season directly, such as "summer moon," "autumn evening," or "winter river," or it may be a word commonly associated with a particular season, as blossoms are associated with spring. Alluding to "accumulated resonances and associations from earlier poetry as well as . . . the Japanese way of thinking about time and change," the *kigo* allows the haiku writer to evoke various seasonal and emotional connotations with a single word (xii).[2]

   In traditional haiku, spring is often characterized by rain, birdsong, and blossoms.[3] There is usually a sense of the hope and rejuvenation that we inherently associate with spring: the arrival of birds that have been absent throughout the winter, the appearance of new growth despite lingering snow. Of the transition from winter to spring, Mizūhara Shūōshi writes:

> Mountain cherry blossoms
> Against the snowy peak—
> Silent harmony in heaven (in Miura 32)[4]

Spring and winter exist for a moment in parallel harmony as cherry blossoms, promising renewal, are silhouetted against a distant reminder of snow. With this juxtaposition, Shūōshi conveys the serene inevitability of seasonal change.

Summer haiku are filled with verdant growth, turbulent storms, and references to the shortness of summer nights. Poets, overwhelmed by heat, write of finding refuge in streams, long afternoon naps, or any hint of coolness. Despite the languor of hot summer afternoons, life and energy are as ubiquitous in these poems as the humming of the cicadas that often inhabit the summer haiku of Bashō:

> Nothing in the cry
> of cicadas suggests they
> are about to die (Bashō 119)

This haiku pairs a powerful articulation of timelessness with the awareness that such timelessness is illusory. For while the cicadas' cry does not suggest their impending death, the poem itself does. Bashō makes the retreat of summer seem increasingly poignant by reminding us, with the song of the cicadas, of moments when summer's warmth and languor seem to defy the progression of days.

As summer retreats, autumn haiku collect remnants of color in vibrant leaves and chrysanthemums, yet there is often a reflection on the inevitable sense of loss the season entails. In a haiku that contains both darkness and color, Buson captures the vanishing hues of autumn:

> The mountain darkening
> and the redness of the maples
> taken away (in Sawa and Shiffert 121)

The redness of the maples, vulnerable to night's darkness, is also vulnerable to winter, the approaching season of darkness. Yet this loss of color is conveyed as a natural process, inextricably woven into the fabric of nature, accompanied by a sense of peace and resignation. Autumn haiku convey a compression of time as summer's seemingly endless hours of daylight are condensed by lengthening nights. Bashō relates an image of such compression in this reflection on an ebb tide:

> Autumnal full moon,
> the tides slosh and foam
> coming in (in Hamill 20)

As the beach retreats beneath the tide, Bashō implies a simultaneous shortening of days, emphasized by the autumnal moon that presides over this poem.

While warmth and daylight decrease, winter haiku acknowledge the presence of cold and empty moments. Death and loneliness are not uncommon subjects in the season occupying the darkest side of the year, as "low vitality and a withdrawnness" create a "contrast to the sensuous outgoing poems of spring and summer" (Shiffert 19). Snow often obliterates the sense of growth and life present in the haiku of warmer months. Even in this dormant season, however, haiku poets recognize seasonal and generational cycles, as Issa writes:

> My father also
> studied these high mountains
> from his winter hut (Issa 121)

As winter provides long hours indoors for reflection and study, Issa considers not only the immediate cycle of seasons but the perpetual nature of this cycle. This perpetuity allows Issa to recognize the ways in which his life reflects his father's, thus acknowledging his participation in a generational cycle that seems to parallel the cycle of seasons.

It is presumptuous of me to generalize about the qualities of each season captured in a genre as subtle and varied as haiku. There are poets who communicate hope on the bleakest winter days, just as there are those who have written spring and summer haiku that seem veiled with a sense of loss, but in a genre that traditionally followed strict conventions, patterns persist. The poems, situated amidst the seasonal cycle of loss and renewal, often reflect the lexicon, character, and cultural associations attributed to each season. While most haiku focus on only a single moment, by heightening the intensity of that moment and placing it within the seasonal flow, these poems convey a reverence for recurrent natural cycles. Traditional haiku poets celebrate this recurrence by including references to nature that situate their poems within a universal context, which is generally a context familiar to both writer and reader. Such composition requires profound attentiveness to the intricacies of the natural world; it implies the importance of knowing a place and understanding the subtleties of its seasonal changes. Haiku poets of the internment camps faced the challenge of writing in unfamiliar places where seasonal changes failed to bring certainty and sameness and where the vocabulary they had once used to describe the natural world was no longer adequate.

THE FIRST season of internment was spring, usually celebrated as a time of birth and new beginnings. Yet for Japanese Americans living on the West Coast, the spring of 1942 brought detention in fifteen assembly centers that "were mostly hastily converted fairgrounds, racetracks, and livestock exhibition halls" (Gesensway and Roseman 43). Many of the living quarters had previously been stables and still held the odors of their former occupants. Although it would seem difficult to celebrate natural beauty and rebirth under such circumstances, many haiku poets in the detention centers seemed reluctant to cast traditional connotations of spring aside. While imprisoned in the Fresno Assembly Center, Reiko Gomyo wrote:

> Vision of loneliness
> I endure
> in the green of spring (in de Cristoforo 193)[5]

The verb *endure* appears in many internment haiku, as internees write of enduring trials such as heat, solitude, and three years' suffering. Gomyo's juxtaposition of endurance against the new growth of spring creates a particularly striking paradox: the tragedy of having simply to endure the season that offers the most promise.

Instead of promise, however, for Japanese Americans, the spring of 1942 offered only the loss of freedom and the loss of loved ones. Families were often separated as Japanese Americans who were perceived to be community leaders, mostly Issei men, were arrested and taken to detention centers. Shiho Okamoto, a Delta Ginsha member for over forty years, was arrested by FBI agents in February 1942. Writing of the experience, he contrasts the horror of his arrest with the promise of a peony bud left behind in his garden:

> Being arrested—
> at home peony bud
> still firm (in de Cristoforo 145)

Okamoto's peony could be read as a *kigo* intended to connote spring, yet it differs from the typical portrayal of flowers in traditional haiku for it appears as a bud, rather than in full bloom. According to the group of Japanese scholars who wrote *Haikai and Haiku*, "Just as a *haiku* expresses the apex of an emotion, so a season word shows a particular thing at its best and most attractive. . . . Flowering trees and plants are conceived as in bloom" (Ichikawa 173–74). In an anthology of Buson's poetry, entitled *Haiku Master Buson* (1978), there are six haiku that contain peonies, and each one is open, displayed in its full glory. Okamoto's peony bud, although clasping the potential for great beauty, seems unable to open in the presence of his unwarranted arrest.

Remembered flowers often appear in internment haiku, echoing the beauty of faraway places as though attempting to erase the desolation of current surroundings. Recalling Shiho Okamoto's arrest, his wife, Kikuha Okamoto, also reflects on their garden:

> Separated year ago today
> Chinese quince
> must be blooming in my garden (in de Cristoforo 145)

While commemorating the flow of seasons beyond the Rohwer Detention Center where she is confined, Kikuha Okamoto does not mention the effects of spring on her immediate environment. As in Gomyo's poem, it seems that spring in the camps is something to be "endured" or perhaps forgotten, as internees imagine a future that might restore their freedom. An anonymous internee, quoted in *Executive Order 9066* (1972) by Maisie and Richard Conrat, claimed that "during the months of confinement, our minds lived in the future" (88). This sentiment is echoed in a haiku written by Neiji Ozawa, from which de Cristoforo derives the title of her anthology:

> From the window of despair
> May sky
> there is always tomorrow (223)

Despite such expressions of faith in the future, the summer of 1942 brought continued imprisonment, rather than freedom, as internees were transferred from the assembly centers to the more permanent relocation centers. The summer was a time of transience and speculation. As Miné Okubo explains in *Citizen 13660* (1946), rumors arose about relocation before any official details were released (109). In a haiku written by Tojo Fujita at the Stockton Assembly Center, even the grass speaks of an unsettled future:

> Small patches
> of untrodden summer grass
> talk of our transfer (in de Cristoforo 115)

Words such as "transfer," "evacuation," "relocation," and "anxious" characterize a syntax of uncertainty that pervades many internment haiku. The poets, echoing Fujita's awareness that further dislocation is imminent, often find parallels in natural cycles to articulate their concern about an obscure future. Upcoming evacuations are reflected by the presence of "early white clouds of fall," conveying change and uncertainty in a haiku by Soichi Kanow (129). Honjyoshi Kunimori, also writing from the Stockton Assembly Center, juxtaposes the threat of evacuation with the scattering of sandalwood flowers (129). The natural environment, which in traditional haiku is generally a source of peace and rejuvenation, is often invoked by internment poets to reflect their feelings of uncertainty and restlessness. Perhaps they sought such images in nature—a distant sky obscured by clouds, or a dispersal of sandalwood flowers—as indications that the uncertainty they faced had parallels in the natural world. Perhaps these parallels provided moments of reassurance, or perhaps they served only as images to convey the poets' frustration at facing evacuations and unsettled futures that lay beyond their understanding or control.

There were ten relocation camps in total, most of which "were located in deserts and swamps, the most desolate, hostile areas of the country" (Gesensway and Roseman 44). Accustomed to the moderate climate of the West Coast, the internees faced extreme weather conditions. Residents of Poston, California, suffered heat prostration, delirium, and unceasing nosebleeds as temperatures soared as high as 125°F. They often slept outside between wet sheets in an effort to survive the heat. In Topaz, Utah, internees faced heat, dust storms, and almost indescribable barrenness; residents looking across the flat terrain could see "apparently forever into the horizon" (Girdner and Loftis 216). The humidity of the swampy lowlands at Jerome and Rohwer, in Arkansas, made the heat of summer and the damp cold of winter feel more extreme. There were no guard towers needed at Jerome because it was surrounded by a swamp full of water moccasins. The high security detention center of Tule Lake was located in desertlike terrain of low and sparse growth, where instead of trees, residents saw only "watchtowers and chimneys" (Girdner and Loftis 218).

Most members of the Delta Ginsha Haiku Kai were interned at the Stockton Assembly Center and later moved to Rohwer. While interned, they actively wrote haiku and continued to hold club meetings. In fact, they celebrated the hundredth meeting of the Delta Ginsha Haiku Kai while at Rohwer. In addition to writing and sharing their poetry, they published two volumes of haiku as a supplement to the *Rohwer Jiho Sha* (the Rohwer camp newspaper), some of which have been translated and included in

de Cristoforo's anthology. In the fall of 1943, when many of the internees at
Rohwer were relocated to the Tule Lake Segregation Center, the poets who
had been transferred organized the Tule Lake Valley Ginsha Haiku Kai and
continued to share their haiku. Most members of the Valley Ginsha Haiku
Kai had initially been interned at the Fresno Assembly Center and were
later relocated to Jerome. Like the Delta Ginsha members, they continued
to meet and read their poetry as members of a haiku club that they renamed
the Denson Valley Haiku Kai.

Although the separation of the two original clubs made it more difficult for members, who had once enjoyed joint meetings, to correspond, de
Cristoforo notes retrospectively that "one beneficial aspect of this scattering
was the variety and power of the haiku the internees wrote. It conveys the
emotional impact of being uprooted, and constitutes a poetry of resistance
to the inhumanity of war" (16). Despite their relocation, members of the
various clubs remained determined to maintain connections with other poets. Their organization and correspondence seems itself a form of resistance
to internment, for they reacted to being "uprooted" by remaining committed or "rooted" to a form of poetry intrinsic to Japanese culture, and to the
haiku clubs themselves, which represented the persistence of friendships
and the fellowship of writers in a time when family members and friends
were continually faced with separation.

Neiji Ozawa, founder of both the Delta Ginsha and Valley Ginsha Haiku
Kai, became ill with tuberculosis following his internment at the Fresno Assembly Center and was moved to the Gila Indian Reservation Sanatorium,
in Arizona, for treatment. Although there were no organized haiku groups
at the Gila Hospital, Ozawa managed to correspond with Delta Ginsha and
Valley Ginsha members in other camps and continued to critique their work
(in de Cristoforo 44). Throughout his hospitalization, Ozawa also continued to write haiku, documenting the storms and sunsets of the surrounding
desert and paying close attention to the changing seasons:

> Even in the desert
> four seasons are seen
> changing into flannel nightshirt (219)

While an initial reading may suggest only Ozawa's surprise when unexpected cold temperatures descend upon the desert, this poem can also be
read as a powerful tribute to the significance of haiku poetry to Ozawa and
other internees. The four seasons, so crucial to a haiku poet's understanding
of the ways in which the natural world illuminates experience, are depicted

by Ozawa as being present "even in the desert." This reference implies that despite the harsh and unfamiliar desert landscape in which Ozawa found himself, the presence of seasons, in conjunction with an art form that honors seasonal change, allowed him to find moments of familiarity and perhaps even solace in the confluence of place and poetry.

The autumn of 1942 was a time of settling into the permanent relocation camps. Arriving at the relocation centers, internees were often dismayed to find the facilities and accommodations as austere and poorly constructed as those they had left behind in the assembly centers. Provided only with army cots for furniture, the internees constructed tables, chairs, shelves, and other items from the camps' scrap lumber piles. The haiku of this first autumn convey the paradoxical experience of adjusting to a new environment while simultaneously longing for home. Despite difficult living conditions, Yajin Nakao writes a somewhat resigned haiku describing his first autumn at Rohwer:

> Getting used to things
> feeling at ease
> trees are turning crimson (in de Cristoforo 141)

While many internees might disagree with the sense of ease that Nakao describes, this poem provides a reminder that each relocation camp became a community and a "home"—for lack of an alternative—to its residents for a period of up to three years. Like Ozawa, Nakao conveys his experience of adjusting to his new surroundings in the context of familiar seasonal change. Although autumn in Arkansas likely differed significantly from his memories of autumn in California, Nakao selects a familiar image—that of trees turning color—to complement his articulation of ease in his new environment. However, while acclimating to his life in Rohwer, Nakao continued to contemplate his home in California:

> Autumn foliage
> California has now become
> a far country (139)

Imbricated with the distancing of Nakao's home in California, the foliage of this poem seems to color, then quickly fade, reflecting the internees' inevitable sense of loss as they witnessed the passing of another season from behind barbed wire.

The arrival of winter increased the sense of isolation in the camps. As temperatures fell below zero, families clustered around whatever sources of heat were available. In Topaz, each family was given a pot-bellied stove and the scrap lumber pile became a coveted source of fuel (Okubo 146, 141). Cold winds blew unceasingly against the poorly insulated barracks and snow came early to many of the camps. While at first a novelty to the former West Coast residents who had rarely seen snow, it soon lost its uniqueness as it claimed the vast expanses of landscape surrounding the camps, making them seem even more hostile, desolate, and featureless. Winter increased feelings of fruitlessness as internees, often confined to their barracks, found their days filled with nothing but the requirements of survival. Of these winter days, Shiho Okamoto wrote:

> Eating and sleeping
> nothing to do
> falling snow disappears into ground (in de Cristoforo 147)

When Okamoto wrote this poem, he related an existence void of productivity. However, although he may have imagined his days as being wasted, like disappearing snowflakes, he has preserved in this haiku both his experience and the apparently ephemeral falling snow. By leaving behind this eloquent reflection, Okamoto has helped future generations to understand the experience of internment, thus ensuring that neither his time nor the snowflakes captured in his haiku were wasted.

While it is evident that many internment haiku draw upon traditional seasonal references, the cycle they portray seems to diverge from the smooth seasonal flow characterized by earlier haiku. In many of the internment poems, the seasonal cycle is distinguished by a focus on memories of past years or uncertainty about the future, as though the poets are reluctant to locate themselves in the present. Other internment haiku seem locked in an oppressive present, such as Okamoto's poem, describing eventless days that obliterate one's faith in time as a force of change. Undoubtedly the cycle of seasons, as it was experienced in the internment camps, must have appeared to offer little hope. Spending as long as three years in the detention centers, internees may have watched spring offer its promise of new life again and again, only to be denied by another summer, autumn, and winter of continued confinement. As the years passed, even spring flowers struggled to bloom. In Tule Lake, Kazue Matsuda, who later became Violet Kazue de Cristoforo, wrote:

> Afternoon sun shining
> this year's moss-rose
> reverted to single petal (in de Cristoforo 233)

In a note accompanying this haiku, she explains "Moss-rose reverts to single petal after a time, thus showing years spent in camp" (233).

In the spring of 1942, de Cristoforo and her family were interned in the Fresno Assembly Center, from which they were subsequently transferred to the Jerome Detention Center in Arkansas, and later, in the fall of 1943, to the Tule Lake Segregation Center in Northern California. While at Tule Lake, de Cristoforo suffered the death of her mother-in-law, and she was separated from her father-in-law, her husband, and her brother, who were sent to Japan. In March 1946, she and her children were expatriated from the United States. She arrived in Hiroshima to find that her parents had been killed in the atomic bombing, their home had been destroyed, and her husband had remarried. Faced with such upheaval and devastation, it is not surprising that she conveys the seasons not with a sense of renewal but rather as a reflection of the physical and psychological ravages of internment.

Although many of the internment haiku contain *kigo* or seasonal references, there are others that do not refer to any season but instead portray the dark, seasonless infinity that internment became for some. These haiku often seem the most desolate, as though even time has abandoned the internees:

> We are silent
> above the window
> empty sky (in de Cristoforo 243)

Written by Hekisamei Matsuda at Tule Lake, this haiku implies an almost complete void. There is no sound, nothing to see beyond the window, and without a seasonal reference, there seems to be no prospect of advancing time.

References to movement and life in internment haiku often exist only beyond the barbed wire fences that surrounded the camps. As with much of the artwork created in the camps, many haiku are bifurcated by the undeniable presence of a fence between the internees and the outside world. Internees would gaze past this fence to witness the beauty of a sunset reflected on a distant mountain, the movement of cars on a nearby highway, or the migration of a flock of geese to farther skies. From Tule Lake, Hakuro Wada wrote:

> Even the croaking of frogs
> comes from outside the barbed wire fence
> this is our life (in de Cristoforo 273)

In classical haiku, the croaking of frogs was usually a reference to spring. By locating this sound outside the fence, Wada implies that the opportunity for renewal lies beyond the internment camp.

The barbed wire fence, confining the internees within a narrow, often hostile space, is also a reflection of the new vocabulary that distinguishes haiku of the internment camps from those written elsewhere. Prevalent in these poems are words such as "war," "barracks," "gate," "mess hall," "guard tower," "sentry," and "segregation." Incorporating the vocabulary of internment, these haiku relate a poignant history of the experience of being imprisoned. Although not as chronologically straightforward or detailed as a narrative history, they convey aspects of daily existence in a form that exemplifies the personal and emotional elements of internment.

The unique sense of movement conveyed by these poems further illustrates the daily realities of the internment experience. With words such as "temporary quarters," "transfer," and "relocation," the poets create a sense of constant expectancy, which lends an unsettled sensation to many of their haiku. The reader of these haiku shares this feeling of uncertainty, as though always waiting to see whether tomorrow will bring continued confinement or an end to the injustice of internment. This paradoxical combination of apprehension and suspended action is further emphasized by the presence of a train in many internment haiku. Other than reminiscences of home or dreams for the future, the train is among the few references in these poems to a world beyond the camps. As most of the internees were moved from the assembly centers to the relocation camps by train, the sound of the train reminds them of the places they came from and of a country that continues to function while they remain confined. The train serves both as a link to the internees' former lives and as a reminder of the distances they have traveled from places they once knew. From Rohwer, Senbinshi Takaoka writes:

> Frosty night
> listening to rumbling train
> we have come a long way (in de Cristoforo 167)

This distance can be read, of course, either literally or metaphorically, negatively or optimistically, as an acknowledgement of the distance that separates the internees from their homes or a tribute to the hardships and challenges they have overcome in seeking to adjust to and inhabit their new environments.

The camps themselves are sometimes named in the poems and, as de Cristoforo notes, the internees created words for the camps using Japanese characters (18). Naming is also significant in internment haiku in terms of the names used to describe aspects of the environments in which the camps were located. Having been moved to unfamiliar surroundings, the poets often lacked the vocabulary to name natural entities such as flowers and plants that they included in their poems. While interned in Rohwer, Kikuha Okamoto wrote:

> In my palm—flower seeds
> you gave me
> with their local names (in de Cristoforo 145)

Do these flower seeds remain unnamed because Okamoto has forgotten the names or because she has no translation for them in Japanese? A haiku by Hekisamei Matsuda, written at Tule Lake, implies a similar lexical uncertainty:

> Spilled seeds
> sprouting tiny leaves
> of unknown flowers (243)

While classical haiku poets tend to be very specific in terms of naming plants, flowers, and other aspects of the natural world, the internment poets faced the challenge of not knowing the names or having no equivalents in Japanese for natural features of their new surroundings.

Despite the difficulties of identifying elements of their unfamiliar surroundings, these poets continued to regard the natural world as a source of meditation and refuge, as had countless generations of haiku poets before them. In the introduction to the second of two volumes of haiku published by the *Rohwa Jiho Sha*, Kyotaro Komuro wrote: "In order for us to transcend our condition we must immerse ourselves in nature, and be grateful to find happiness in the life of haiku poetry" (qtd. in de Cristoforo 89). While the internment poets' immersion in nature and haiku may have allowed them briefly to "transcend" the hardship and tedium of years spent imprisoned, it also encouraged them to engage deeply with their emotional responses to exile and imprisonment and thereby to create a unique and poignant record of the internment years.

The significance of nature in this response makes internment haiku particularly appropriate for ecocritical consideration. The study of these haiku intersects with many current areas of interest in ecocriticism and also suggests new possibilities for ecocritical study. Much recent ecocritical writing has focused on the role of the natural world in allowing us to regard a place we live in as "home." The internment haiku provide a unique counterbalance to this work, as they help to illuminate the role of the natural world in a place not home, but exile, and the ways in which immersion in the natural world can help one to express a reaction to being unjustly taken from one's home. As ecocritics consider this articulation of exile, we are simultaneously encouraged to explore the confluence of literature, history, and nature, theorizing the significance of the natural environment in the creation of literary accounts of history.

Reading the haiku of the internment period, it is difficult to determine whether the poets wrote out of a desire for solace or escape, an effort to remember home or come to terms with exile, or an attempt to record their experience of profound historical injustice. Although any or all of these incentives may have contributed to the writing of internment haiku, I believe that these poems were written primarily for the solace and fulfillment that they offered the individual poet at the time of conception. The poets may have shared them with friends or read them aloud at haiku club meetings, but it seems unlikely that they would have imagined the future publication of these haiku in *May Sky* or that they would have considered the possibility that their poetry would find readers generations away. Such a thought would have seemed improbable to the Japanese Americans who had witnessed the suppression of their culture as a result of war. While there was likely no conscious effort on the part of the internment haiku poets to join the ranks of American nature writers, they deserve to be included in this increasingly diverse and varied group. Faced with harsh and unfamiliar environments, these poets turned to what they knew: to an art form endemic to their culture and to the inevitable seasonal progression that allowed occasional glimpses of the familiar. They turned to nature—both to remember their home places and to begin to know the places in which they found themselves. While interned in the Tule Lake Segregation Center, Shonan Suzuki wrote:

> Moon shadows on internment camp
> I hear the cries of geese
> again this year (in de Cristoforo 261)

These geese, reminiscent of those that visit the pages of Aldo Leopold or Terry Tempest Williams, are part of the spirit of place. Yet for Suzuki, their calls seem bittersweet. Echoing memories of the previous year, these calls are part of the natural cycle of seasons that allows a place to become familiar, but they are also a confirmation of another year spent behind barbed wire.

Suzuki's poem implies imprisonment, as the barracks, guard towers, and fences cast their shadows in the moonlight, but it also alludes to freedom, as the cycle of the seasons continues, and the geese fly unimpeded across the sky.

Haiku have been described as a convenient art form for the internment period because they take little paper and can contain in a few words an insight or emotion that might occupy pages if written in prose. Their conciseness emphasizes the value of each word. As Bashō once told one of his disciples, when a verse has only seventeen syllables, "not a single word should be carelessly used" (qtd. in Yasuda 32). The haiku form also reflects the internment experience itself. Its constrained length resembles the enclosures within which the internment poets were confined. And true to the extent of emotion that can be conveyed using the haiku form, the internment haiku seem to expand outward to encompass the internees' ordeals within the camps and their memories and dreams beyond the barbed wire limits. While haiku reveal the depth of wisdom and emotion that can emerge in only a few words, the internees revealed the depth of endurance, patience, and hope that could emerge from within a small, fenced enclosure. The internment haiku deserve wide readership and recognition: for their aesthetic and emotional value, for their momentary yet vast glimpses of the natural world, and for their illumination of the internment experience and its effects on a group of nature poets as they sought to come to terms with an unexpected land.

NOTES

1. In this essay, I use the term *Japanese Americans* to refer to U.S. citizens of Japanese ancestry and Issei.

2. The *kigo* often seems to elude translation, and although the words themselves may translate into other languages, the cultural associations that accompany these words are largely untranslatable. For a selected list of *kigo* traditionally associated with each season, see *Haikai and Haiku*, 176–79.

3. As Yasuda notes, "The very use of the words *imply*, *suggest*, and *associate* [or in this case, *characterize*] raises an interesting question, which can illuminate the difference between the Japanese grasp of the seasonal sense and a Western one." In Japan, "the sense of season is so implicated in natural objects" that the *kigo* or seasonal references *are* the seasons they represent (46). Thus, according to the Japanese understanding of seasons, rain, birdsong, and blossoms *are* spring, rather than simply characterizing it.

4. As I do not read Japanese, I have relied on English translations of haiku while researching and writing this essay. Many translators preface haiku collections with

an admission of the inadequacy of translation in this genre. Inevitably, the reader of a translation experiences the poem through the window of the translator's interpretation. Due to the brevity of haiku and the diversity of interpretation a single poem can evoke, various translations of a single haiku often differ significantly. For those familiar with Japanese, many anthologies of translated haiku provide the original version in Japanese characters for each poem. Many also provide a version in romanji (the romanized form of Japanese) so that readers can construe the sound of the original haiku.

5. Most of the haiku written by the Delta Ginsha and Valley Ginsha poets were composed in the kaiko style, which relaxed the syllabic restrictions of classical haiku but continued to focus on "observation of nature . . . and elegant usage of words correlated with the season" (de Cristoforo 23). The haiku anthologized in *May Sky* were originally written in Japanese and translated into English by de Cristoforo. For each haiku, she provides the original Japanese characters, the romanji, and an English translation.

WORKS CITED

Bashō, Matsuo. *Narrow Road to the Interior and Other Writings*. Trans. Sam Hamill. Boston, Mass.: Shambhala, 2000.

Conrat, Maisie, and Richard Conrat. *Executive Order 9066: The Internment of 110,000 Japanese Americans*. Los Angeles: California Historical Society, 1972.

de Cristoforo, Violet Kazue, ed. and trans. *May Sky: There Is Always Tomorrow, an Anthology of Japanese American Concentration Camp Kaiko Haiku*. Los Angeles, Calif.: Sun and Moon Press, 1997.

Gesensway, Deborah, and Mindy Roseman. *Beyond Words: Images from America's Concentration Camps*. Ithaca, N.Y.: Cornell University Press, 1988.

Girdner, Audrie, and Anne Loftis. *The Great Betrayal: The Evacuation of the Japanese-Americans during World War II*. London: Macmillan, 1969.

Hamill, Sam, trans. *The Sound of Water: Haiku by Basho, Buson, Issa, and Other Poets*. Boston, Mass.: Shambhala, 1995.

Hass, Robert, ed. and trans. *The Essential Haiku: Versions of Basho, Buson, and Issa*. Hopewell, N.J.: Ecco Press, 1994.

Ichikawa, Sanki, ed. *Haikai and Haiku*. Tokyo: Nippon Gakujutsu Shinkōkai, 1958.

Issa, Kobayashi. *The Spring of My Life: And Selected Haiku*. Trans. Sam Hamill. Boston, Mass.: Shambhala, 1997.

Miura, Yuzuru, ed. and trans. *Classic Haiku: A Master's Selection*. Boston, Mass.: Tuttle, 1991.

Okubo, Miné. *Citizen 13660*. 1946. Reprint Seattle: University of Washington Press, 2001.

Sawa, Yuki, and Edith Marcombe Shiffert, eds. and trans. *Haiku Master Buson: Translations from the Writings of Yosa Buson—Poet and Artist—with Related Materials*. San Francisco, Calif.: Heian International Publishing Company, 1978.

Shiffert, Edith Marcombe. Introduction. *Haiku Master Buson: Translations from the Writings of Yosa Buson—Poet and Artist—with Related Materials*. San Francisco, Calif.: Heian International Publishing Company, 1978. 4–23.

Yasuda, Kenneth. *The Japanese Haiku: Its Essential Nature, History, and Possibilities in English, with Selected Examples*. Rutland, Vt.: Tuttle, 1957.

ROBERT T. HAYASHI

Beyond Walden Pond

Asian American Literature and the Limits of Ecocriticism

IN THE LATE Kashmiri poet Agha Shahid Ali's long poem "In Search of Evanescence" he writes: "India always exists / off the turnpikes / of America" (41). The poem is a multilayered personal narrative that recounts the author's travels in America and the twisted strands of memory and personal loss that are both a part of the American landscape and shaped by it. In fact, the entire collection of which "In Search of Evanescence" is a part, *A Nostalgist's Map of America*, recounts the author's journeys across America as he retranscribes the history of its places through the lens of his Indian past and his newer American cultural identity. One of the poem's unique qualities is Ali's use of the oeuvre of Emily Dickinson as a kind of touchstone. He incorporates, alludes to, and reshapes lines of her poems in a fashion similar to a DJ sampling his favorite classic cuts in a remix. Although this work offers much to our understanding of American places and the literary canon's presentation of them, I doubt that many ecocritical scholars or, more important, teachers of literature and the environment would consider Ali's brilliant work for inclusion in their scholarship or syllabus.

The absence of Asian American authors from the field of ecocriticism is part of the field's more general inability to address seriously issues of race and class, as has been pointed out by other scholars.[1] Despite the fresh perspective ecocritical inquiry has offered, its reliance on canonical authors—Willa Cather, John Muir, Aldo Leopold, Annie Dillard, and of course Henry David Thoreau—continues to limit its discoveries and its relevance. Moreover, the field's historical dependence upon "nature" as the de facto definition of environment has further limited the incorporation of other voices. This tendency is part of a larger failure to investigate the experiences of racial and ethnic minorities in relation to America's environmental history, as noted, for instance, by Carolyn Merchant in her recent presidential address to the American Society for Environmental History.

Merchant notes: "We especially need more research on the roles of African Americans in the southern and western U.S. environment and in early urbanization and more research on Asian and Hispanic perceptions of nature" (381). In fact, whether in the arena of public policy or intellectual inquiry, most conversations about the environment have failed to consider the experiences of the working class and nonwhites. As Edwardo Lao Rhodes notes in *Environmental Justice in America*, "Just as people of color until recently have not had a major presence in any part of the environmental movement, explicit reference to race, ethnicity, class, or to issues concerning the poor simply has not appeared in modern natural resources and environmental agendas" (31).

The environmental justice movement does represent a paradigmatic shift, a more expansive vision of environmental issues and relevant constituencies and one wedded to issues of social justice. It has helped uncover the unequal distribution of environmental dangers and benefits, especially as it relates to public health. However, environmental justice is most oriented toward the mediation of current environmental risks and injustices and to the prevention of future ones. This orientation can reinforce an ahistorical perspective by looking at race and environment from a limited framework that maintains primary focus on recent environmental degradation and on protection from environmental hazards. As Julie Sze notes in a recent essay, "The current singular emphasis on public policy and on remediation of environmental harms necessarily narrows environmental justice as an analytic frame because it truncates theory and action/practice" (166).

For example, how can one discuss current groundwater pollution in an all-black rural community in Tennessee without first exploring the process by which slavery and Jim Crow laws arranged the economic and political system that supported American apartheid and organized a landscape segregated along borders of class and race? Or without exploring how the larger society's views of the environment "naturalized" this process? And what of the community's views of its environs, natural and man-made, if one can distinguish the two? How do they correspond with or conflict with the views of the dominant society? What are the relevant environmental issues as these individuals see them? These communities warrant attention, but too often policy shapers and scholars have viewed their experiences from frames of reference that prevented these groups from articulating their concerns and perspectives, including how they define the term "environment." This hypothetical example illustrates the need to consider both a reorientation of the field and a wider range of texts within ecocritical inquiry, including nonliterary ones, to explore fully present-day issues and the historical connection between race and environment in America.

In his essay "Toward an Environmental Justice Ecocriticism," T. V. Reed argues for such self-examination within the field of ecocriticism. Reed argues not only for the study of "other than white traditions in nonfiction nature writing" but also of "the cultural assumptions in various environmental rhetorics," including science. Reed's call for a critical self-exploration of rhetorics and epistemology within environmental studies is especially apropos. He notes that he envisions ecocriticism incorporating theoretical perspectives from other fields, such as critical race theory, political ecology, postcolonial theory, and cultural studies. Sze advocates that the environmental justice movement further broaden its perspective by including approaches from literary studies. Yet I am wary if the toggling of multiethnic literature to environmental justice remains its only major point of entry in ecocriticism. I argue that an even more expansive list of disciplinary approaches be a part of this project and that the dominant Weltanschauung of ecocritical inquiry can continue to limit what Reed and others envision. Ecocritical inquiry still remains rooted in American environmentalism and constrained by limitations that stifle its evolution. Having evolved from the dialectic between the conservation and preservation of natural resources, American environmentalism is steeped in an ethos that values untainted nature above all else, including people, especially those whose lives seem most in conflict with its protection. As Edwardo Lao Rhodes opines:

> A major reason for the modern agenda's neglect can be traced back to the foundation philosophy and early beginnings of the modern environmental movement. . . . Many of the questioned behavior and policies encountered in environmental organizations have less to do with some deliberate racism or social elitism in the movement and more to do with these organizations having evolved from an ethos that was indifferent to the needs of the poor and minorities. (1–2)

Just as the environmental movement's reliance upon wilderness to save natural spaces limits its effectiveness, denying alternative definitions of wilderness, the traditional activist orientation of the environmental justice movement to policy issues of ecological protection and public health limits its reach. As Sze notes, "the environmental justice literature generally does not substantively address the historical constructions and cultural discourses of mainstream environmentalism's representations of 'nature' " (166). Both

Merchant's and Reed's calls to include nonwhite views of nature to expand our understanding of the environment are symptomatic of this historical assumption that nature is equivalent to environment. Activists and scholars can more accurately define the environment and its relevant public issues by considering how ethnic/racial minorities have defined, experienced, apprehended, and represented it. This means considering a wider range of texts, disciplinary approaches, and epistemological assumptions.

In general, the inclusion of multiethnic literature and the traditionally interdisciplinary methodology of its study can move ecocritical inquiry into more salient discussions of current environmental issues by exploring the historical link between the social and natural realms. Some scholars have explored the nexus between ecocriticism and postcolonial theory, a perspective that considers the social and political realms that works reflect. Yet ecocriticism's common focus on natural environments can still limit these innovative explorations.[2] Even writers and teachers influenced by the environmental justice movement and its attendant scholarship commonly neglect to consider the role of Asians in American places because of the movement's emphasis on issues of access to environmental benefits and exposure to health threats. Although Asian Americans are by no means free of such problems, their literature less directly addresses obvious examples of environmental racism or inequity, and so these texts may be easily overlooked by the ecocritic. One author who has been discussed in this light is Karen Tei Yamashita, but it is precisely because her work does explicitly address issues such as rainforest degradation and corporate power that Yamashita is relevant to ecocritical inquiry.[3]

With their common themes of immigration and acculturation, many Asian American literary works may seem unfit for ecocritical inquiry. Yet even works that stress such typical themes have much to say about how Asian Americans have experienced, described, and shaped their environments. The environmental issues that most attract ecocritical inquiry, however, are often only part of a larger constellation of long-term social justice issues found in minority communities and the literatures they produce.[4] The failure of white environmentalists to acknowledge these concerns is one reason why environmental groups have long had trouble recruiting significant minority support. The larger incorporation of Asian American literature and history into the general study of the environment addresses some of the limitations outlined and offers new possibilities for a field that, like Asian American studies, has grown out of a political perspective that now seems a tenuous and limited means by which to define it.[5] What can

Asian American literature reveal to the student and scholar of American places? I outline a few possibilities by discussing a brief sampling of works.

The Canon and Layers of Place

In his famous essay "Solitude," a *de rigueur* starting point for many environmental literature classes, Henry David Thoreau asserted the universal value of self-reflection that one alone in nature enjoys. He posited that the liberating effects of solitude in nature were such that his home at Walden was "as much Asia or Africa as New England" (130). Reading the works of Asian American authors, such as Agha Shahid Ali, illustrates how only one who is not from Asia or Africa could claim that this small New England pond could be as much a part of India or Japan as Massachusetts. Asian American literature spins the telescope around by forcing readers to experience American places from a perspective that often contradicts the cultural values traditionally defining them, such as solitude, transcendence, or preservation. It forces a critical self-examination of the literature and scholarship that has defined what the land has meant to us. The American landscape, as in Ali's poetry, becomes a multifaceted and multilayered place, one more faithful to historical reality and the range of traditions that have shaped the environment. As he writes in his poem "Leaving Sonora,"

> Certain landscapes insist on fidelity.
> Why else would a poet of this desert
> go deep inside himself for shade?
> Only there do the perished tribes live.
> The desert insists, always: Be faithful,
> even to those who no longer exist. (Ali 29)

In this poem, Ali resurrects the past lives of ancient Indian peoples as he simultaneously observes the lights of present-day Tucson, while "go[ing] deep inside himself." A Kashmiri immigrant's self-exploration connects him not only to home but also to the landscape of the American Southwest and to the Hohokam, who precede him.[6] It is a marked contrast to the dominant tradition of American nature writing, which often assumes a historical perspective and promotes personal growth via encounters with "untouched" nature. Ali's view reminds us of the range of cultural traditions that continue to shape the environment. As philosopher Edward Casey notes:

> Places gather things in their midst—where "things" connote various animate and inanimate entities. Places also gather experiences and histories, even language and thoughts. Think only of what it means to go back to a place you know, finding it full of memories and expectations, old things and new things, the familiar and the strange, and much more besides. (24)

Reading Asian American literature is a means to revisit known places but in such a fashion that the familiar path may become strange, something new.

The few investigations of environment, or of place, within Asian American literary criticism discuss place more as a process than as a locale. This is most often characterized as the experience of displacement of Asians in America: the struggle to establish, find, and maintain literal as well as cultural and social roots in America, while retaining those of somewhere else. In "South Asian American Writers: Geography and Memory," Ketu Katrak notes, "the migratory nature of many of these voices opens up new areas of imaginative exploration—returning home through the imagination, recreating home in narrative, creating a simultaneous present, of being here and there" (125). Katrak discusses how Ali's work is characterized by this collapsing of discrete units of time, place, and history that stands in opposition to the common American perspective of valuing specific places defined as outside of human influence. She rightfully cautions that her claims relate to the cultural production of a specific class of individuals only—expatriate academics—who naturally define their new homelands in a fashion not applicable to all who classify as South Asian; or, I would add, to all in the even broader classification of Asian American. Nevertheless, Ali's contemporary work does suggest a sometimes radical arc within Asian American literature, not only offering new perspectives on the relationship of the self to the environment but also expanding critical understanding of the more traditional American literary canon's evolution.

Race and Class and Asian American Places

Twenty years after Thoreau's famous stay at Walden, a group of seventy-five Chinese laborers passed through his transcendent New England landscape on their way to work in a strike-ridden shoe factory in North Adams, Massachusetts. Had they stopped at Walden Pond, how would these Chinese laborers have portrayed Thoreau's refuge? Would it have reminded them of Guadong province? Would Walden have been seen as a part of

China, the way that Ohio was a part of Ali's India? Would they have quoted Confucius, as Thoreau did in "Solitude"? Would it be a place of sanctuary for them, or of fear?

The geographic mobility of these California workers appears to belie the generally restricted nature of life for Chinese immigrants in America during the nineteenth century and that of later Asian immigrants. As historian Patricia Nelson Limerick notes, Asian Americans have experienced "a landscape of restriction—in prohibitions on alien land ownership, in housing segregation, and in episodes of harassment when they crossed certain boundaries of space and behavior" (1035). These men crossed the continent, however, because of their value as cheap labor, as replacement workers for the white strikers, and they were met at the train station by a jeering mob who hurled stones at them. They required police protection while in the commonwealth. Asian Americans' letters, poems, and fiction recount this denial of the American landscape's expansive promise of individual freedom and wealth and call into question ecocriticism's continued reliance on common ideas of who an American is and what American places mean. The experience of Gold Mountain is one separate from that of the Frontier, the Garden, or the Sublime. The earliest roots of Asian American literary production are evocative reminders of this alternative vision that remains obscured by following traditional lines of inquiry.

After 1910, Chinese immigrants arriving in the port of San Francisco were detained at the Angel Island Immigration Station. At Angel Island they were examined and questioned by immigration officials, and at times this process took several weeks or even months to complete. In the meantime, the immigrants remained housed in crude barracks on the island, where many of them recorded their feelings in short poems that they scrawled on the barracks walls. For many of the Chinese, their experiences had disillusioned them, despite early optimism that America would offer them the kind of monetary and social rewards the image of Gold Mountain promised.

> Instead of remaining a citizen in China, I willingly became an Ox
> I intended to come to America to earn a living.
> The Western styled buildings are lofty; but I have not had the luck to live in
>   them.
> How was anyone to know that my dwelling place would be a prison? (Hom 40)

Although mostly absent from discussions of the American environment—its history and cultural valence—Asian Americans and immigrants of other races were often the very engine of environmental change, the oxen this anonymous poet described. They were the land's miners, railroad workers, farm hands, and fishermen: its workers. In his essay "Are You an Environmentalist or Do You Work for a Living? Work and Nature," the prominent environmental historian Richard White critiques the tendency of Americans to separate labor, and laborers, from their views of nature and to valorize a pure nature reserved for recreation or personal discovery— wilderness. This privileging of wilderness not only hides the nearly ubiquitous connection between human labor and the natural environment; it also silences the views of those who most impact the environment through their work. This is especially the case for urban dwellers, whose experiences and views of nature are only now finding a voice, as entities like the environmental justice movement call attention to the current state of urban spaces.

IT IS TRUE that some canonical American nature writers have celebrated labor. Thoreau farmed and wrote about the land near Walden, and another equally canonical nature writer, Wendell Berry, has written about farming and its influence on his thinking and writing. However, neither man relied on agriculture, especially from the bottom rung on its wage scale, for his livelihood. Like Aldo Leopold, they practiced agriculture as an avocation, and as White observes, their views generally propose some form of "good" agricultural practice that is a counter to the destructive modernist practices of today's farming. The reliance on this binary of good and bad land use practices causes scholars to overlook the issues of power and choice that have played out on the American landscape. In her seminal work on Asian American views of the American West, Patricia Limerick questions what the historical perspective on Asian participation in the development of the railroad system should be: "How do we appraise the Chinese 'contribution' to that disruption?" she asks (1032–33). Reading the works of Asian American authors is a critical step to answering this question, for it reminds us that unlike other shapers of the American landscape, these individuals often had little say in what their "contribution" would be.

In her critically acclaimed and popular work *China Men*, Maxine Hong Kingston recounts the history of Chinese men in America through a unique collection of myths, personal narrative, and historical documentation. In the section "The Grandfather of the Sierra Nevada Mountains," she recounts the story of Ah Goong, a Chinese immigrant who works on the Union Pacific Railroad. In the late 1880s, the railroad industry provided one of the few work opportunities open to Chinese immigrants, who received far less pay than white workers and who endured inhospitable, often dangerous work conditions.

Living in isolated all-male railroad camps far from home, Ah Goong finds solace in nature but suffers its challenges as well. He recognizes two stars that represent ill-fated lovers from Chinese lore, and also the familiar magpie, and they operate as symbols of his longing for home as he toils in a harsh and alien landscape. Kingston reinforces the connection between the American social world and the Chinese men's relations to its natural one in her chapter "The Laws," immediately following "The Grandfather of the Sierra Nevada Mountains." She chronologically lists a detailed series of discriminatory acts by local, state, and federal legislatures and courts that affected Chinese people in the United States. Their experiences with the American environment, as Kingston's text infers, were shaped by American institutions and by definitions of race that controlled social and economic mobility. Like other Chinese immigrants, Ah Goong was subject to anti-miscegenation and immigration laws that denied him the possibility of citizenship and marriage. When he is lowered down cliffsides to place dynamite into the granite face as part of the work involved with blasting a path into the mountains, Ah Goong masturbates, "fucking the world," in an act symbolic of his sexual and political irrelevance (133). In the same mountains where John Muir scrambled over dangerous passes testing his manhood, Ah Goong could only realize the loss of his. As Rachel Lee notes, Kingston's text provides a provocative nexus between "the American tradition of frontier expansion construed as sexual aggression" and the contrasting "tradition of Asian American writing focused upon male impotence" (151).[7]

Kingston's character, unlike Muir's narrated self, is also a communal voice. Although the narrator describes Ah Goong as her great grandfather, the narration of his personal history after his railroad years becomes a brief chronology of a generalized Chinese American history, written in the mythic tone typical of Kingston:

> Ah Goong would have liked to have a leisurely walk along the tracks to review his finished handiwork, or to walk east to see the rest of his new country. But, instead he was Driven Out, he slid down mountains, leapt across valleys and streams, crossed plains, hid sometimes with companions and often alone, and eluded bandits who would hold him up for his railroad pay and shoot him for practice like they shot Injuns and jackrabbits. . . . Good at

hiding, disappearing—decades unaccounted for—he was not working in a mine when forty thousand Chinamen were Driven Out of mining. He was not killed or kidnapped in the Los Angeles Massacre, though he gave money toward ransoming those whose toes and fingers, a digit per week, and ears grotesquely rotting or pickled, and scalped queues were displayed in China-towns. (146–48)

Ah Goong's story illustrates the racial segregation of the American city, workplace, and wilderness and the physical violence used by whites to maintain it. Reinserting these "China Men" back into the historical record allows them then to reclaim the land, but one antithetical to its traditional image; and the book fittingly opens with a Chinese explorer, Tang Ao, discovering America, referred to here, however, as "the Land of Women" (3–5).[8]

Kingston's work focuses on the unique experiences of Chinese men in America, but it also reveals the broader subject position of Asians on Ameri-can soil. *China Men*'s narrator begins her story in Stockton, California, where her family lives among other Asians: Filipinos and Japanese. She notes of the Japanese section of town, "Then we passed the Japanese's closed up house, nobody home for years" (12). What the girl's observation reveals, of course, is that these residents of Stockton were among the thousands of Japanese Americans relocated during World War II, forced to leave behind homes and businesses and live in concentration camps in isolated rural re-gions of the United States. Later, Kingston's narrator reveals her distrust of her Japanese American neighbors, using the same kind of reverse logic that characterized the anti-Japanese rhetoric of the time:

> They gave us their used comic books, and were the only adults who gave us toys instead of clothes for Christmas. We kids, who had peasant minds, sus-pected their generosity; they were bribing us not to lynch them. The friendlier they were, the more hideous the crimes and desires they must have been cov-ering up. (273–74)

What is significant about this passage is the narrator's expression of a panethnic consciousness, the awareness that Chinese and Japanese are all suspect in the eyes of Americans and share equally tenuous ground. She continues, "My parents gave them vegetables; we would want them to be nice to us when the time came for us Chinese to be the ones in camp" (274).

Asians, and other minorities, were denied the perquisites of American identity because of their inherent unfitness for inclusion, their "natural" inferiority and foreignness that would allegedly contaminate its purity. Legal codes, political speeches, newspaper editorials, and even the works of canonical American nature writers have represented this perspective of Asians, and other minorities, as unwanted foreign pests, as weeds. In this sense, the doctrine of America as pure wilderness was a means to exclude them. Though constituting a diverse range of ethnic and cultural identities in the United States, Asian immigrants shared a socially constructed identity as "mongolians" or "orientals," which equated with limited social status including, until 1952, the inability to become "naturalized" citizens. Ironically, after two centuries of European-introduced diseases had swept across the Americas and decimated native peoples, Americans viewed Asian immigrants as threats to the land's well-being. In the late 1800s, for instance, Japanese and Chinese immigrants were driven out of several Idaho towns in response to a feared outbreak of cholera. A local newspaper article of the time expressed the fear: "The feeling in this town and vicinity is deep and people are determined to protect their wives and little ones from the dreaded scourge" (*Idaho Daily Statesman*). Anti-miscegenation laws relied on the rationale that the inclusion of Asian blood in the American stock would warp and pollute it, and metaphors of nature and allegedly scientific reasoning justified this exclusion. A more recent example of this bias is the anti-immigrant stance publicly taken by Edward Abbey, who, along with some members of the Sierra Club, bemoaned the environmental impact of illegal Mexican migration along the United States–Mexico border.

The inclusion of Asian American and other nonwhite perspectives provides a necessary critique of the historical class and racial positioning of canonical writers and the traditionally narrow concerns of American environmentalism they have espoused. Considering their writings leads to a questioning of ecocriticism's investment in equating the environment with nature and opens new avenues to explore the connection between the social world and the natural world in both abstract and material terms. The words of Asian Americans are tangible reminders that any environmental issue is best understood within such a framework and is necessary to build viable cross-racial coalitions that advocate social justice in all environs. The American environmental movement has been plagued by a lack of minority participation, due in part to the limited perspective of its predominantly white leadership, which fails to consider alternative definitions of what an "environmental" issue is. A disturbing implication of deep ecology, for instance, is its failure to address directly the troubling legacies of capitalism and racism that afflict undeveloped nations like Mexico as well as American urban spaces.[9]

The perspective of Kingston's narrator provides such an opportunity to reconsider representations of American environments, the events surrounding them that complicate their meaning, and the influence of historical consciousness upon how we understand them. The railroads that define the landscape of Stockton connect her not to the mythic story of American nation-building, or the more contemporary regret for its environmental impact, but to a family and group history marked by class struggle and racial inequality that were also part of America's geographic expansion. As she considers her ancestor's legacy, she notes, "Grandfather left a railroad for a message: We had to go somewhere difficult. Ride a train. Go somewhere important. In case of danger, the train was ready for us" (126).

Place and Tradition

Kingston's story of Ah Goong provides an additional critique of the traditional view of regions such as the Sierra Nevadas as sublime or pristine—as part of what Wallace Stegner termed "our geography of hope" (447). The increased incorporation of Native American authors into ecocriticism is, in part, an acknowledgment of this general oversight and relates to T. V. Reed's call to look beyond dominant cultural tropes. However, as Reed points out, this inclusion often takes the form of a simplistic valorization of "wise" Indian land use—as if Indians neither played any part in actually shaping the land before Europeans nor have any relevance as individuals today. As discussed earlier, environmental studies ignores or even bemoans the role of Asian laborers, like Ah Goong and the Chinese shoe factory workers. But as he works for three costly years tunneling into a mountain, a perspective on the environment is revealed to Ah Goong that is reminiscent of the way Aldo Leopold comes to appreciate the natural world in his famous piece "Thinking Like a Mountain," considering the detached and long-range perspective of a mountain. Kingston writes: "Ah Goong understood the immovability of the earth. Men change, men die, weather changes, but a mountain is the same as permanence and time . . . 'I felt time,' he said. 'I saw time. I saw world.'" (135). What differentiates Ah Goong's insight from Leopold's, however, is that it is a recognition of the human toll of American labor history, not just an acknowledgment of its natural history. The land is full of stories, full of ghosts—not a once virginal place outside of culture. The Sierras made famous by the manly prose of John Muir and the beautiful photographs of Ansel Adams, which helped inspire the American preservation movement, remind Ah Goong instead of childhood scenes of hell that he saw at a Taoist monastery. Their significance to him is the result of a mixture of painful memory, embodied experience, and a cultural heritage that binds California to China.

Kingston's reference to Taoism in this section points to another benefit of placing Asian American experience within the general discussion of American responses to the environment. It points to the prominent role religious perspective has played in the lives of many Americans, despite the often irreligious or nontraditional religious views of canonical nature writers. How Buddhism, Hinduism, or Confucianism has impacted Americans' relation to their environment is found in the work of ecocritical scholars, but mainly in relation to works by authors such as Gary Snyder or Thoreau, who quotes Confucius in "Solitude." How the specific cultural and religious contexts of Asian immigrants and their descendants have impacted their views of the American environment and their interaction, shaping, and expressions of it remains unexplored.

This is not to propose that all Asian American responses to the environment have been influenced primarily by these belief systems. It is important to note that some Asian immigrants were also Christians, even before coming to the United States, and have seen the handiwork of Christ in the American landscape. The qualities that have most characterized American identity have been shared by Asians but, like the landscape itself, often refashioned into something different, something Asian *and* American. How Asian and American cultural strands have influenced one another is another line of inquiry worth greater attention from ecocritics. A fine example of a work that illustrates this interrelation is David Mas Masumoto's memoir *Epitaph for a Peach*, a chronicle of one season on Masumoto's family farm, where he wages a quixotic fight to farm organically a peach variety out of step with the demands of America's consumer society.

Despite obtaining a degree from Cal-Berkeley, Masumoto returns to his family's eighty-acre peach and raisin farm, where he continues the family's farming legacy and finds inspiration for his book—a mixture of nature writing, social commentary, and family history. As he notes early in the work, "In the process of exploring the landscape I discover a little bit more of who I am" (19). In this connection between self-identity and his environment, Masumoto presents a familiar trope of American nature writing. His eco-friendly stewardship of his land also echoes the writings of

Thoreau, Leopold, and Berry. However, as he notes, "My peaches are like the traditions of the homeland—you don't simply leave them behind, you carry them with you like historical baggage" (20). And part of Masumoto's "historical baggage" includes a family lineage of rural peasantry in Japan, one that informs his treatment of the migrant workers he employs on his farm. He notes how they are blamed "for many of society's problems," while labor activists and other social critics never question "the exploitation of urban laborers, the people who work behind closed doors in restaurant kitchens, mow lawns, or clean rooms and offices after hours" (22). Echoing the views of historian Richard White, he derides environmentalists both for their failure to appreciate the difficult decisions those who depend on the land for their livelihood have to make and also for the limited concern they show those who toil in the land for their benefit.

Masumoto notes that while his life as a yeoman farmer is often reminiscent of "a Norman Rockwell painting," his Japanese cultural identity is a significant influence on not only how he treats the workers on his land but on the land as well. (119). Through his labor *in* nature, Masumoto realizes that nature is not a force to conquer, but one to adapt to, and a Japanese saying about the strength and flexibility of bamboo functions as a symbol of this perspective and a model for him to emulate. In the section "Obon," Masumoto recounts the Japanese Buddhist festival that commemorates the dead, a period when spirits are believed to return to visit their families. As it is for many American Nikkei, Obon is now more of a secular ritual for Masumoto, but the ties that bind him to his grandparents, who settled here after the painful dislocation of World War II, are reaffirmed during the festival.[10] Masumoto imagines their spirits returning to visit him and his children. Their presence and the history they incorporate are a part of his farm, as is the scrap heap of the farmer who preceded his father and the story it tells. He notes:

> I'll consider myself a better farmer when I have a clearer sense of history about
> a place, when I understand the knowledge of a farm's hills and the sweat and
> blood left behind. Until then I'm just managing a piece of dirt and probably
> still foolishly believing I rule the earth. (113)

Reading the works of authors such as Masumoto, Kingston, and Ali and especially those of first-generation Asian immigrants reminds us that, as Limerick has written, "the complete story of the investment of human consciousness in the American landscape requires attention to the whole set of participants. . . . With anything less, the meaning of the landscape is fragmented and truncated" (1026). The inclusion of Asian American voices addresses an ongoing limitation on how we portray and understand the American environment and reveals how the environmental movement still too often "just manages a piece of dirt." It highlights the problematic assumptions of those too often given the role as spokespersons of a narrowly defined tradition. It questions their hegemony and the manner in which both writers and critics have too often cared more for plants than for people, especially those who came later to America.

In his famous tract *A Sand County Almanac*, Aldo Leopold wrote about the eradication of the perennial *silphium* from his native Wisconsin. The following analogy is both an accurate prognostication and a disturbing example of the invisibility of Asians in discussions of the American environment. I close with his words, rhetoric that serves as perhaps the best example of the too-often ignored link between environment and race that ecocriticism, in even its most revolutionary approaches, fails to recognize. It displays views about race that, at the least, provided a frame for the canonical author's understanding of his environment and those with whom he shared it.

> The erasure of a human subspecies is largely painless—to us—if we know little enough about it. A dead Chinaman is of little import to us whose awareness of things Chinese is bounded by an occasional dish of chow mein. We grieve only for what we know. (52)

NOTES

1. In her introduction to *The Ecocriticism Reader*, Cheryll Glotfelty notes: "Ecocriticism has been predominantly a white movement. It will become a multi-ethnic movement when stronger connections are made between the environment and issues of social justice, and when a diversity of voices are encouraged to contribute to the discussion" (xxv). Elizabeth Dodd made similar observations in 1999. See her article, "Forum on Literatures of the Environment."

2. See David Mazel, "American Literary Environmentalism as Domestic Orientalism," and Christine Gerhardt, "The Greening of African American Landscapes: Where Ecocriticism Meets Post-Colonial Theory."

3. See Julie Sze, "From Environmental Justice Literature to the Literature of Environmental Justice." See also Molly Wallace, "A Bizarre Ecology: The Nature of Denatured Nature," *ISLE* 7, no. 2 (Summer 2000): 137–53.

4. An excellent articulation of this point is Andrew Hurley's book, *Environmental Inequalities*. Hurley details how the black community of Gary, Indiana, was more invested in job equity and adequate housing than such environmental issues as air quality and preservation of recreational spaces. Such issues were part of a larger

struggle to obtain social equity in a climate dominated by racist public and private institutions that denied these individuals equality in the workforce and in the larger Gary community.

5. Asian American literature is an offshoot of Asian American studies, a project realized by a panethnic coalition of Asian American activists in the 1960s and 1970s who sought social justice and greater representation in the academy. Asian American literature, therefore, has been tied to a political consciousness that critics often utilize in assessing the relative merit or "authenticity" of Asian American literary production. The increasing heterogeneity of Asian Americans and their cultural production, however, challenges this means of defining the field and any theoretical framework that seeks to contain it. For an excellent discussion of the theoretical challenges of defining Asian American literature, see Susan Koshy, "The Fiction of Asian American Literature."

6. The Hohokam were a prehistoric people residing in south-central Arizona, from approximately 300 B.C. to the mid-fifteenth century.

7. Annette Kolodny, in *The Lay of the Land*, discusses the Euro-American tradition of gendering the American landscape, a process that she argues served to rationalize its conquest by Euro-American men, as a kind of "psycho-sexual drama." Asian American studies scholars, including David Eng, have discussed how the social, economic, and legal status of Asian men in the United States has often denied them the status and perquisites of American masculine identity. See David Eng, *Racial Castration*. While Kolodny argues in her later text, *The Land Before Her*, that women settlers of the Great Plains held different views than men, her claims rely on the writings of white women only. A similar exploration of early Asian American women's views of gender and environment can provide a more complete understanding of the general claims made by Kolodny.

8. Kingston, in fact, has stated that *China Men* was her attempt to "claim America." See Timothy Pfaff, "Talk with Mrs. Kingston."

9. See Michael Bennett's essay, "Manufacturing the Ghetto: Anti-Urbanism and the Spacialization of Race." In his essay, Bennett argues that ecocriticism and the larger environmental justice movement must address the panoply of issues that plague American urban environments, including the repercussions of the racial segregation that increasingly defines them.

10. *Nikkei* is a general term, used as an adjective or noun, that refers to people of Japanese ancestry who immigrated from Japan and their descendants.

WORKS CITED

Ali, Agha Shahid. *A Nostalgist's Map of America*. New York: W. W. Norton, 1991.

Bennett, Michael. "Manufacturing the Ghetto: Anti-Urbanism and the Spacialization of Race." In *The Nature of Cities: Ecocriticism and Urban Environments*, ed. Michael Bennett and David W. Teague. Tucson: University of Arizona Press, 1999. 169–88.

Casey, Edward S. "How to Get from Space to Place in a Fairly Short Stretch of Time."

In *Senses of Place*, ed. Steven Feld and Keith Basso. Sante Fe: School of American Research Press, 1996. 13–52.

Dodd, Elizabeth. "Forum on Literatures of the Environment." *PMLA* 114, no. 5 (1999): 1094–95.

Eng, David. *Racial Castration: Managing Masculinity in Asian America*. Durham: Duke University Press, 2001.

Gerhardt, Christine. "The Greening of African American Landscapes: Where Ecocriticism Meets Post-Colonial Theory." *Mississippi Quarterly: The Journal of Southern Cultures* 55, no. 4 (Fall 2002): 515–33.

Glotfelty, Cheryll, ed. *The Ecocriticism Reader: Landmarks in Literary Ecology*. Athens: University of Georgia Press, 1996.

Hom, Marlon K., trans. *Songs of Gold Mountain*. Berkeley: University of California Press, 1987.

Hurley, Andrew. *Environmental Inequalities: Class, Race, and Industrial Pollution in Gary, Indiana, 1945–1980*. Chapel Hill: University of North Carolina Press, 1995.

Idaho Daily Statesman. 27 July 1892. Unpaginated and untitled.

Katrak, Ketu. "South Asian American Writers: Geography and Memory." *Amerasia Journal* 22, no. 3 (1996): 121–38.

Kingston, Maxine Hong. *China Men*. New York: Vintage International, 1989.

Kolodny, Annette. *The Land Before Her: Fantasy and Experience of the American Frontiers, 1630–1860*. Chapel Hill: University of North Carolina Press, 1984.

———. *The Lay of the Land*. Chapel Hill: University of North Carolina Press, 1975.

Koshy, Susan. "The Fiction of Asian American Literature." *Yale Journal of Criticism* 9 (1996): 315–46.

Lee, Rachel. "Claiming Land, Claiming Voice, Claiming Canon: Institutionalized Challenges in Kingston's *China Men* and *Woman Warrior*." In *Reviewing Asian America*, ed. Wendy L. Ng, Soo-Yung Chin, James S. Moy, and Gary Okihiro. Pullman: Washington State University Press, 1995. 147–59.

Leopold, Aldo. *A Sand County Almanac*. New York: Ballantine Books, 1970.

Limerick, Patricia Nelson. "Disorientation and Reorientation: The American Landscape Discovered from the West." *Journal of American History* 79, no. 3 (December 1992): 1021–49.

Masumoto, David Mas. *Epitaph for a Peach*. New York: HarperCollins, 1996.

Mazel, David. "American Literary Environmentalism as Domestic Orientalism." *ISLE* 3, no.2 (Fall 1996): 37–45.

Merchant, Carolyn. "Shades of Darkness: Race and Environmental History." *Environmental History* 8, no. 3 (July 2003): 380–94.

Pfaff, Timothy. "Talk with Mrs. Kingston." In *Conversations with Maxine Hong Kingston*, ed. Paul Skenazy and Tera Martin. Jackson: University Press of Mississippi, 1998. 14–20.

Reed, T. V. "Toward an Environmental Justice Ecocriticism." In *The Environmental*

Justice Reader, ed. Joni Adamson, Mei Mei Evans, and Rachel Stein. Tucson: University of Arizona Press, 2002. 145–62.

Rhodes, Edward Lao. *Environmental Justice in America*. Bloomington: Indiana University Press, 2003.

Stegner, Wallace. "Wilderness Letter." In *Literature of the Environment*, ed. Lorraine Anderson, Scott Slovic, and John P. O'Grady. New York: Longman, 1999. 442–47.

Sze, Julie. "From Environmental Justice Literature to the Literature of Environmental Justice." In *The Environmental Justice Reader*, ed. Joni Adamson, Mei Mei Evans, and Rachel Stein. Tucson: University of Arizona Press, 2002. 163–80.

Thoreau, Henry David. *Walden*. Ed. J. Lyndon Shanley. Princeton: Princeton University Press, 1989.

White, Richard. "Are You an Environmentalist or Do You Work for a Living? Work and Nature." In *Uncommon Ground: Rethinking the Human Place in Nature*, ed. William Cronon. New York: W. W. Norton and Company, 1996. 171–85.

To Name Is to Claim, or Remembering Place

Native American Writers Reclaim the Northeast

RELYING ON THE assumption (left unspoken) that the cliff dwellers in what is now southwestern Colorado abandoned their city because of a long-term drought, Wallace Stegner writes in the introduction to *Where the Bluebird Sings to the Lemonade Springs* that contemporary western cities facing the possibility of drought "might ponder the history of Mesa Verde." Then, as if the former inhabitants of Mesa Verde have no history after all, Stegner turns immediately to this generalization: "all western places are new" (xvi). In a chapter entitled "A Sense of Place," he actually offers a definition of what it is that makes a place a place: "a place is not a place until people have been born in it, have grown up in it, lived in it, known it, died in it—have both experienced and shaped it, as individuals, families, neighborhoods, and communities, over more than one generation. . . . No place, not even a wild place is a place until it has had that human attention. . . . No place is a place until things that have happened in it are remembered in history, ballads, yarns, legends, or monuments" (201, 202). Elsewhere in the book, Stegner mentions in passing Louise Erdrich, Scott Momaday, Leslie Marmon Silko, James Welch, and an unnamed Crow friend, but—as is evident from his passing reference to Mesa Verde—his formulation of what makes a place a place essentially writes Native American historicizing out of the history of the West.[1] At the same time, however, he perhaps unwittingly provides a means for reclaiming place. To be born in it, live in it, or to remember it is to claim it, he avows.

Taking as a point of departure the attitude about place expressed by Stegner in the context of the West, this essay suggests that in the East, also, "things that have happened" are "remembered in history," in Native American history, even though those histories have been essentially ignored by the dominant culture over the past four to five hundred years. After glancing briefly at examples of how the dominant culture has embraced an almost total disregard of Native histories and Native historicizing, I turn to the essay's main argument: that many Native American poets of the Northeast attempt through their writing to reclaim the land and history that was denied their ancestors beginning at least as early as the seventeenth century; through their verbal art, they reassert themselves into the history of New England from which they were essentially written out, and they thus reclaim their place: personally, historically, geopolitically. And further, by asserting a history, these poets also claim a future. In this sense they refute those historians, anthropologists, and archeologists who imply "that Indians lack not only a past of their own but a present and a future as well" (Salisbury 46).

There is, of course, a well-established argument that Native Americans have been written out of the historical record. In his study of Puritans and Indians, *New English Frontier: Puritans and Indians, 1620–1675* (1965), for example, Alden T. Vaughan assumes "the total absence of Indian sources" and implies (without acknowledging) the bias of his endeavor: "I have concentrated on the acts and attitudes of the Puritans toward the Indians and have not, for the most part, attempted to account for the actions and reactions of the natives" (vii). Even though more recent historians have offered correctives to Vaughan, others have continued to disregard and discount Native views of history. Clifford Trafzer writes, for example, that many scholars claim that "oral history taught by American Indian elders is mere myth, fable, and fairytale" (485).[2] The suggestion that Native histories have been ignored and written out is important to an understanding of how contemporary (or recent) Native American and First Nations peoples retell and revise that history, challenge the paradigm, and thus reclaim not only a history but a place as well and, ultimately, a future.

One example of how one might counter the dominant culture's perspective with an Indian perspective comes from Cherokee poet Jimmie Durham as he remembers Columbus Day:

> In school I was taught the names
> Columbus, Cortez, and Pizarro and
> A dozen other filthy murderers.
>
> . . .
>
> No one mentioned the names
> Of even a few of the victims. (128)

Durham proceeds to identify some of those victims: Chaske, Many Deeds, Greenrock Woman, Laughing Otter, and "that young girl who danced so gracefully" (128). In a similar vein, Onondaga-Micmac poet and visual artist Gail Tremblay notes that mainstream American culture explains Indians

> to its children in words
> that no one could ever make
> sense of. The image obscures
> the vision, and we wonder
> whether anyone will ever hear
> our own names for the things
> we do. (Tremblay 2)

Of the self-proclaimed democratic poet Walt Whitman, Mohawk poet Maurice Kenny writes this: "Everything America produced or which produced America was allowed a pentameter in Whitman's work—but only rarely the American Indian, the indigenous native to the land, what the Native American sons and daughters know as Mother Earth." As Kenny points out, "Indians neither produced nor were produced by Whitman's hero, America, and merited only a veiled apparition or pitiful elegy" ("Whitman's Indifference" 29).

If Whitman, the apologist for democracy, is one example, Catharine Maria Sedgwick, spokesperson for the Native American, is another. Her novel *Hope Leslie* (1827) takes as one of its heroines a Native American named Magawisca, daughter of a Pequot chief. Yet despite Sedgwick's stated intentions to do right by the Native Americans, her opening passages comparing the Puritans' and Pequots' homes dehumanize and animalize the Native Americans. In characterizing her Puritan heroes, she writes: "They were pilgrims, for they had resigned, for ever, what the good hold most dear—homes. Home can never be transferred; never repeated in the experience of an individual." In this context, compare this description of the "pilgrim's" home with that of the Algonquins' a few pages later: "She [Magawisca] is the daughter of one of their chiefs, and when this wolfish tribe were killed, or dislodged from their dens, she, her brother, and their mother, were brought with a few other captives to Boston" (18, 21). Sedgwick's Indians live in dens, not homes, and true to that abode, the tribe itself is characterized as wolfish. Thus even Sedgwick, as an author who attempts to set the record straight, cannot avoid the ethnocentric biases of her social, cultural, and temporal moment in history.

Sedgwick's description of the wolfish clan in its den contrasts sharply with a description of an Iroquois home by Mohawk writer Maurice Kenny in *Tekonwatonti/Molly Brant* shortly after the Iroquois (according to Kenny's narrative) had arrived in what was to become their *home* in the Mohawk Valley:

these new people built a kindling
fire under a pot,
within a wide circle
and hung the bow and quiver
by the door of the lodge.
Home.
Haudenosaunee. (21)[3]

A sense of home and that home's connection to his Mohawk ancestry are important to Kenny's writing. He begins an autobiographical sketch for the volume *I Tell You Now*, for instance, with a statement about the importance of "dealing directly with either home in northern New York state and the Adirondacks or directly with Iroquois (Mohawk) ancestry or culture, which [he has] written about over many years" (Kenny, "Waiting at the Edge" 39). In another autobiographical sketch, *On Second Thought*, Kenny writes that after he was in legal trouble for missing too much school, his father took him *home*: "My father appeared before the court and asked permission to take me home. . . . I stayed in his house. His home remained my home." While at home, the young Kenny wandered in the hills nearby: "The hills and rivers helped heal my dark soul and damaged mind. . . . I listened to chicory on the winds, I smelled the ripe wild strawberries, I observed the flight of birds, especially the red-tailed hawk." Later in the same memoir, he writes that his father "taught respect for bear and wolf, but he also taught respect for wild iris, or blue flag, for trillium and cattail" (*On Second Thought* 17–18, 56).

In this way Kenny essentially fuses the concepts of home, nature, and his father's teachings. By extension, of course, one can read that by turning to his Mohawk father he is consciously embracing his heritage, associating a sense of home or of place with that heritage, and insisting that along with the cultural world, the natural world is an integral part of that geophysical place. He lives in it, and he gets to know it through its weather, its flora, and its fauna.

In many of Kenny's poems it is difficult to separate the speaker from the natural world of which that speaker is a part. In a poem actually titled "Home," for instance, Kenny sets himself in place, writing of going "home" to the Adirondacks. Here again the speaker expresses a sense of ambivalence toward his home, or a sense of displacement and consequent yearning. He travels "north by the star" toward a geophysical home, but the place has been changed by the tourist industry. The Adirondacks have evidently been "forgotten in the rush for camp-sites" and both the wolf and bear are missing from home. He laments the butchering of a bear "who will not share the berry picking / with the girls of June this year" ("Home" 29). Despite the speaker's ambivalence, a sense of place does figure prominently in Kenny's poetry. Time and again he makes the point emphatically that he has, or had, or will have a home in the homelands of his Mohawk ancestors. In this sense, in the sense of telling or describing that homeland, he is claiming or reclaiming a place. In Stegner's phraseology he is remembering in history what has happened in a particular landscape, and he is thus giving place human attention, remembering it in stories, making place a place by giving it a history.

Kenny's most extended effort at reclaiming the history, people, and landscape of the Northeast is his book-length collection *Tekonwatonti/Molly Brant: Poems of War* (1992). As Patrick Barron points out in his long essay (essentially summarizing Kenny's book-length poetic history), the "driving theme and intent of [the book] is to reconstruct the times, life, and land of the influential yet largely forgotten Mohawk woman, Molly Brant" (31). Barron sums up by stating that Kenny "has boldly and convincingly reawakened awareness of and interest in Tekonwatonti's life" (60). Kenny does indeed rescue the forgotten biography of this woman and her century (she lived from 1735 to 1795), and as he remembers the person and her century, he reclaims a homeland, writing the Mohawks back into history.

One way in which Kenny reclaims a place is by beginning his account well before American Indian contact with European immigrants, a maneuver through which he insists on an existence and thus a history and a homeland before Mohawk contributions were written out of what was later or is even now taken for the established record of the Northeast. He begins by describing a beginning:

> Water was first
>
> Morning rolled
> fog steamed
> from mud
> where pollywogs
> wiggled.

> And legends began . . . (19)

In this prefatory poem to *Tekonwatonti/Molly Brant*, Kenny introduces the water creatures, plants, birds, and land creatures: "Feet touched the earth on turtle's back," he begins:

and finally at last
words echoed through the forest .

. . .

after the miserable trek
east
through cold and snow
and hunger
sun swept
the river valley. (20–21)

Traveling from the west, argues Kenny, the "People of the Longhouse, the Haudenosaunee," arrive and settle (21). They make a home; they have come to stay. In making historical an argument that the Mohawks came from the west, that is, by traveling eastward, into their homelands in what is now upstate New York, he historicizes that migration, and at the same time he counters the doctrine of Manifest Destiny, a doctrine that insists on a Eurocentric god's sanction of the westward movement across the North American continent.[4]

There are indeed numerous passages in Kenny's book that one could draw on to make the point that Kenny is rewriting history by placing the Mohawk woman Tekonwatonti at the center of eighteenth-century America. In the "Woman/Warrior" section, for example, Molly (the first-person speaker) reminds the reader (and the assumed eighteenth-century white audience) of her role, the Mohawk role, the Iroquois Confederacy's role, in providing a blueprint or a paradigm for the subsequent Constitution of the Thirteen Colonies:

If you would listen with clean ears,
and I could scratch these sureties
onto birchbark or rock,
you would remember always
where your freedoms and liberties
first captured your attention. (130)

In this passage Kenny not only places his speaker Tekonwatonti at the center of American history; he also acknowledges the Iroquois as responsible for the creation and existence of one of the most central and most prized documents of the United States, the Constitution itself. In a sense the controversy about whether the Iroquois provided the underlying principles of the Constitution is finally immaterial to the poem.[5] Of importance is that the poem places Tekonwatonti at the center of this history; that it tells a story otherwise not acknowledged; that it reminds its auditors of Tekonwatonti's role in the Indian wars; that it finally challenges and thus rewrites history. And Tekonwatonti reminds the reader both of the importance of remembering and of the dangers of forgetting:

> A people who do not remember:
> *rain which falls upon a rock.* (130)

In the epilogue Kenny turns to the voice of the Ottawa chief Pontiac, who in a Whitmanesque style reminds his audience of where and how his power and spirit reside. Through the use of the imperative voice, Kenny (or Chief Pontiac as speaker) insists that the history be chronicled and remembered:

> Tell this to the historian
>   who chronicles
> Tell this to the general
>   who believes me dead
>
> I sing you
> I blood you
> I am the bone of your thought. (192)

In placing the story of Tekonwatonti before his readers, Kenny makes at least two obvious and important points. First, the appearance of Tekonwatonti (Molly Brant) on the historical scene, as it were, demands that her place in history be acknowledged. In reclaiming her, he reclaims the historical and political space as well as the literal landscape upon which she lived. Second, since the publication of Kenny's almost epic poem in 1992, two book-length histories of the long-neglected and almost-forgotten Molly Brant have appeared in print.[6] This attention to Molly Brant revives her as an important historical figure. Her story demonstrates that the Northeast has had human attention, that Native Americans are not only remembered in history but actually made that history. Tekonwatonti was born in this place, lived in it, and died here. By giving her voice, Kenny has shown that the place has a history and has thus made that place the home of his Mohawk ancestors as he has made it his own home:

> My blood flows through their history . . .
> they cannot deny my place though
> my name was canceled and my flesh left to rot
> under the peach tree with the fallen fruit. (174)

ANOTHER MOHAWK writer who lays claim to the historical Northeast is Beth Brant. She suggests in her short story "Wild Turkeys" that "everyone should know where they are from, where home is" (*Food and Spirits* 39), and part of that understanding of home, she suggests, comes through language. In writing about Beth Brant, Linda Cullum, for example, suggests that by sharing her stories Brant creates or makes her "own 'place' out of words" (139). Although she was born in Detroit, Michigan, Brant recalls that one of her first memories is of her Mohawk grandfather telling her stories in Mohawk: "teaching me to count, to say special words" ("Beth Brant" 30).

In her prose poem "Native Origin" Brant takes a reader inside a long-house into the very center of that cultural life, and she thereby reclaims a place as she asserts a history. The speaker of the poem celebrates the minu-tia of drinking coffee and preparing for a specific ritual among several of the "old women" inside the longhouse: "The old women are gathered in the Longhouse. First, the ritual kissing on the cheeks" (33). Blended with Brant's description of the mundane, however, are her carefully articulated interjections. It is through these interjections and subsequent descriptions of the women's actions that the speaker of the poem offers the reader an insight into the significance of the ritual. As the ritual takes shape through words, the history is reclaimed: "One grandmother sets the pot over the fire that has never gone out. To let the flames die is a taboo, a breaking of trust" (33). To state that the flame has never gone out is to insist that there has been no break in the continuity of life from Mohawk mother to Mohawk daughter.

Although the speaker does not make it explicit, the poem seems to be the ritual welcoming of a child: The women "are together to perform a ceremony. Rituals of women take time. There is no hurry." One woman presents a cradleboard and the women sing of a little baby that will "Ride on Mother's back." Another woman presents a turtle rattle: "the daugh-ter shakes the rattle, and mother and she-turtle live again" (33–34). These lines again suggest continuity from mother to daughter and the refusal of death. But the image also evokes another origin story, that of turtle bringing dirt and establishing earth, that of turtle being the mother of mothers. Here again, then, the poem constitutes a reclaiming in that it articulates place with a story, in this case, a story of origins. According to one version of the Iroquois creation account, turtle carries the woman/mother earth upon which the earth rests: "The tradition of the Nottowegui or Five Nations says, 'that in the beginning before the formation of the earth; the country above the sky was inhabited by Superior Beings, over whom the Great Spirit presided. His daughter having become pregnant by an illicit connection, he pulled up a great tree by the roots, and threw her through the Cavity thereby formed; but, to prevent her utter destruction, he previously ordered the Great Turtle, to get from the bottom of the waters, some slime on its back, and to wait on the surface of the water to receive her on it. When she had fallen on the back of the Turtle, with the mud she found there, she began to form the earth, and by the time of her delivery had increased it to the extent of a little island' " (Klinck and Talman 88).

In his poem "Turtle," Peter Blue Cloud makes reference to this creation story, giving voice to turtle:

> I am turtle
> and the earth I carry is but
> a particle in the greater Creation. (84)

According to Blue Cloud, turtle declares that patience is a salient characteristic of the creation:

> Patience was given me by Creation. . . .
> I am turtle,
> and await the council of my tribes. (84)

Beth Brant's poem "Native Origin" similarly evokes and draws on the creation story. The speaker implies the importance of patience in general as it is fundamentally important to this creation story.

Like several other poets who have northeastern ancestry, Brant fuses the historical sense of place with an awareness of the human connection to the nonhuman world. In this instance, the movement of the poem is toward the oldest grandmother's untying of a pouch that she wears around her neck. She opens the pouch and empties "a fistful of black earth. It smells clean, fecund." This fistful of earth reverberates in many directions at once. It harkens immediately back to the notion of turtle and that particular story of the origin; and at the same time it symbolizes ideas of fertility and spiritual health. In that the earth comes from the pouch that the woman wears between her breasts, it also evokes images of a newborn's breastfeeding: "The pouch lies between her breasts, warming her skin. Her breasts are supple and soft for one so old. Not long ago, she nursed a sister back to health" (34). The image thus also looks forward, suggesting the future of a nursing babe.

In addition to evoking images of the coming generation, the image ties the grandmother, the mother, and the baby very directly to the literal earth. From the humble beginnings of women boiling and sipping bitter coffee, the poem ends with a suggestion of cosmic implications. When the women have finished performing the ritual, they walk outside: "They go out into the night. The moon and stars are part of the body of Sky Woman. She glows on, never dimming. Never receding" (34). The reader has thus, in a sense, come full circle, or rather perhaps full spiral, from the specific and local of the fire that never goes out to the stars that never recede. Like the fire, like the stars, like the mothers and daughters, and by implication, like the Mohawk Nation itself and the literal earth, the stars never dim. The women "tend the fire, and wait" (34). Like turtle, they demonstrate their patience, and like turtle they have brought forth life and earth in a particular place.

IN THE introduction to her poetry in Joseph Bruchac's collection *Songs from This Earth on Turtle's Back*, Wisconsin-Oneida poet Roberta Hill Whiteman expresses her disappointment with the economics and politics of the late-twentieth-century world (rampant commercialism, unemployment, alcoholism, pollution), writing this: "The only strength I find comes from the myths of our people. As in the Popul Vuh, I believe it is the artisan's responsibility to help the earth overcome such dreadful tyranny. It is the artisan's responsibility to sing the sky clear so that we can walk across the earth, in a place fit for flowers" (*Songs from this Earth* 273). Her use of "artisan" with its somewhat archaic meaning of "craftsperson" is interesting in that in addition to poets and other artists, she thereby includes those skilled in the mechanical and fine arts, a suggestion that the responsibility of walking carefully across the earth belongs to everyone. Certainly the responsibility is not limited to poets and other fine artists.

As in her comments in the introduction, in her poem "In the Longhouse, Oneida Museum," Whiteman links an almost nostalgic sense of the past with a concern for the health of the natural environment. Addressing the longhouse of the title, she compares the house she grew up in with what she imagines the longhouse to be:

> What autumn wind told me you'd be waiting?
> House of five fires, they take you for a tomb,
> but I know better. When desolation comes,
> I'll hide your ridgepole in my spine
>
> and melt into crow call, reminding my children
> that spiders near your door
> joined all the reddening blades of grass
> without oil, hasp or uranium. (16–17)

The poem's speaker finds that the existence of the longhouse, albeit in a museum, gives her a sense of history and with that sense of history comes the promise of a feeling of power, a sense of place. In contrast to the longhouse, the hall of her tenement

> . . . reveals a nameless hunger,
> as if without a history, I should always walk
> the cluttered streets of this hapless continent. (16)

In the poem "Speaking through the Generations," Whiteman acknowledges a debt to the past and to the land; she promises, in a sense, to honor that debt. By evoking the spirit of the grandmothers and the centrality of the earth to all she does, she reinscribes the Native American presence in the Northeast regardless of where the children of those grandmothers may find themselves living at the end of the twentieth century: "We'll remember your generosity, grandmothers":

> Although we've been scattered, we keep alive
> the memory of your voices, speaking
> through the generations.

In addition to linking the past and present by an acknowledgment of debt, the speaker of the poem acknowledges the human link to the earth by suggesting a reciprocity: past and present are mutually interdependent, as are the earth and human beings:

> On this earth, our Turtle Island, we know our needs
> dovetail the needs of those to come
> and the needs of those who've gone.

Whiteman's speaker is not more specific about what those needs are than to note that when

> frost clouds the bean vine and corn,
> and starvation wakes us with its cranky burden,
> we'll remember your generosity, grandmothers.
> (*Philadelphia Flowers* 48)

With an image of destruction in another poem in the same collection, "Unbinding Anger," the speaker again emphasizes the link between humans and the natural environment, this time by a kind of double negative: With boots "on our voice boxes, they ripped apart / clans as they did the Great Wood" (49). Here the poet decries the violence perpetrated against her grandfathers and elders, linking this with violence against nature—the Great Wood—in a somewhat ecofeminist turn. In this context, she implies the ecofeminist argument that the same colonial mindset that motivates oppression and even annihilation of certain peoples also motivates the destruction of the nonhuman natural world. Despite her anger, however, this poem, like so much of her poetry, seeks, finds, and establishes hope and looks to the future despite her "colonized histories":

> Our children search their marrow
> for strange paths into tomorrow.
> They dare to find that place
> where the voices that judged
>
> our worth before we lived it
> recede into the mists
> of our colonized histories.

It is the image of love that sustains the speaker, and that love is bound inextricably with the earth itself:

> When I feel alone, it twirls
> the earth's boundless green energy above me. (50)

In "Lynn Point Trail" Whiteman again fuses human love with love for place as she reveals her own hope for the future through her children. The speaker, like her daughter, longs somewhat nostalgically for a home in the natural world:

> I, too, wish we could have lived
> Near the tilted horizon. (*Star Quilt* 76)

The fir trees, ferns, cuckoo's call, and shells all suggest the closeness that she and her daughter feel for the earth, and their longings turn to hope:

> With songs for granite and bluer skies,
> children gathered rain-eroded shells.
> Let these rocks be eggs until the tides
> scorch them, or until the heart reveals
> at last the grace we lost. (77)

ABENAKI POET Joseph Bruchac begins to reclaim a history when he problematizes a too simplistic commemoration of one set of grandparents having arrived at Ellis Island:

> Yet only one part of my blood loves that memory.
> Another voice speaks
> of native lands
> within this nation.

The phrase *within this nation* refers on the one hand to the United States, the nation resulting from invasion and imposing ownership upon the land, but on the other hand the phrase *within this nation* suggests the Abenaki (Wabanaki) Nation:

> Lands invaded
> when the earth became owned.
> Lands of those who followed
> the changing Moon,
> knowledge of the seasons
> in their veins. ("Ellis Island" 33)

In this poem, Bruchac fuses nation, land, and landscape and thereby suggests their interconnectedness. In these few lines he not only suggests that interconnectedness but also calls into question the concept of private ownership of land in the first place.

LIKE BRUCHAC, Peter Blue Cloud demands a revisionist history of his ancestors' homeland when he reminds his readers of Native American survivors. In his poem "Bear: A Totem Dance as Seen by Raven," for example, despite the sorrows and the anguish of the past, he stands as living proof that his people have survived but have not forgotten, cannot forget:

> And the death of a village is a great sorrow,
> and the pain of the survivors
> is a great anguish
> never to heal. (86)

In the poem "Turtle" Blue Cloud again reminds his readers of great anguish. Turtle as speaker declaims thus:

> such pains that exist for this moment,
> which slay so many of the innocent
> cannot but end in pain repeated
> as all are reflected twins to self. (84)

But finally, there is hope for the future, and that hope lies in continuing to reclaim the history and the land, "chant to the four directions":

I am turtle,
and death is not yet my robe,
for drums still throb the many
centers of my tribes. (84)

Blue Cloud's poem "The Old Man's Lazy" is very much a poem about place, about reclaiming a particular space. The title comes from an agent's characterization of the speaker. He is deemed lazy because he has not repaired a fence, a fence originally built by the speaker's white neighbor. Once the neighbor disappears, the fence

lies on the ground like
a curving sentence of stick writing.

And according to the speaker of the poem, the fence tells a different story each day:

the rain and wind and snow,
the sun and moon shadows,
this wonderful earth,
    this Creation.
I tell my grandchildren
many of these stories,
    perhaps
this too is one of them. (98)

In this poem, Blue Cloud clearly links the story (written by the fence) with the earth, with the past, and through the grandchildren, with the future. In this sense he gives the place, his place, human attention; he claims it, gives it a history and a future.

Taken together, these poems begin to gain momentum in a push toward reasserting a claim to the Northeast. What European colonists and historians began and continue to write out of history, Maurice Kenny, Beth Brant, Roberta Hill Whiteman, Peter Blue Cloud, and other Native American poets begin to write back in. These poets recreate the landscape and people that landscape with Native American heroes and heroines. Tekonwatonti/Molly Brant once again walks to the Mohawk River. Whiteman evokes the "laughter" that "measured harmony and strife" and recalls the promise of recapturing a lost grace. Blue Cloud listens to the earth's story and looks to the grandchildren. In such ways, Native American writers anticipate Stegner's definition of how to make place; they give that place human attention and thereby make it again their own. As we can see in

Peter Blue Cloud's poem, "Turtle," place exists for Native Americans in both time and space. Turtle carries the earth on her back, and the children who are the future want to know the past. They take their place:

> . . . a young
> child smiles me of tomorrow,
>   "and grandparent,"
> another child whispers, "please,
> tell again my clan's beginning."(84)

NOTES

1. Stegner does devote one paragraph to Native American writing. He writes that "studies could be made . . . of the literature of the West, and of special groups of writers such as Native Americans who are mainly western. The country lives, still holy, in Scott Momaday's *Way to Rainy Mountain*. It is there like a half-forgotten promise in Leslie Marmon Silko's *Ceremony*, and like a homeland lost to invaders in James Welch's *Winter in the Blood* and Louise Erdrich's *Love Medicine*" (113). This acknowledgment of Native American writers "who are mainly western" ignores any eastern writers and *ipso facto* denies them the opportunity of claiming a history or a place.

2. Clifford E. Trafzer makes this point in his essay "Grandmother, Grandfather, and the First History of the Americas" (485). See also Arnold Krupat, "American Indian History," in his *Red Matters* (57–60), where he offers several examples of how Native American histories have been discounted.

3. Kenny glosses the word *Haudenosaunee* as "People of the longhouse, later known as the Iroquois Confederacy" (*Tekonwatonti/Molly Brant* 199).

4. See Kehoe, *North American Indians*: "Because the Iroquois and the Cherokee seem to intrude into a huge region otherwise entirely Macro-Algonkian, early scholars assumed that Iroquoians had migrated eastward from their nearest Siouan relatives in the western and upper Mississippi Valley. . . . [Archeological evidence] has convinced most contemporary scholars that the ancestral Iroquois were Owasco, and that therefore the historic Iroquois territory was Iroquoian from at least A.D. 1200, and very possibly earlier" (218).

5. There are those who argue that the constitutional principles of the Iroquois Confederacy did not after all influence the framers of the constitution of the United States. Such detractors, Kenny and others point out, ignore the fact that Franklin himself acknowledges the debt. For a discussion of the issue of how the Iroquois Confederacy influenced the character of the U.S. Constitution, see Gail Landsman, "Informant as Critic" (160–76).

6. See Lois Huey and Bonnie Pulis, *Molly Brant: A Legacy of Her Own* (1997),

and Thomas Earle, *The Three Faces of Molly Brant* (1996). Chapters in two recent collections have also been devoted to Molly Brant: Lois M. Feister and Bonnie Pulis,
"Molly Brant: Her Domestic and Political Roles in Eighteenth-Century New York,"
and James Taylor Carson, "Molly Brant: From Clan Mother to Loyalist Chief."

WORKS CITED

Barron, Patrick. "Maurice Kenny's *Tekonwatonti, Molly Brant*: Poetic Memory and
    History." *MELUS* 25, no. 3–4 (Fall–Winter 2000): 31–64.
Blue Cloud, Peter. "Bear: A Totem Dance as Seen by Raven." In Niatum, *Anthology*,
    85–87.
————. "The Old Man's Lazy." In Niatum, *Anthology*, 96–98.
————. "Turtle." In Niatum, *Anthology*, 83–84.
Brant, Beth. "Beth Brant." In Bruchac, *Songs*, 30.
————. *Food and Spirits*. Ithaca: Firebrand, 1991.
————. "Native Origin." In Bruchac, *Songs*, 33–34.
Bruchac, Joseph. "Ellis Island." In Hobson, *Remembered*, 33.
Bruchac, Joseph, ed. *Songs from this Earth on Turtle's Back: Contemporary American In-
    dian Poetry*. Greenfield Center, N.Y.: Greenfield Review Press, 1983.
Carson, James Taylor. "Molly Brant: From Clan Mother to Loyalist Chief." In *Sifters:
    Native American Women's Lives*, ed. Theda Perdue. New York: Oxford University
    Press, 2001. 48–59.
Cullum, Linda. "Survival's Song: Beth Brant and the Power of the Word." *MELUS*
    24, no. 3 (Fall 1999): 129–40.
Durham, Jimmie. "Columbus Day." In Niatum, *Anthology*, 128.
Earle, Thomas. *The Three Faces of Molly Brant: A Biography*. Kingston, Ont.: Quarry
    Press, 1996.
Feister, Lois M., and Bonnie Pulis. "Molly Brant: Her Domestic and Political Roles
    in Eighteenth-Century New York." In *Northeastern Indian Lives, 1632–1816*, ed.
    Robert Steven Grumet. Amherst: University of Massachusetts Press, 1996. 295–
    320.
Hobson, Geary. *The Remembered Earth: An Anthology of Contemporary Native American
    Literature*. Albuquerque: University of New Mexico Press, 1979.
Huey, Louis, and Bonnie Pulis. *Molly Brant: A Legacy of Her Own*. Youngstown, N.Y.:
    Old Fort Niagara Association, 1997.
Kehoe, Alice B. *North American Indians: A Comprehensive Account*. Englewood Cliffs,
    N.J.: Prentice Hall, 1981.
Kenny, Maurice. "Home." In Hobson, *Remembered*, 29.
————. *On Second Thought: A Compilation*. Norman: University of Oklahoma Press,
    1995.
————. *Tekonwatonti/Molly Brant, 1735–1795: Poems of War*. Fredonia, N.Y.: White
    Pine Press, 1992.

―――. "Waiting at the Edge: Words toward a Life." In *I Tell You Now: Autobiographical Essays by Native American Writers*, ed. Brian Swann and Arnold Krupat. Lincoln: University of Nebraska Press, 1987. 37–63.

―――. "Whitman's Indifference to Indians." In *The Continuing Presence of Walt Whitman*, ed. Robert K. Martin. Iowa City: University of Iowa Press, 1992. 28–38.

Klinck, Carl F., and James Talman, eds. *The Journal of Major John Norton*. 1816. Reprint Toronto: Champlain Society, 1970.

Krupat, Arnold. *Red Matters: Native American Studies*. Philadelphia: University of Pennsylvania Press, 2002.

Landsman, Gail. "Informant as Critic: Conducting Research on a Dispute between Iroquoianist Scholars and Traditional Iroquois." In *Indians and Anthropologists: Vine Deloria, Jr., and the Critique of Anthropology*, ed. Thomas Boils and Larry J. Zimmerman. Tucson: University of Arizona Press, 1997. 160–76.

Niatum, Duane, ed. *Harper's Anthology of Twentieth-Century Native American Poetry*. San Francisco: HarperSanFrancisco, 1988.

Salisbury, Neal. "American Indians and American History." In *The American Indian and the Problem of History*, ed. Calvin Martin. New York: Oxford University Press, 1987. 46–54.

Sedgwick, Catharine Maria. *Hope Leslie*. 1827. Reprint New Brunswick: Rutgers University Press, 1987.

Simmons, William S. "Cultural Bias in the New England Puritans' Perception of Indians." *William and Mary Quarterly* 38 (January 1981): 56–72.

Stegner, Wallace. *Where the Bluebird Sings to the Lemonade Springs: Living and Writing in the West*. New York: Random House, 1992.

Trafzer, Clifford E. "Grandmother, Grandfather, and the First History of the Americas." In *New Voices in Native American Literary Studies*, ed. Arnold Krupat. Washington, D.C.: Smithsonian Institution Press, 1993. 474–87.

Tremblay, Gail. *Indian Singing*. Corvallis: Calyx Books, 1998.

Vaughan, Alden T. *New England Frontiers: Puritans and Indians, 1620–1675*. Boston: Little Brown, 1965.

Whiteman, Roberta Hill. "In the Longhouse, Oneida Museum." In Bruchac, *Songs*, 273.

―――. *Philadelphia Flowers*. Duluth: Holy Cow! Press, 1996.

―――. "Roberta Hill Whiteman." In Bruchac, *Songs*, 272–73.

―――. *Star Quilt: Poems by Roberta Hill Whiteman*. Minneapolis: Holy Cow! Press, 1984.

Lynching Sites

Where Trauma and Pastoral Collide

I STUMBLED UPON a column in the *Kansas City Star* a while ago about a restaurateur, Myra Harper, who decided to name her new place Strange Fruit Restaurant and Smoothie Bar after the signature song of her favorite singer, Billie Holiday. Appropriately, the restaurant would be setting up shop in the 18th and Vine District, legendary hotbed of jazz in Kansas City, redeveloping around the American Jazz Museum and the Negro Leagues Baseball Museum. But the name Harper chose stirred up a mild hubbub in Kansas City, with a number of people disturbed at her naming a restaurant after a graphic song about lynching. "Granted," one letter said, "lynchings are a horrible and repulsive historical fact, which can't be ignored but it's hardly an appropriate name for an eatery. I hope the owner will consider a name change." Some supported the choice and others said they would not personally choose the name but acknowledged Harper's reasons. Harper felt that the name Strange Fruit not only honors Holiday but is "indelibly linked to American history as the voice of protest and hope. I want to capture people's interest and provide them with access to eating healthier food" (qtd. in Penn).

On the one hand we have fruit and its associations, from health to fecundity, but on the other hand those associations are strained by the brutal historical facts of lynching. The Kansas City story is rich with a very instructive irony, an irony that exists in the two words of the song's title "Strange Fruit," and in the song's lyrics, which contrast a "pastoral" South with gruesome images of mob murder. And it is the same irony that permeates any picture or image of a rural lynching and makes that image, if this is possible, all the more horrifying. It is in these images from remote lynching sites—whether they are in photographs or in words—that the traumatic and the pastoral collide.

The term *pastoral*, of course, has a range of meanings, from the specialized to the general. At its narrowest, *pastoral* refers to that class of poems, based on the *Idylls* of Theocritus, in which rustic shepherds speak to one another about love and death. At its broadest, *pastoral*, especially as an adjective, is commonly applied in flexible ways to texts or images that idealize nature, simplicity, or withdrawal from complexity of city life. Leo Marx's term *pastoral ideal* is one such enlarged use that refines our understanding of the psychological and intellectual impulses behind not only pastoral verse but all kinds of texts and cultural expressions. More recently, Terry Gifford, in his fine book *Pastoral*, describes the broad use of *pastoral* as "an area of content" in a way that I find helpful. "In this sense," he says, "pastoral refers to any literature that describes the country with an explicit contrast to the urban." For Gifford "delight in the natural" also figures into the pastoral, but that delight, when it is viewed skeptically, engenders a third kind of pastoral in his scheme, the "pejorative" use of *pastoral*, which sees the "pastoral vision" as "too simplified" or too idealized (2). I wish to use *pastoral* mainly in its broadest sense as an idealization of the natural, the rural, and the withdrawal from the busy life, yet most of the texts I am exploring here carry with them a pejorative understanding of pastoral, an understanding that is informed by an unsettling irony, the sharp contrast between the pastoral ideal and the violent reality of lynching. Occasionally, I employ the narrower sense of pastoral by examining how some of the classic tropes of pastoral verse have curious parallels in texts about lynching.

The first time I really took note of the clash between the beauty of nature and the trauma of lynching was in Toni Morrison's *Beloved*. The main character Sethe has deeply ambivalent memories of the landscape around Sweet Home, the plantation in Kentucky from which she escaped. Indeed, her struggle with traumatic memory is arguably the overriding theme of the novel. In one of her many bouts with "rememory," Sethe finds herself sorting through recollections, and she pictures "Sweet Home rolling, rolling, rolling, out before her eyes, and although there was not a leaf on that farm that did not make her want to scream, it rolled itself out before her in shameless beauty." She wishes to scream from the pain, yet she cannot help but picture a scene that stretches out vistalike in her mind. The passage goes on to show how appalled she is by her memory and how the impulse to admire natural beauty ends up compounding her pain:

> It never looked as terrible as it was and it made her wonder if hell was a pretty place too. Fire and brimstone all right, but hidden in lacy groves. Boys hanging from the most beautiful sycamores in the world. It shamed her—remembering the wonderful soughing trees rather than the boys. Try as she might to make

it otherwise, the sycamores beat out the children every time and she could not forgive her memory for that. (6)

Sethe (or Morrison) links a classic image of pastoral beauty, the "lacy groves," with the explicit images of sycamores, which her memory has forced into her consciousness, suggesting that both the trope and the trauma have persistent influence over the mind. Sethe appears to have internalized a pastoral ideal, but her difficulty with it reveals a pejorative attitude toward the pastoral impulse.

The song "Strange Fruit" also uses pastoral in the pejorative sense, and far more explicitly. The song places lynching inside a southern white culture that was partly defined by its nostalgic devotion to pastoral values. Although Billie Holiday's artistry made the song into an antilynching anthem, the lyrics were originally written around 1936 and the tune in 1938 by Abel Meeropol (under the pen name of Lewis Allen). Both Holiday's performance and Meeropol's composition shed light on the song's arresting challenge to the South's pastoral self-image. First with the text, Meeropol juxtaposes images of death against natural images in lines like "Blood on the leaves and blood at the root / Black bodies swinging in the southern breeze." But he also chose to name the connection explicitly and to identify the South with the pastoral so that he could exploit the bitter hypocrisy of lynching against a backdrop of purported gentility and agrarian simplicity. The second stanza of the song uncovers the comparison plainly:

> Pastoral scene of the gallant south,
> The bulging eyes and the twisted mouth,
> Scent of magnolias, sweet and fresh,
> Then the sudden smell of burning flesh. (qtd. in Margolick 15)

It is hard to imagine a more cherished symbol of the southern reverence for nature than the magnolia, a tree and flower associated with a beauty distinct to the region, with gentility, and in some quarters with the idealization of white womanhood and the accompanying sense of purity. "Strange Fruit" is an antilynching song, but it deepens its protest by alluding to the cultural values that should, but do not, prohibit brutalities like lynching. Not only do these cultural values fail to stop lynching, but indeed, they were used by some to promote it. Whether or not Meeropol intended this full irony, his words remind the audience that lynching was a culturally accepted practice, part of the same value system that idealized soft breezes, magnolia trees, gallantry, and politeness.

Commenting upon lynching in Mississippi during Jim Crow, Neil R. McMillen demonstrates rather convincingly that perpetrators, as recently as 1939, felt little need to hide their involvement in lynching, and he finds it astonishing that "so many lynchers felt at liberty to operate so openly in the confidence that their deeds were sanctioned by the community and beyond the reach of law or even serious public censure" (229). Many lynchings were reported in newspapers in grisly detail and with a kind of festive fascination with the victim's pain. The participants did not disguise themselves, and in fact lynchings were attended like social events with people drinking, being photographed next to the corpse, and taking away the victim's body parts as souvenirs. The recent book *Without Sanctuary: Lynching Photography in America* documents the lynching era in photographs, many of which are postcards people bought and sent to relatives and friends. More than tolerated, mob violence against blacks was condoned by many—including politicians, people in law enforcement, whites both rich and poor. It is important to note that lynching was not confined to the South, nor were black men the only victims. But the problem was huge in the South, where it had significant cultural implications, and by far most of the victims were black men.

McMillen and other historians tend to agree that a likely objective of lynching was social control of blacks. It sent a message to African Americans that if they overstepped their social-caste boundaries (even with such acts as failing to address a white man as "sir"), they were in grave danger. Policing these social boundaries with mob violence, lynching was a form of terror, which Richard Wright refers to in *Black Boy* as the "white death," omnipresent in the Mississippi of his youth (172). While lynching likely served this form of social control, the protection of white womanhood was frequently cited as a justification for lynching. The brother of Wright's friend was taken out on a country road and shot by whites because they accused him of "fooling with a white prostitute" (171). In the period from 1882 to 1930, lynchers most often cited the crime of murder as the reason they took the law into their own hands, but sexual assault was the second most cited justification, accounting for about a third of all justifications given (Tolnay and Beck 92). In 1882 a note pinned to the body of a black lynching victim read: "Our mothers, wives, and sisters shall be protected, even with our lives" (qtd. in Tolnay and Beck 64). A postcard from 1902 portrays on one side a burnt corpse hanging from pine trees, and on the other appears the following inscription: "*Warning* The Answer of the Anglo-Saxon race to black brutes who would attack the womanhood of the South" (Allen, plates

59, 60). Without assuming that these sentiments were universally held even in the South, it still seems clear that lynching was to a large degree a socially sanctioned tool supposedly to uphold cultural values like chivalry. In such a cultural context, Meeropol's lyrics were driving at the core of the issue. His line "Pastoral scene of the gallant south" not only offers the pastoral ideal as a contrast to lynching, but it implies how pathologically twisted the cultural value of gallantry had become.

"Strange Fruit" is first and foremost an antilynching protest song, but it also participates, at least obliquely, in what Terry Gifford has termed the antipastoral tradition, which asserts that "the natural world can no longer be constructed as 'a land of dreams,' but is in fact a bleak battle for survival" (120). Like some antipastoral poems, the song "Strange Fruit" presents audiences with a view that is radically different from what they initially expect. Billie Holiday's performances of "Strange Fruit" are legendary, according to David Margolick, whose book chronicles the history of the song. Music critics too numerous to name speak in hyperbolic language about the impact of Holiday's interpretation of the song. For instance, jazz critic Benny Green says, "When Billie Holiday sings the phrase 'pastoral scene of the gallant South,' civilization has said its last word about the realpolitik of racial discrimination in all its forms and degrees" (qtd. in Margolick 65). Rhetorically and symbolically the song is a heavy club, and Billie Holiday wielded it with memorable force.

Reportedly she performed it for the first time at a party in 1938. One witness claims that the party had been quite lively, but after Holiday sang the song, it became positively quiet, funereal. The song soon became a standard in her performances at the progressive, integrated nightclub Café Society. "Strange Fruit" would be the last song in her set. The lights would go down except for a single spotlight on her face. Holiday and club owner Barney Josephson decided that Holiday would walk off the stage immediately after the song and not come back for any encore, no matter how loud the applause. After her performance the nightclub would go still, and, in the words of Josephson, the audience would have "their insides burned with it" (qtd. in Margolick 50), not the typical goal for a nightclub act. Although Holiday chose her venues for the song cautiously, she inevitably ran into audience members who reacted very strongly against the song. Margolick describes a party where a number of people walked out on the song, saying, "We don't call this entertainment." One woman caught Holiday in the powder room and screamed, "Don't you sing that song again! Don't you dare!" (89).

Even sound recordings hit people hard. When Warren Morse played the record for a group of undergraduate students in Missouri, one young woman "broke down and started sobbing" (68). These anecdotes about Billie Holiday have striking resonance with Gifford's story about Ted Hughes and his relentless performing of an antipastoral poem in which the lamb must be decapitated during its birth. An audience of university students, perhaps expecting something more typically pastoral, became angry and vocally critical of Hughes at his reading. Both Holiday and Hughes seem to know and accept that by crossing certain conventions they will shock and even antagonize their audiences (137–38). In these instances the "anti" in antipastoral disturbs some people by going sharply against what they expect in these conventional contexts—pastoral poem, jazz song—which are themselves then sites of disjunction.

The antipastoral message in "Strange Fruit" relies mainly on the power of symbols (magnolias, blood) and themes (gallantry, pastoralism) and therefore operates at a fairly high level of generality. Richard Wright's poem "Between the World and Me," however, operates at a very fine level of specificity, employing both narrative movements and intricate details, many of which achieve symbolic value as well. This poem too participates in an antipastoral mode, but Wright goes beyond symbolism to a rich layering of particulars to understand lynching at a deeply psychological level.

In this poem, first published in *Partisan Review* in 1935, Richard Wright uses the abandoned scene of a lynching to show the terrifying and demoralizing affect lynching had on him and other blacks in the Jim Crow South. Wright crafted the poem's narrative structure to mirror this identification with the lynched victim. The first line opens as a walk in the woods, but before the first line is complete, the speaker has "stumbled suddenly" upon something that startles him and grabs his attention. The poem's details mount up, and incrementally the reader comes to understand that the speaker has discovered the violent remains of a lynching, which—like many lynchings—was a party for its perpetrators, who had left a flask, cigarette butts, lipstick, and peanut shells in the "trampled grass." Following the description of the aftermath, the bones and ashes reanimate into a human being and then enter into the speaker's flesh. In the final stanza, the speaker becomes the lynched victim, narrating his own brutal agony, his skin peeled by the hot tar, feathers stabbing his flesh, the cool dousing of gasoline just before he is lit on fire. In the final line, the speaker is reduced to the remains: "Now I am dry bones and my face a stony skull staring in yellow / surprise at the sun" (lines 51–52).

The "whore's lipstick," the flask, and the shells are all part of a longer list of objects in the poem. Thomas G. Rosenmeyer identifies the catalogue as "the single most effective and congenial" trope in the traditional pastoral lyric. He says: "The loving enumeration of allied propositions or goods documents the discreteness of the herdsman's sensory experience and his detachment in pleasure" and gives "proof that the grove is harmonious" (256–57). As one might expect, the catalogue in Wright's poem shows the violence that disturbed whatever harmony may have existed in this clearing. In the space of fifteen lines, Wright lists about twenty items like the following: "white bones," "charred stump," "torn tree limbs," "tiny veins of burn leaves," "scorched coil of greasy hemp," "vacant shoe," "empty tie," "ripped shirt," "lonely hat," and so on (lines 6–20). This inventory is certainly antipastoral in the way it builds evidence of violence and discord. As with pastoral literature, "Between the World and Me" uses many natural images—grass, wind, sun, woods, darkness, water. But those images, even if they suggest natural vigor, are often quickly tainted by the grisly reality of the lynching. For example, one sentence begins with "morning air" but ends with a skull: "And through the morning air the sun poured yellow surprise into the / eye sockets of a stony skull" (19–20). In the poem's middle stanza, where the scene comes alive with auditory imagery, a peaceful wind yields to baying hounds:

> The sun died in the sky; a night wind muttered in the grass and fumbled the
> leaves in the trees; the woods poured fourth the hungry yelping of hounds;
> the darkness screamed with thirsty voices; and the witnesses rose and lived.
> (25–28)

Just when a conventional observation of nature begins to develop, it is pulled away, deemed improper or impossible in a world where lynching takes place. Even the terrifying hounds lack nourishment, with their "hungry yelping" and "thirsty voices." No semblance of tranquility can last long in this world of terror, where violence and predation hold sway. The most arresting example of this confiscation of the pastoral comes in the opening line where the first-time reader is searching for the overarching tone of the poem. It begins:

> And one morning while in the woods I stumbled suddenly upon the thing,
> Stumbled upon it in a grassy clearing guarded by scaly oaks and elms.
> And the sooty details of the scene rose, thrusting themselves between the world
>   and me . . . (1–5, Wright's ellipses)

To begin, the speaker is in the woods, but on the other hand, his mode of locomotion is not to walk or ramble but to stumble. He is taken off guard by "the thing," the "sooty details" of which become the focal point of the poem. Modulating back to the pastoral, the speaker finds himself in a clearing, under the protective canopies of oaks and elms, no less. Then come more "sooty details" that take hold of the poem for good.

It is impossible to say how deliberate this choice of natural detail is and impossible to say whether the opening line is meant to hint at pastoral retreat, but we know a few things about Wright's youth and his reading that suggest he was aware of a kind of pastoral impulse. First of all, Wright was a voracious reader, and even if he were not explicitly invoking the tradition of pastoral poetry, he must have had some sense of the pastoral impulse as it existed in American culture generally and in literature explicitly. Indeed, Wright could not easily have avoided coming in contact with the pastoral ideal if it lurks, according to Leo Marx, in Herman Melville, Walt Whitman, Henry James, Robert Frost, and Mark Twain, among others (16). In *Black Boy* Wright lists a number of books that were part of his earliest reading, including Gertrude Stein's *Three Lives*. Wright tried to emulate Stein's imagery in his self-designed writing exercises, the purpose of which "was to capture a physical state or movement that carried a strong subjective impression" (Wright, *Black Boy* 280). The longest story in *Three Lives*, "Melanctha," about a black girl in a "southern" locale, has scenes of pastoral retreat to the country-side. Jeff and Melanctha "sat in the bright fields and they were happy, they wandered in the woods and they were happy" (161, 149). This escape to the woods seems to bring greater clarity to their relationship. It is reasonable to say that Wright had pastoral examples available to him, one of which he studied closely.

Wright also reports a nonliterary connection with the natural world, one that offered him solace in difficult times, particularly as a child. There are two key moments in Wright's autobiography *Black Boy* when young Richard, facing bleak circumstances at home, turns rather startlingly to focus on simple natural details as a source of comfort. In the opening chapter of the book Richard is four, and with Granny ill in bed, he is admonished to stay quiet. Out of a mixture of boredom and four-year-old curiosity, he lights the lace curtains on fire; the flames spread and set the house on fire. Wright reports that his mother is relieved to find him safe but instantly punishes him with such a severe beating that he loses consciousness and takes days to recover. As he comes out of the illness and the trauma, he shifts into a long series of natural observations:

I was chastened whenever I remembered that my mother had come close to killing me.

Each event spoke with a cryptic tongue. And the moments of living slowly revealed their coded meanings. There was the wonder I felt when I first saw a brace of mountainlike, spotted, black-and-white horses clopping down the dusty road through clouds of powdered clay. (7)

This passage goes on to add twenty-two more short paragraphs, each introducing a rural or wild image with the repeated opening *there was* or *there were*. The passage has a rhythmic and lyrical quality as it steps out of book's typically riveting narrative into the stillness of *to be*. The paragraphs describe physical details and emotional responses to those details. In stark contrast to the malicious and confining stories of Wright's Jim Crow South, such passages seem to be an oasis of meditation: "There were the echoes of nostalgia I heard in the crying strings of wild geese winging south against a bleak, autumn sky" (8). Not all the images are as agreeable as migrating geese, and some have tinges of violence to them, but they all involve plants, animals, and other natural details and all seem to avail Richard of emotional responses denied him in his day-to-day reality.

The second moment in *Black Boy* is patterned just like the first. Richard is eight years old. He unwittingly blurts out an insult to his grandmother and is hit by Granny, threatened by his grandfather, and finally beaten by his mother. Again, bewildered by his own behavior and the violent reaction by adults, he seeks meaning in natural images:

. . . and I resolved that in the future I would learn the meaning of why they had beat and denounced me.

The days and hours began to speak now with a clearer tongue. Each experience had a sharp meaning of its own.

There was the breathlessly anxious fun of chasing and catching flitting fireflies on the drowsy summer nights. (45)

A series of eighteen small paragraphs make up this passage, again the stasis of *there was* followed by mainly natural details. Richard normally found a great deal of comfort in his mother but was in constant tension with Granny. On the heels of a traumatic beating by the adults to whom Richard would expect to turn for safety, he turns to the physical richness of the world around him for meaning and solace. In both cases those details have a "tongue" that manages to talk to him and offer "meaning."

After he is eight years old and has become more aware of the hostility of southern whites, this sort of passage never appears again in either *Black Boy* or the second part of his autobiography, *American Hunger*. So when it comes to the poem "Between the World and Me" it is reasonable, I think, to attribute some significance to the poem's setting in the woods and to other details of nature in the text. It may also follow the pattern of *Black Boy*: after an attempt to connect to nature, the effort fails. "Between the World and Me" does have some relationship to the pastoral, but not a conventional one.

As the speaker of the poem is drawn toward the victim, he separates from the world. One would have to ignore most of Wright's work and severely narrow the poem's frame of reference to claim that the *world* of "Between the World and Me" is simply the natural world. In *Black Boy*, for instance, Wright finds himself alienated from much of his family, from their brand of Christianity, from other children, from the principal of his school, from whites, and from blacks who do not share his interest in books, and all these make up the world from which he feels estranged. Similarly in *Native Son*, Bigger Thomas is alienated from his neighborhood, his family, from the white power establishment, and from his own girlfriend Bessie. But Wright does put this psychic alienation in concrete terms in such passages from *Black Boy* as "Emotionally, I was withdrawn from the objective world" (278). For Wright the "world" can mean many things, but it seems reasonable to assert that the physical world of nature is an important aspect of the world to which Wright sought to be connected.

Just as Wright's autobiography seems to leave nature behind as Richard experiences more and more cruelty from white society and from certain relatives, "Between the World and Me" also leaves the pastoral behind. The walk in the woods promises an escape, and that promise is jerked away. This poem offers not so much an antipastoral but what I might call a curtailed pastoral. In this curtailed pastoral, Wright may not really be challenging the validity of pastoral ideal as much as he is simply excluded from it. The trauma of lynching sets up a barrier to the pastoral that is so firm that Wright may not even be able to test the validity of the pastoral view. He is denied access. In the poem, nature does not prove to be hostile to itself, but humans have brought their hostility to nature, so much so that Wright's speaker has no opportunity for the *otium* (Rosenmeyer 67–68), the pastoral withdrawal from civilization, no escape really, except perhaps, as in Wright's case, *to* a city in the North.

Denied to the speaker, is the pastoral impulse denied to other blacks in the South as well? Is it reasonable to extend the speaker's psychic experience to encompass other African Americans? David P. Demarest finds such widening right in the poem itself, saying that the speaker's transformation into the victim connects him to all African Americans. The speaker begins with a walk in the woods, "enjoying the kind of personal contemplation that should be every man's birthright," but as he becomes the victim, this "lynching wrenches him into a group identity he cannot deny" even in his isolation (238). Trudier Harris agrees with Demarest that the lynched man's suffering, being embedded in history, is the suffering, the trauma, of all black people in America (104). Beyond the poem, Wright himself sees the traumatic results of racial violence in other American blacks. In a seminal passage from *Black Boy*, Wright sums up the psychological results of the narrative of his life in the South, explaining how all this brutality affects him personally and blacks generally:

> A dim notion of what life meant to a Negro in America was coming to con-
> sciousness in me, not in terms of external events, lynchings, Jim Crowism, and
> the endless brutality, but in terms of crossed-up feelings, psyche pain. I sensed
> that Negro life was a sprawling land of unconscious suffering, and there were
> but a few Negroes who knew the meaning of their lives, who could tell their
> story. (267)

For me three important ideas flow out of Wright's description of psychic pain: one is that he believes the suffering afflicts virtually all blacks in America at that time. Second, Wright also believes that it is experienced largely on an unconscious level. And third, a few people are able to bring the trauma into conscious awareness and tell the story behind this pain.

Regarding the first point, can trauma be suffered by a group? Many believe it can. Judith Herman, in her landmark study *Trauma and Recovery*, says that "entire communities" and countries can suffer from post-traumatic stress. Herman suggests that the Los Angeles riots were prompted by the acquittal of the police officers who beat Rodney King but were truly fueled by the trauma of long-term, systematic oppression. African Americans were outraged when bystanders (the jury) identified with the perpetrators rather than the victim. Following on Herman's work, J. Norman Reid in "Trauma Theory and Racially Divided Communities" believes that trauma theory can be used in public policy to heal racial divisions and begin to help communities in formerly slave-holding areas to improve their lives. And once again, returning to Richard Wright's experience and to the stated purpose of lynchers themselves, it is reasonable to see the trauma of lynching as a familiar ordeal to African Americans, particularly in the Jim Crow South. Many surely had the kind of terrifyingly close connections to racial killing reported by Wright in *Black Boy*: the brother of his friend was murdered by whites out on a country road (171); Wright's Uncle Hoskins was shot and killed by whites because of his business success (54).

The second point from Wright's discussion of psychic pain is that it dwells in the unconscious. In "Trauma and the Conservation of African-American Racial Identity," Sheldon George maintains that the trauma of slavery is experienced by African Americans consciously, where it can be used as a political tool, but he insists that it also inhabits the unconscious in a very potent way. George explores why writers like W.E.B. Du Bois and Lucius Outlaw wish to preserve the concept of race even though they understand that race has no basis in biology. In addition to their conscious use of race for its political utility, Du Bois, Outlaw, and others conserve race, he says, because of their unconscious attachment to the trauma of slavery. George relies on Jacques Lacan's special concept of the *real*, that part of our psychic makeup that lurks beyond the reach of symbolization, outside of expression, yet exerting a substantial influence over us. The *real* at once is excluded from consciousness and yet inserts its burden upon our psyche. For those who identify themselves as African American, says George, the *real* contains the "intrusive traumatic past" of slavery. The historical connection to slavery may live in Du Bois and others on a conscious and discursive level at the same time as it occupies this central place in the *real*, where the "intrusive traumatic past" of slavery asserts itself (58). If I can go back for a moment to Toni Morrison's *Beloved*, Sethe's struggle with the persistence of her "rememory" is a close analogue to the phrase "intrusive traumatic past." Interestingly, both the lynching images and the pastoral scenes from her memory bubbled up intrusively into her consciousness.

For George, the trauma of slavery works as the very glue of racial identity. Locating this trauma in the *real* as George does is reminiscent of Wright's "sprawling land of unconscious pain," the traumatic origin of which is Jim Crowism and lynching, extensions of slavery's oppressive reign. To the extent that George is right about the "psychological link to the trauma of slavery," the trauma of lynching and racial violence in the wake of slavery must also have an enduring effect on African American identity. George closes his discussion by saying that the way to craft a more productive relationship with this trauma is to "assemble and articulate the narrative of one's story" (71). And this brings me to Wright's third point about psychological pain: that telling the story is essential and that something important happens when people bring trauma out of the unconscious in order to grasp "the meaning of their lives" and they enfold and unfold it in narrative.

Herman says that the recovery from trauma tends to progress in three stages, frequently moving back and forth recursively. First the traumatized individual must find "safety." In the case of abuse, for example, the victim must get out from under the power of the abuser. The second stage is "remembrance and mourning," and the third "reconnection with ordinary life" (155). Literature, music, photographs, and other kinds of artistic expressions often perform the work of this second stage. The photographic collection *Without Sanctuary*, Richard Wright's *Black Boy*, "Between the World and Me," and his short story "Big Boy Leaves Home," Toni Morrison's *Beloved*, Billie Holiday's rendering of "Strange Fruit," and even Myra Harper's naming of her restaurant are all efforts to tell the story, efforts to move the recovery process forward. Each of these narratives has no doubt been met with resistance, sometimes quite public in the cases of Holiday and Harper, but for others the resistance is less public, coming from readers or viewers, some of whom are in full sympathy with the message. The message, especially when it is a detailed narrative, is a hard one. Look what was done. Look how people suffered. And look what we humans are capable of. My students, black and white, have told me how difficult it was for them to engage in the concreteness of some of these narratives. Herman insists, however, that when sufferers of post-traumatic stress tell their story as part of the recovery process, they tell it in detail and often repeat the telling almost ritually. I think of Holiday's singing "Strange Fruit" night after night. The victims, says Herman, have "an intense reliving experience" but can do so in safety (183).

Billie Holiday, as I noted earlier, chose her venues carefully because there were times when telling the story was not safe. And Richard Wright published "Between the World and Me" after he had moved to Chicago and out of the South, where he continually felt threatened by whites. One way to understand "Between the World and Me" is to see the poem as a turning point for Wright, the moment when he had found enough safety, in Chicago, to be able to tell the story. It coincides with the poetic moment in which he has found his aesthetic power, according to Trudier Harris. The significant accomplishment of this poem, she says, is that Wright turned suffering and violence into an aesthetic form. As the speaker crafts the story, imagining himself as the victim and "recreating the death," he "thereby becomes the artist" and "enables the reader to witness the horror" (104). The detailed telling of the story opens the way over time for reconnection. In creating the poem, perhaps Wright is beginning to exercise the traumatic stress that stands between him and the world.

Richard Wright's life, in relationship to his work, follows a trajectory that first separates from and later begins to reconnect with, among other things, the world of nature and the solace he once found there. Attempting in his own way to get himself free of the imprisoning influence of racial trauma, he moved away from Mississippi to Memphis, then completely away from the South to Chicago, then to New York, and finally away from the United States to France. In a scene from a documentary film on Richard Wright, his daughter is standing in the garden in his home outside Paris some years after his death, and she points up to a second story window where Wright had his desk. She notes that her father worked by that window so that he could always look out and see his garden. Toward the latter part of his life he had perhaps come to enjoy some sense of pastoral withdrawal, and his leaving the United States may have been the only way he could leave the memory of racial trauma far enough behind.

It is, I think, significant that one finds elements of the pastoral ideal and what seem to be pastoral tropes in these works that delve into the horror of lynching in America. The connection at least asks us to consider whether the pastoral ideal is easily embraced by everyone, and it suggests that those who identify themselves as African Americans may have reason to greet the pastoral ideal with some ambivalence and may be motivated to revise it. In the recently published anthology *The Colors of Nature: Culture, Identity, and the Natural World*, Al Young questions the focus of mainstream environmental thought.

In "Silent Parrot Blues," Young finds that his careless landlord, named Valve, leaves a South American parrot to languish in a dark, stuffy room near the laundry and that the landlord's neglect has made the bird sick. Young and his neighbor Briscoe discuss the parrot's plight, noting that it parallels their own. The irony they both see immediately is that publicly decrying the treatment of the bird would be the most effective way to expose the landlord's neglect of his human tenants. Referring to the mistreatment of animals, Briscoe reminds Young that "white people don't like that shit." In other words, people who ignore distressed humans would become outraged at the inhumane treatment of this exotic bird. "In fact," says Briscoe, sharpening this incongruity, "they're prepared to make your ass extinct in a minute before they'll let anybody fuck with a timberwolf" (116). And Young draws this conversation to a close with Briscoe signifying on the trope of extinction, "Shee-it, the black male—we're an endangered species, too, you know" (117).

One way Young revises environmental consciousness is to emphasize "work" rather than "recreation" as the means through which his ancestors connected to nature. He associates recreation with romanticism, individualism, the rejection of "city life," and the tendency "to exoticize nature" (118). Young veers away from the conventional pastoral escape while he aims toward engagement in community. He is certainly not unique in emphasizing community and interrelatedness, but his motivation stems from his and Briscoe's experience of racism. In the same anthology with Young, bell hooks also names work as the activity that has connected her and her family to nature. But unlike Young, she offers a rather straightforward pastoral appeal to the soothing power of nature. She says that even in the face of racism and domination by whites, rural black people during the time of her growing up sought "the wild spirit of unspoiled nature" as a strengthening force (68). hooks is less inclined than Young to revise the pastoral wholly.

The pastoral ideal plays a significant part in American identity and cultural values. It does manifest itself in some odd and contradictory ways, such as magazine and television ads that use a wilderness backdrop to promote gas guzzlers. But such paradoxes attest to the resilience and centrality of the pastoral ideal and to the complex way we incorporate it. According to Lawrence Buell, critics have been hard at work rethinking this "pastoral ideology" in America, especially rethinking the notion that the pastoral ideology opposes the established power structure (the machine versus the garden). Instead, says Buell, critics are considering how the pastoral is in line with power—that is, how it is "hegemonic"—and further, they are asking as Al Young does whether the pastoral leaves out many people who are not white.

The narratives of lynching and nature that I have taken up (and there are more examples) contribute to this conversation about pastoral ideology. As we try to understand the role of the pastoral in American identity, the connection to trauma in the work of African Americans should complicate and enrich this understanding and perhaps remind us that the most fruitful answers, and indeed the most fruitful questions, must have a high degree of nuance.

WORKS CITED

Allen, James, ed. *Without Sanctuary: Lynching Photography in America*. Santa Fe: Twin Palms, 2000.

Buell, Lawrence. "American Pastoral Ideology." *American Literary History* 1, no. 1 (Spring 1989): 1–29.

Demarest, David P. "Richard Wright: The Meaning of Violence." *Negro American Literature Forum* 8, no.3 (Autumn 1974): 236–39.

George, Sheldon. "Trauma and the Conservation of African-American Racial Identity." *JPCS: Journal for the Psychoanalysis of Culture & Society* 6, no. 1 (Spring 2001): 58–72.

Gifford, Terry. *Pastoral*. New York: Routledge, 1999.

Harris, Trudier. *Exorcising Blackness: Historical and Literary Lynching and Burning Rituals*. Bloomington: Indiana University Press, 1984.

Herman, Judith. *Trauma and Recovery*. New York: Basic Books, 1992.

hooks, bell. "Earthbound: On Solid Ground." In *The Colors of Nature: Culture, Identity, and the Natural World*, ed. Alison H. Deming and Lauret E. Savoy. Minneapolis: Milkweed, 2002. 67–71.

Lacy, Madison Davis, producer. *Richard Wright: Black Boy* (videorecording). Mississippi Educational Television/BBC production. San Francisco: California Newsreel, 1994.

Margolick, David. *Strange Fruit: Billie Holiday, Café Society, and the Early Cry for Civil Rights*. Philadelphia: Running Press, 2000.

Marx, Leo. *The Machine in the Garden: Technology and the Pastoral Ideal in America*. New York: Oxford University Press, 1964.

Morrison, Toni. *Beloved*. New York: Penguin, 1987.

McMillen, Neil R. *Dark Journey: Black Mississippians in the Age of Jim Crow*. Urbana: University of Illinois Press, 1990.

Penn, Steve. "This Fruit Tastes Sour to Some." *Kansas City Star*, 29 October 2002. B1.

Reid, J. Norman. "Trauma Theory and Racially Divided Communities." Proceedings of the International Community Development Society Conference, Cleveland, Mississippi, 22 July 2002. http://www.comm-dev.org/new/index.html (accessed May 2002).

Rosenmeyer, Thomas G. *The Green Cabinet: Theocritus and the European Pastoral Lyric*. Berkeley: University of California Press, 1969.

Stein, Gertrude. *Three Lives*. New York: Albert and Charles Boni, 1927.

Tolnay, Stewart E., and E. M. Beck. *A Festival of Violence: An Analysis of Southern Lynchings, 1882–1930*. Urbana: University of Illinois Press, 1995.

Wright, Richard. "Between the World and Me." 1915–16. Rpt. in *The Heath Anthology of American Literature*, vol. 2., 4th edition, ed. Paul Lauter. Boston: Houghton Mifflin, 2002.

———. *Black Boy*. New York: HarperPerennial, 1998.

———. *Native Son*. New York: HarperPerennial, 1998.

Young, Al. "Silent Parrot Blues." *The Colors of Nature: Culture, Identity, and the Natural World*, ed. Alison H. Deming and Lauret E. Savoy. Minneapolis: Milkweed, 2002. 113–24.

PART 2

The Solid Earth!
The Actual World!

Environmental Discourse and Practice

Composition and the Rhetoric
of Eco-Effective Design

IT IS NOT every day that judging a book by its cover turns out to be the best form of literacy criticism, but that is what William McDonough and Michael Braungart would have us do with their book *Cradle to Cradle: Remaking the Way We Make Things*. Even before you begin reading, you know there is something weighty, something substantial, about the book. It is heavy for its size, and the pages are a bit thicker than normal. On the cover you notice a small round graphic in the bottom right corner with the words "Water Proof Durabook" inscribed in it, indicating that the book is particularly well suited for reading in the hot tub or at the beach. You get the sense that the medium is the message, and that the book's argument begins when you pick it up.

Cradle to Cradle is an argument for eco-effective design, an approach assuming that the environmental problems we face today are ultimately a result of poor design choices. It is not enough to consume less and recycle more; we need nothing less than a second Industrial Revolution, one patterned on the effectiveness of nature. If we use nature as our design model, the authors argue, it is possible that "the production and consumption of goods can be a regenerative force" rather than a destructive one.

McDonough and Braungart make it clear that eco-effective design is important not just in a technical sense—because it saves energy or creates healthy relationships between products and the environment—but because it is more rhetorically effective than much mainstream environmental discourse. In this sense, it presents both a challenge to and source of common ground for ecocompositionists and ecocritics who see rhetoric as playing a central role in finding solutions to our current environmental crisis. However, by communicating their vision of the future in a book that is attractive, durable, and infinitely recyclable, they also remind us that it matters what material form this argument takes and that reading and writing are ultimately products of design. McDonough and Braungart present eco-effective design as a concept that has implications not just for the products and buildings we make but also for the rhetorical artifacts we create, and not just for traditional design fields like architecture and engineering but also for humanities fields like composition and rhetoric.

As recent work by such scholars as David Orr, Gunther Kress, and Mike Sharples suggests, ecocomposition and ecological design may already be kindred fields. When examined in light of scholarship that increasingly views "writing as design," the rhetoric of *Cradle to Cradle* reveals design principles that could inform an eco-effective approach to composition, one that views writing as a form of sustainable design. Moreover, while ecocomposition—and ecocriticism more generally—tend to be closely aligned with the biological sciences, McDonough and Braungart's approach suggests that ecological design could also serve as a source of metaphors, terms, and practices capable of broadening our ability to help our students imagine and design more hopeful futures in their writing.

Eco-Effective Rhetoric

Like most environmentalists, McDonough and Braungart do not shirk from laying out the bad news, and like many composition instructors, they ask us ask tough questions about how culture gets constructed and to whose advantage. Take a look at things around you, they write. As descendants of the Industrial Revolution, we have come to accept as normal an industrial paradigm in which our products, routinely made with toxic chemicals, hurtle through their short lives toward landfills, there to wait until our grandchildren are forced to deal with them. And recycling is no solution since most products are not meant to be recycled; their "cradle to grave" design means their materials will eventually end up in the landfill like everything else. Such a system of production creates the environmental problems we face today—pollution, deforestation, species extinction, global warming—and it bequeaths even worse problems to future generations.

However, McDonough and Braungart highlight not only the design problems behind such issues but also the rhetorical problem that they observe in some environmental discourses. To an audience of average consumers, the message sounds something like this:

> Stop being so bad, so materialistic, so greedy. Do whatever you can, no matter
> how inconvenient, to limit your "consumption." Buy less, spend less, drive

less, have fewer children—or none. Aren't environmental problems today—global warming, deforestation, pollution, waste—products of your decadent Western way of life? If you are going to help save the planet, you will have to make some sacrifices, share some resources, perhaps even go without. And fairly soon you must face a world of limits. There is only so much the Earth can take. (6)

McDonough and Braungart's response to this rhetoric is, "Sound like fun? We have worked with both nature and commerce, and we don't think so." Clearly, their strategy in this passage is both to reflect the tone of much environmentalist rhetoric back to those who dish it out (even when it might step on toes), and to reach out to the nonenvironmentalist who has been on the receiving end of such an address. The primarily negative rhetoric of much environmental discourse may leave an audience feeling convicted but not necessarily inspired to act in positive ways. Moreover, as Timothy Luke has argued, convincing individual consumers that they can change the world through their choices can obscure the very narrow range of environmentally sound options that producers actually offer them. Even if we do manage to hold producers responsible for their products, we still fail to offer solutions that allow companies to meet the bottom line. In the end, such rhetoric also fails to invite participation by the very ones who could have a significant impact in designing a more sustainable future, people such as industrialists and businesspeople.

Throughout *Cradle to Cradle*, McDonough and Braungart are less interested in laying blame than in trying to imagine how we can go forward. Look at the cherry tree, they say. It produces an extravagant number of flower petals just to be assured a few seeds will take root. The tree's abundance serves not only to meet its needs but to nourish everything around it by enriching the soil, providing shade, generating oxygen (78–82). When we follow nature's model of good design, we eliminate the concept of waste—in nature, waste equals food—and we imagine products that are designed from the beginning with their future uses in mind. In this industrial ecology, "biological nutrients" are designed to decompose and enrich the environments where they are disposed of and "technical nutrients" are materials that circulate in a closed industrial loop without losing quality (the book *Cradle to Cradle* itself is an example of this). They envision buildings that, like trees, produce more energy than they consume and purify their own wastewater; products like carpets and shoes made from material that can be infinitely recycled, so that companies will want their products back when consumers finish with them; a newly designed Styrofoam substitute that not only biodegrades when discarded but is implanted with indigenous seeds that begin to grow after the product breaks down. And all of this can be done in ways that make for good business at that same time as improving the long-term health of communities and ecosystems (92–117).

Sound like science fiction? It would, if the authors failed to offer concrete, real world examples to back up their vision as more than just pie-in-the-sky idealism. At a recent talk William McDonough gave to a packed auditorium of MBA students at the Harvard Business School, he described example after example of recent projects that succeeded at once in saving companies money, increasing productivity, and adding to health of local environments, from the redesign of the Ford headquarters in Detroit to construction of an upholstery producer's factory that lets off water cleaner than the tap water coming in (McDonough, "Triple Bottom Line"). But like good science fiction, McDonough and Braungart's vision of the future is mind-bending; it has the ability to help us imagine how things could be different, to create a new vision of the future. *Cradle to Cradle* functions as the kind of near-future narrative that Derek Owens points to as an important genre for helping students begin engaging critically with the future (Owens 109).

McDonough and Braungart are highlighting the rhetorical qualities of design that Richard Buchanan argues are central, not secondary, in all design practice. In Buchanan's words, "the skillful practice of design involves a skillful practice of rhetoric, not only in formulating the thought or plan of a product, through all of the activities of verbal invention and persuasion that go on between designer, managers, and so forth, but also in persuasively presenting and declaring that thought in products" (Buchanan 109). In the case of *Cradle to Cradle*, the rhetoric of both text and product serves to create a broader tent for dealing with our environmental crisis, one that aims to include industrialists, engineers, and businesspeople.

Writing as Design

According to Richard Buchanan, designers and rhetoricians have much to learn from one another: "If designers can benefit from explicit talk about rhetorical concerns, those who are interested in rhetoric can benefit even more from studying how design continues to influence and shape society by its persuasive assertions" (109). In his book on ecological design and education, *The Nature of Design*, David Orr reinforces the connection between traditional design fields like architecture and graphic arts and the humanities by stressing the role of human intentions in ecological design, describing environmental problems as being "mostly the result of a miscalibration between human intentions and ecological results" (13–14). Like McDonough and Braungart, Orr believes we need nothing less than a design revolution, one that "must aim to foster a deeper transformation in human intentions and the political and economic institutions that turn intentions into ecological results" (23). Ecocritics have been making a similar argument for some time now, asserting that the environmental crisis is not just a scientific issue that involves providing more evidence of global warming, species extinctions, or pollution. Rather, it is an issue of cultural ideologies that shape the decisions people make. Orr suggests that the same is true for the more applied fields of technology and design, and that we will begin to design more sustainably only if design includes reflection on the ecological implications of the technologies we use, the products we make, and the buildings we construct.

Many scholars both in design fields and in composition-related disciplines have begun to recognize a fruitful overlap in their research. Like Richard Buchanan, Malcolm McCullough has highlighted the rhetorical nature of design and has further argued that design should be considered a liberal art, since "good design is felt to be communicative" and "critical and cultural narrative remain essential to significant design" (168). In McCullough's field of interaction design, the relationship between technologies, users, and places is a central concern, and understanding the implications of such a relationship requires more than just technical expertise. Ellen Strain and Gregory VanHoosier-Carey point out the need for humanities scholars to see design as a significant part of their work, arguing that "we need to acknowledge the continuity between design efforts and the long-standing traditions of humanities work and to understand the practical initiatives of humanities-based computing as legitimate scholarly work" (276). More specifically, scholars in various fields have begun to explore the notion of "writing as design": Donald Norman, in a chapter titled "Design as Writing, Writing as Design," identifies analogies between principles of user-centered design and writing; Andrew Dillon, in "Writing as Design: Hypermedia and the Shape of Information Space," asserts the need to view content creation (writing) as intimately connected to interface design rather than as a separate activity; and in his chapter "Writing as Design," Mike Sharples identifies important parallels between the ways designers think and the way writers create textual artifacts. While these pieces vary in the connections they make between design-related fields and the humanities, the number of intersecting articles in recent years indicates an important trend.

Gunther Kress and Lester Faigley assert that the notion of "writing as design" arises from significant changes in literacy practices, changes caused by the growth of new communication technologies and by cultural and economic globalization. In Kress's estimation, the changes have two primary characteristics: "the broad move from the now centuries-old dominance of writing to the new dominance of the image . . . and the move from the dominance of the medium of the book to the dominance of the medium of the screen" (1). Faigley points out that while "images and words have long coexisted on the printed page and in manuscripts," and "literacy has always been a material, multimedia construct," it is only recently that computers have made it possible to "exploit the rhetorical potential of images combined with words" in a way that few could do in the past (Faigley 175). According to Kress, what this reality requires from us is "the facility for *design*" and an ability to work with "the varying affordances of the modes and facilities of the new media of information and communication." According to Kress, "anything and everything is now subject to design," whether it be the message, the mode (word, image, moving image), or the medium (computer screen, paper, television), such that "what used to be called 'stylistic choices' are now design decisions" (49).

Ultimately, the notion of writing as design may be most useful for the way it reminds us that every verbal artifact we create is meant *to do something in the world*. As obvious as this may seem, it is surprising how easily both students and teachers lose sight of it in a classroom setting. Mike Sharples points out that the most obvious lesson we have to learn from designers is "that texts, and other external representations, are artifacts that can be shaped and revised," and in this sense, Bryan Lawson's definition of design, with only nominal revision, can serve as a useful definition of writing: "a conscious and creative communication with and through materials to achieve a human effect" (Sharples 60). Viewing writing as design can help reinforce the rhetorical nature of composition while also encouraging us to take responsibility for our design decisions.

As the metaphor of "writing as design" gains currency in composition and literacy studies, it becomes apparent that many naturally occurring bridges already exist between an ecological design and composition studies. *Cradle to Cradle* helps solidify these connections by offering a design language that applies both to traditional fields of design and to composition.

In the same way that designers depend on a shared "terminology or meta-language" to do their work, writers need a similar design language "to talk to themselves and others about the process of writing and the properties of texts" (Sharples 63–65). In reality, there are several design languages specific to writing, such as rhetoric, literacy theory, and cognitive psychology, and scholars and teachers of English frequently range farther afield to draw on many other disciplines in order to understand better the process of reading and writing. In recent years, ecocriticism and ecocomposition have emerged as approaches that draw on scientific discourse in ecology and biology for their terms and metaphors. In his introduction to *Ecocomposition: Theoretical and Pedagogical Approaches*, Sid Dobrin describes ecocomposition as a place where ecology and rhetoric and composition can converge, and he wonders why the field of "composition and rhetoric has embraced the metaphors of space and place, but has been limited in its adoption of ecological methodologies" (Weisser and Dobrin 12). Without ignoring the impressive range of theoretical approaches in this volume, it is safe to say that the discourse of the life sciences—biology and ecology—tends to play a central role in the theoretical orientation of ecocomposition and ecocriticism.

However, McDonough and Braungart's argument in *Cradle to Cradle* would suggest that we need more than this to address fully the rhetorical challenges we face. Since little precedence currently exists for viewing writing as design, and since eco-effective design has such a clear rhetorical focus, the design principles of eco-effective design seem relevant to compositionists who take seriously the role human intentions play in our environmental crisis. As I argue in the following discussion, eco-effective rhetoric seeks to produce texts that are designed with the future in mind, that grow out of a deep engagement with place and pay close critical attention to technologies we use and design. While these points clearly do not exhaust the implications of eco-effective design for composition, they do suggest ways that ecocomposition could benefit from adding such design to its store of theoretical and pedagogical resources.

Designing for the Future

For those involved in ecocomposition and sustainable pedagogy, the future is ultimately what is at stake in how we teach our students to write. We urge our students to think critically not only about how our choices affect the health of ecosystems and communities right now but also about how they will impact future generations. We try to raise students' awareness of how the products we buy and the places we design have a way of connecting the global to the local in complex ways, and we encourage students to develop research skills that enable them to trace out the often hidden, global effects of local places and products. Because such cultural criticism often involves presenting students with bad news about environment degradation or global injustices, we face a dilemma similar to what McDonough and Braungart highlight in *Cradle to Cradle*—namely, that just communicating bad news often is not enough in itself to motivate others to change their attitudes or behavior. As Paula Mathieu and James Sosnoski point out in their essay "Enacting Culture: The Practice of Comparative Cultural Study," teaching cultural criticism can pose rhetorical challenges because it often conveys an underlying message that students need to give things up, to "abnegate their entire way of life and exciting cultural practices." This often stems from urging them to identify the negative aspects of culture (often as determined by the professor) without offering them viable alternatives, without asking students "to choose the cultural practices that benefit them," and without encouraging students to see themselves as agents of change in culture (Mathieu and Sosnoski 328). It is no wonder that students may either become defensive, feeling that their way of life is under attack, or succumb to despair, feeling as if the problems presented are insurmountable and their responses are insignificant.

Mathieu and Sosnoski propose "rhetoricizing critique" by having students "enact culture" rather than simply stopping with criticism, by having students participate in the "the development of a new practice or the remodeling of [an existing] one" (330). This contrast between criticizing culture and "enacting culture" closely resembles the difference Gunther Kress sees between critique and design. In his view, critique is most appropriate for "periods of relative social stability" when it has the "function of introducing a dynamic into the system," while design is better suited for periods of widespread change, when "the rules of constitution both of texts and of social arrangements are in crisis: they are not settled, but in process of change." In Kress's words, "Critique is anchored to the ground of someone's past agendas; design projects the purposes, interests, and desires of the maker into the future. Design is prospective not retrospective, constructive not deconstructive, utopian and not nostalgic" (50). If, as Bryan Lawson argues, "any piece of design contains, to some extent, an assertion about the future," then emphasizing design rather than critique makes it more likely that criticizing culture will always involve imagining positive design alternatives as well (Lawson 169). In other words, cultural criticism remains implicit in the process of design in a way that can diffuse defensiveness and despair while attempting to foster a hopeful, productive engagement with culture.

This design philosophy was evident in Paula Mathieu's course, "Reading, Writing, and Enacting Cultures," a pilot composition course taught at the University of Illinois, Chicago, that "involved students in reshaping specific, local, cultural practices in which they were positioned as subjects" (331). For their final class project, students chose to create a website that responded to a perceived lack of information provided by the official university website. Students researched questions about the University of Illinois–Chicago community, compared the UIC website with other university sites, and then published their results on an alternative site called "The Missing Links," accessible from the English department website. A related assignment asked students to write an essay in which they imagined their ideal university, an assignment that invited students "to escape the purely negative space of critique by asking them to imagine better ways to teach and learn" (334). In Mathieu's assessment, "students developed their desires and critiques through the process of writing," and "the act of comparison, either concrete or utopian, became a process of critical creation, through which students were able to form and test critiques in the light of their desires for a better place to live and work" (335–36).

The rhetorical artifacts designed in this course are significant not only because they allow students to imagine alternative futures, but also because they take an electronic form that can circulate beyond the classroom and can affect a broader audience than just their teacher. If eco-effective texts are designed to imagine alternative futures, then perhaps we need to pay more attention to the futures of these texts themselves. In other words, is it important to be asking, "Where do composition papers go to die?" The answer could be as straightforward as researching a university's recycling policy and discovering the quantity of papers consumed by students and faculty. However, woven in with these material considerations are broader rhetorical issues. Since the production of texts requires valuable resources of time, money, and materials, eco-effective design would have us ask how the rhetorical artifacts we create, circulate, and teach work to promote sustainability and address the environmental crisis we face. To this end, we need to design texts with a lifespan that more closely resembles the life cycle of an eco-effectively designed product. Too often we ask students to design texts with a natural lifespan of fifteen weeks, as if a kind of planned obsolescence is built into our assignments. Like the products McDonough and Braungart describe, most academic writing assignments have a "cradle to grave" design—they travel from student to teacher and then, after one final contact with the student, they proceed directly to the academic landfill—the waste basket. By contrast, eco-effective texts are designed to be used and reused, to be circulated among students and other classes, and to serve as an ongoing resource in the lives of the authors themselves, providing ideas and inspiration throughout their college education and beyond.

Design from Place

In the context of increasing residential mobility, rapidly transformed physical environments, and quickly changing technologies, students need more than just "freshman orientation" to figure out where they are. For many of us, a deep sense of place is no longer something we inherit simply by residing in the same place over time; rather, it is something we must actively construct. Fortunately, in recent years several place-based approaches have emerged within the field of composition and rhetoric—geographic approaches, ecocomposition, service learning, community literacy, regional studies—approaches that take seriously the relationship between literacy, identity, and place and that view the question "Where am I?" as central to the intellectual project of the university. Similarly, eco-effective design draws on the local for resources and ideas in order to make products and buildings that are fully native to that place. As McDonough and Braungart put it:

> In our minds, all sustainability is local. On one level, that suggests a rich engagement with one's place, an attitude toward design that draws information and inspiration from the nearby living world. But it can also mean that one develops an appreciation for the distant effects of local actions and the local effects of distant actions. ("Extravagant Gesture" 26)

In the same way McDonough and Braungart design buildings that take both form and function from local environments, we can ask students to engage in the production of local knowledge that intimately shapes the texts they design. Eco-effective rhetoric fosters a deeper sense of place by having students draw on local materials for their writing, whether that means writing about where they are from—hometowns, neighborhoods, summer vacations—or the communities in which their university is situated. In both cases, design grows from a careful attention to place and produces something that tends to nourish local environments and those who inhabit them.

This emphasis on place is closely related to what Sim Van Der Ryn and Stuart Cowan define as another central principle of ecological design, that *everyone is a designer*. According to their definition:

> Ecological design suggests a deeply participatory process in which technical disciplinary languages and barriers are exchanged for a shared understanding of the design problem. Ecological design changes the old rules about what counts for knowledge and who counts as a knower. It suggests that sustainability is a cultural process rather than an expert one, and that we should all acquire a basic competence in the shaping of our world. (147)

In the context of composition, we must assume this "world" that we shape refers not just to the physical places we create or the products we make but also the rhetorical artifacts we design. Places are designed not just through blueprints and bulldozers but also through texts that express human intentions, desires, and visions of the future. For every subdivision, highway, or public park, there are thousands of pages of words put to paper: memos, policy statements, legislative bills, science fiction novels, academic essays, websites. Composition takes seriously the rhetorical web that shapes the design of any physical place or product.

For a place-based composition course to reflect the "participatory process" of ecological design, students and teachers alike must begin to view themselves as designers. Before students can design eco-effective texts, teachers must design eco-effective courses. As Strain and VanHoosier-Carey have argued, creating engaging courses in the humanities involves a process that closely resembles interactive design. Whether or not it uses new technologies, a well-designed course involves presenting complex material to students in such a way that they do not just passively receive knowledge but actively shape the experience of the class and the knowledge the course creates (278). Derek Owens has identified one of the central design problems teachers face in creating an eco-effective course: "For me the challenge becomes how to create a classroom environment where students have the freedom to pursue writing projects that matter to them, and yet where, as an instructor, I not only remain energized by their questions and pursuits but also consider the ongoing conversations to be of paramount importance to my students' short- and long-term survival" (7). For Owens, the solution to this challenge must involve getting students to write about work, place, and the future and then to take seriously the knowledge they create. Writing about place in this context is not simply an academic exercise but a way to "serve the larger academic and public realms by making available student testimonies about their environments" (7).

These testimonies are so important that, as C. Mark Hurlbert has argued, "we need to learn much, much more from the people we teach and who are right there, in the exactly proper position to teach us things so important that to ignore them is to commit an act of cruelty" (69). This is particularly the case when students testify about the unhealthy places and cultures they have experienced. In *Letters from the Living*, Michael Blitz and C. Mark Hurlbert describe the Interstate Neighborhood Project, a collaborative project they designed to enable urban students in New York City and students at a university in rural Pennsylvania to share writing about life in these places. In order to explore the meaning of "neighborhood," they conducted both primary and secondary research and then produced a collaboratively authored book documenting their findings. Blitz and Hurlbert intended that during this process students "would try to identify and investigate critical issues in their neighborhoods, and finally, they would collaborate to design or describe plans for better neighborhoods" (95–96). At the end of the semester, one of Blitz's students summarized her experience of the project this way: "Until now, I didn't even know I lived anywhere. I mean, it's like I wasn't anywhere. Now I think about it and I see this place I live in and the place I go to school in. And I could see why some places fall apart. The people in them don't even know they're there" (132). These reflections suggest the effect eco-effective design in composition can have, as it informs both course design and textual production: designed artifacts foster both a more meaningful sense of place and deeper insight into how places are designed.

Technology

While *Cradle to Cradle* is a book about technology, McDonough and Braungart do not subscribe to a blind faith in technological progress. Instead, they share the view of Malcolm McCullough when he observes: "Humanity naturally adapts to being in the world by using technology. The sustainability of our species depends on the appropriateness of our adaptation" (211). According to *Cradle to Cradle*, the Industrial Revolution largely offers examples of inappropriate technological adaptation. In McDonough and Braungart's view, our problem is not that we lack the technology to redesign how we make things; rather, we lack the imagination and the will to use the design intelligence we already have. They issue a challenge to both environmentalists and designers of all kinds to reimagine the possibilities for human innovation and creativity: "In the midst of a great deal of talk about reducing the human footprint, we offer a different vision. What if humans designed products and systems that celebrate an abundance of human creativity, culture, and productivity? That are so intelligent and safe, our species leaves an ecological footprint to delight in, not lament?" (15–16). In other words, for McDonough and Braungart the problem has less to do with technology than with our design values, and the solution is not to withdraw from technology but to engage with it more fully, redesigning everything we can with greater ecological intelligence.

However, by designing a book using materials that exemplify eco-effective design, McDonough and Braungart also present a challenge to composition scholars. In McDonough and Braungart's assessment, neither traditional books nor recycled books are designed as intelligently as they could be, nor as they need to be in our current environmental context. Though they could have put forth a strong argument in the form of a traditional book, they chose instead to design the physical medium and the verbal argument such that the two reinforce each other in profound ways. Because the technology of reading matters for them, their book succeeds in making visible what would be transparent to most readers—the material design of the text. In doing so, they have achieved what most in the "Computers and Writing" field of composition see as one of their primary goals in fostering critical technological literacy: to help readers (or, in the case of teachers, students) recognize the writing technologies they use *as technologies* that are neither natural nor neutral.

Were McDonough and Braungart hired as consultants to analyze the field of composition, they might identify an unproductive split between ecocomposition and technoliteracy, between those who care about the environment and those who focus on new technologies. In McDonough and Braungart's view, these are shared projects. They might inquire to what extent are computers and writing scholars addressing the environmental consequences of the digital media we use? To what extent are ecocompositionists moving beyond technological critique by helping students imagine positive design alternatives?

An eco-effective approach to writing technologies might involve examining the affordances within new media to discover how they can support the design qualities mentioned earlier—an orientation toward the future and an attention to place. Eco-effective design, then, attempts to foster a deeper sense of place while encouraging a critical attitude toward where new technologies might be leading us. It is not enough simply to adjust to new technologies; rather, we must also wrestle with the long-term implications of current ways of being in the world by cultivating a productive tension between *kairos* and *chronos*, between the tyrannical timeliness of technology and the broader prospects for a sustainable future (Orr 72). Part of this process might be to ask how new media and online technologies can connect us to place rather than disconnect us? As Mitchell Thomashow has argued, the Internet can play an important role in helping us understand the connections between our local environments and such global phenomena as climate change, as long as we find ways to modulate our perceptual pace by both exploring places via the Web and observing places at a walking pace (139–40). If we ask students to create local knowledge using a range of writing technologies, both new and old, we cultivate a healthy tension between the experience of place and the experience of technology that encourages more critical engagement with both.

Perhaps the most profound ecological lesson we could teach our students would be by enabling them to compose using a writing technology designed as elegantly and eco-effectively as the book *Cradle to Cradle*. Does it matter that the computer I write with is composed of a "witch's brew of toxic chemicals and [is] designed without recycling in mind," a box of toxins that caused pollution when it was created and will likely cause pollution when its lifespan is over, possibly contributing to environmental degradation in a poor community overseas? ("Exporting Harm" 3). For McDonough and Braungart, the answer would surely be yes. Designing an eco-effective computer may be beyond the technical reach of composition scholars, but imagining design alternatives certainly is not. Until we can write with ecologically friendly computers, our job is to communicate this vision through the texts we design.

Designing Hope

Though not a book of composition theory, *Cradle to Cradle* offers a model of eco-effective rhetoric for those of us trying to help our students imagine and design more hopeful futures in their writing. McDonough and Braungart are struggling with the same issues many of us face as teachers and scholars committed to issues of sustainability and environmental responsibility: namely, how do we respond to the world's overwhelming environmental and social problems in positive, life-affirming ways? Ultimately, this can only happen, in McDonough and Braungart's view, when eco-effective design fosters creativity, fecundity, and risk. When a reporter once asked him a question about sustainability, McDonough responded, "I'm not really into sustainability," and posed a question of his own: "Are you married?" When the reporter responded he was, McDonough asked, "How would your wife feel if you described your marriage as 'sustainable'?" His point, of course, was that such a descriptor lacked any sense of passion, excitement, fecundity, or fun, something that matters deeply for the authors of *Cradle to Cradle*.

Fortunately, this also matters to many teachers who encourage their students to be creative, to take risks, to have fun with their writing. As teachers, few of us want students to produce texts that are simply efficient; this is what students are aiming for when they ask us, "What do I have to do to get an A in this class?" But getting beyond "efficiency" takes on added urgency when we consider that our students' ability to imagine more sustainable futures might depend on it. As we put books in our students' hands and ask them to design texts of their own, perhaps we should be asking ourselves the important questions that conclude *Cradle to Cradle*:

> How can we support and perpetuate the rights of all living things to share in a world of abundance? How can we love the children of all species—not just our own, for all time? Imagine what a world of prosperity and health in the future will look like, and begin designing for it right now. What would it mean to become, once again, native to this place, the Earth—the home of *all* our relations? This is going to take us all, and it is going to take forever. But then, that's the point.

If we feel we must give students some bad news to help them think critically about the world, then it is also our job to offer them a bit of hope, the kind of hope that emerges from good design.

I like to imagine the first-year writing students whom I teach picking up *Cradle to Cradle* at the bookstore, thumbing through it quizzically, wondering how this book relates to writing. I can also imagine the benefits of spending a semester convincing them that it does relate. But even if I never teach *Cradle to Cradle* in a writing course, it ought to inform the way I think about composition because it performs what Annette Kolodny has argued is important rhetorical work: finding new languages to address environmental issues, languages that break down rhetorical barriers and meet people where they are. For this to happen, those of us in ecocomposition may need to expand our vocabulary to include not only the discourse of the natural sciences but also the language of ecological design. If McDonough and Braungart can use the rhetoric of eco-effective design to enlist the energies of businesspeople, industrialists, and designers in shaping a sustainable future, then we should feel hopeful that something similar can happen in our classes.

WORKS CITED

Blitz, Michael, and C. Mark Hurlbert. *Letters for the Living: Teaching Writing in a Violent Age*. Urbana, Ill.: National Council of Teachers of English, 1998.

Buchanan, Richard. "Declaration by Design: Rhetoric, Argument, and Demonstration in Design Practice." In *Design Discourse: History, Theory, Criticism*, ed. Victor Margolin. Chicago: University of Chicago Press, 1989. 91–109.

Dillon, Andrew. "Writing as Design: Hypermedia and the Shape of Information Space." In *Writing Hypertext and Learning: Conceptual and Empirical Approaches*, ed. Rainer Bromme and Elmar Stahl. Boston: Pergamon, 2002. 63–72.

Faigley, Lester. "Material Literacy and Visual Design." In *Rhetorical Bodies: Toward a Material Rhetoric*, ed. Jack Seltzer and Sharon Crowley. Madison: University of Wisconsin Press, 1999. 171–206.

Kalantzis, Mary, and Bill Cope. *Transformations in Language and Learning: Perspectives on Multiliteracies*. Australia: Common Ground, 2001.

Kolodny, Annette. Plenary Session: Tribute to Annette Kolodny. Conference of the Association for the Study of Literature and the Environment, 20 June 2001. Northern Arizona University, Flagstaff.

Kress, Gunther. *Literacy in the New Media Age*. London: Routledge, 2003.

Lawson, Bryan. *How Designers Think: The Design Process Demystified*. Boston, Mass.: Architectural Press, 1997.

Luke, Timothy. "Green Consumerism: Ecology and the Ruse of Recycling." In *In the Nature of Things: Language, Politics, and the Environment*, ed. Jane Bennett and William Chaloupka. Minneapolis: University of Minnesota Press, 1993. 154–72.

Mathieu, Paula, and James J. Sosnoski. "Enacting Cultures: The Practice of Comparative Cultural Study." In *The Relevance of English: Teaching That Matters in Students' Lives*, ed. Robert Yagelski, Scott A. Leonard, and Richard M. Ohmann. Urbana, Ill.: National Council of Teachers of English, 2002. 324–43.

McCullough, Malcolm. *Digital Ground: Architecture, Pervasive Computing, and Environmental Knowing*. Cambridge, Mass.: MIT Press, 2004.

McDonough, William. "Cradle to Cradle and the Triple Bottom Line." 14 April 2003. Harvard Business School, Allston, Mass.

McDonough, William, and Michael Braungart. *Cradle to Cradle: Remaking the Way We Make Things*. New York: North Point Press, 2002.

Norman, Donald. *Turn Signals Are the Facial Expressions of Automobiles*. Reading, Mass.: Addison-Wesley, 1992.

Orr, David. *The Nature of Design: Ecology, Culture, and Human Intention*. New York: Oxford University Press, 2002.

Owens, Derek. *Composition and Sustainability: Teaching for a Threatened Generation*. Urbana, Ill.: National Council of Teachers of English, 2001.

Puckett, Jim, Leslie Byster, Sarah Westervelt, Richard Gutierrez, Sheila Davis, Asma Hussein, and Madhumitta Dutta. "Exporting Harm: The High-Tech Trashing of Asia." 25 February 2002. Basel Action Network and Silicon Valley Toxics Coalition. http://www.svtc.org/cleancc/pubs/technotrash.pdf.

Schoenberger, Karl. "Where Computers Go to Die: Poor Cities in China Become Dumping Ground for E-waste." *Mercury News* 23 November 2002, http://www.mercurynews.com/mld/mercurynews/4591233.htm (accessed 29 September 2004).

Sharples, Mike. *How We Write: Writing as Creative Design*. New York: Routledge, 1999.

Strain, Ellen, and Gregory VanHoosier-Carey. "Eloquent Interfaces: Humanities-Based Analysis in the Age of Hypermedia." In *Eloquent Images: Word and Image in the Age of New Media*, ed. Mary Hocks and Michelle Kendrick. Cambridge, Mass.: MIT Press, 2003. 257–81.

Thomashow, Mitchell. *Bringing the Biosphere Home: Learning to Perceive Global Environmental Change*. Cambridge, Mass.: MIT Press, 2002.

Van Der Ryn, Sim, and Stuart Cowan. *Ecological Design*. Washington, D.C.: Island Press, 1995.

Weisser, Christian, and Sidney Dobrin, eds. *Ecocomposition: Theoretical and Pedagogical Approaches*. Albany: State University of New York Press, 2001.

A Mosaic of Landscapes

Ecological Restoration and the Work of Leopold, Coetzee, and Silko

ALTHOUGH THE GOAL of most ecological restoration projects is to return the landscape to its condition prior to European contact, less attention has been paid to the ecological implications of cultural restoration movements that involve restoring the rights and sovereignty of the people who may have lived at the restoration site before the arrival of Europeans. Most recent attempts to define ecological restoration avoid the unsettling questions of cultural restoration, with limited references to the human presence in the landscape and ambiguous allusions to the importance of human preferences in shaping what occurs there. The Society for Ecological Restoration (SER), for example, defines ecological restoration as "the process of assisting the recovery of an ecosystem that has been degraded, damaged or destroyed."[1] Those works that do acknowledge the influence of cultural narrative and human history on the landscape, such as *The Sunflower Forest*, by the influential restorationist William Jordan III, or Eric Higgs's recent *Nature by Design*, promote "historical fidelity" to the ecology of the restoration site without considering what this adherence to the past might mean in the context of indigenous displacement and loss of sovereignty.[2]

For the ecological restorationist, immersed in the selection of native plant species and the management of habitat, the implications of such histories might seem outside the professional and ecological boundaries of the project. Yet the cultural nature of the ecological restoration process demands a reckoning with such issues, to view the restoration site as part of what Joni Adamson, in *American Indian Literature, Environmental Justice and Ecocriticism: The Middle Place* calls "that contested terrain where interrelated social and environmental problems originate" (xvii). This applies particularly when we are, as Jordan suggests, in the process of creating and performing rituals that will define a new series of ethical relationships with the land.[3] The assumption of power and control over the landscape inevitably troubles the restorationist, because the ethic upon which restoration is based is communal and nonhierarchical. We inevitably find ourselves making decisions and taking responsibility for what happens in the world when we would prefer not to, when we would prefer to let nature take its course.

Ecological restoration, as currently conceived, demands firm guidance from above. Yet it could offer us the chance to step down from the high seat of power, if we were to cede some of the rights of ownership and control to the people who existed there first. How can we invite into these new rituals a sense of what it means to be indigenous to these very same landscapes for thousands of years? How can ecological restoration, as a ritualized form of ecological redress, deal with the questions of indigenous history and sovereignty and become a framework of restitution for rights denied and peoples displaced? One way to look for such practices is to examine the cultural impact of ecological restoration narratives, such as Aldo Leopold's *A Sand County Almanac*, and simultaneously to consider the ecological implications of such cultural restoration narratives as J. M. Coetzee's *Life and Times of Michael K* or Leslie Marmon Silko's *Gardens in the Dunes*. These narratives exemplify the ambivalent, often paradoxical and competitive relationship to the restoration space and help characterize the drive that seeks to restore in certain locations and not others, or to engage in certain restoration practices but not others, or to imagine certain outcomes and prohibit others.

Restoration, as a narrative of emancipation, self-realization, nostalgia, and return, is itself such an integral, dialectic counternarrative to the progressive development of modernity that its presence is nearly ubiquitous, but as an *ecological* manifestation its expression until recently has been limited.[4] Ecological restoration is a particular expression of cultural restoration that has manifested itself most fully in those places with unassimilated divisions between an indigenous culture and a European, colonial culture. As Higgs points out, the desire to return to conditions prior to European contact is primarily a preoccupation in those areas where such a disturbance, and continued colonization, has taken place.[5] Thus the ecological restoration narrative expresses certain desires and anxieties while avoiding and disguising others, such as the highly troubling question of land rights. The relationship of the return journey to the process of restoration is one such point of anxiety. The return journey calls attention to an act of creative belonging that undermines the authenticity, and thus the legitimacy, of the restoration process, and therefore the whole question of how the restorationist arrived at the restoration site is often a missing sequence in the restoration narrative. Such is the case with the foundational ecological narrative *A Sand County Almanac*, which I juxtapose here with restoration narratives that come from outside the traditional boundaries of ecological restoration.

Despite clear distinctions between the book's three sections, and the fact that the book was assembled in large part after Leopold's death, the *Almanac* has rarely been viewed as the product of two distinct periods in Leopold's life. Born in Iowa, Leopold joined the westward expansion of the American frontier and spent the first half of his career exploring the territory that eventually became New Mexico and Arizona, a period chronicled in the second portion of the book. Then he returned to the Midwest, purchased a worn-out farm, and began the philosophical and practical work of ecological restoration for which he is famous, a period that appears in the first section of the book. The chronology of the work is thus strangely discontinuous—the "homecomer" is already situated in place when the almanac begins.[6]

Leopold spent nearly half his adult life in the Southwest, and at first glance his sojourn there appears to reflect a deepening commitment to the regional community and the land. In almost every cursory respect, the southwestern Leopold appears to be the quintessential re-inhabitory bioregionalist, rooting himself in the political, economic, and biotic communities of his adopted location.[7] So why did he leave? What was missing from the re-inhabitation of New Mexico that could be found in Wisconsin? Curt Meine, his biographer, suggests that Leopold himself never offered a full explanation, and certainly the *Almanac* offers no explicit justification for the move. To understand it, we must look at the implications of his beliefs within the context of the Southwest at the time. Leopold believed that "a thing is right when it tends to preserve the integrity, stability, and beauty of the biotic community. It is wrong when it tends otherwise" (225). He may very well have viewed his work as a professional forester in the region as untenable on these terms. Acting under the wise use mandate of Gifford Pinchot, the early Forest Service sought to improve the management of forest resources, and management often meant making resources available for the economic demands of "Progress," not preserving their integrity, stability, and beauty. In Leopold's view, this ideology of economic growth extinguished much of the region's cultural distinctness and charismatic megafauna.

At some point, Leopold must have decided that in accordance with his own developing land ethic, his continued presence in the region did not make sense. An admission of this sort appears in "Pioneers and Gullies," an article published in 1924, as Leopold prepared to make the move back East:

> To a degree we are facing the question of whether we are here to "skin" the Southwest and then get out, or whether we are here to found a permanent, civilized community with room to grow and improve. We cannot long continue to accept our losses without admitting that the former, rather than the latter, is by way of becoming the real result of our occupancy. (*Round River* 110)

Erosion becomes the central metaphor for his stay in the Southwest, explored most fully in a 1933 essay titled "The Virgin Southwest," in which Leopold reads the landscape back to the Spanish importation of herd animals as an erosion of cultural and ecological value. The essay concludes hopelessly that "real harmony" with the southwestern landscape demands an impossible cultural and ethical shift (179). This wasting away of cultural and ecological capital erodes the premise of re-inhabitation; rather than building up a relationship to place over time, the outsider causes the ecology of the place to change so dramatically that whatever bonds were established at the start cannot be maintained. In the *Almanac* essay "Escudilla," Leopold connects the signs of erosion to the colonization of wild areas and regional cultures, and laments his own role in the process, admitting that "we, too, were the captains of an invasion too sure of its own righteousness" (137). Given this powerful sense of loss, it would hardly be surprising if Leopold felt trapped by the loss of the sublime, on one hand, and the spiritual inadequacy of "Progress," on the other. He was unable to maintain a re-inhabitory identity in this landscape.

Leopold's return to the Midwest was thus a rejection of frontier conquest and re-inhabitation in favor of an exploration of the forgotten, overlooked, and underimagined. His leaving also suggests that moving to a new bioregion entails more than the discovery and celebration of the adopted region's biological and cultural resources. It requires an economic, ethical, and most important, ecological integration into the landscape that Leopold did not ultimately perceive as possible for himself in the Southwest.

Despite the apparent rejection of southwestern colonization, the *Almanac* makes clear that the move back to one's "homeland" does not require the same kind of sensitivity to the rights of previous occupants that might apply to the occupation of a southwestern frontier. The midwestern landscape, in

Leopold's view, was a nearly abandoned ruin, the secret ecological fragments of which could be discovered and pieced back together to approx-
imate a whole ecosystem. This reweaving of the old ecological fabric de-
manded human intervention, and because the damage had already been
done, it provided the opportunity for human integration into the ecological
community without an accompanying sense of guilt. When *A Sand County
Almanac* focuses on Leopold's activities at the Sauk County farm, the narrator frequently imagines what has been lost, but unlike his acknowledgment
of culpability in "Escudilla," he does not take responsibility for midwestern
biological and cultural losses, and he never implicates himself in the historical narrative that included the destruction of the prairie as both ecosystem
and homeland. Coming back, therefore, did not liberate Leopold from the
sense of loss, but in returning to an already despoiled land he was freed
from the sense of having caused it, and from the feelings of helplessness
that might otherwise arise.

Contesting Land Rights on the Farm

The nature of Leopold's originary claim to the Midwest does not appear
in the *Almanac*, presumably because such a claim can be asserted so easily
from inside the hegemonic system, by purchasing property and pointing to
the presence of one's forebears, that it requires no defense. Yet as the South
African novelist J. M. Coetzee's apartheid-era *Life and Times of Michael K*
indicates, the questions of where you come from, and where you belong,
are embedded in a system of property rights that is neither politically inert
nor transparent. In fact, the very land acquisition process through which
Leopold glides so swiftly that it barely deserves mention becomes the focal point of indigenous land rights movements, for the narrative of land
possession suddenly appears as a series of political obstacles, questionable
naturalisms, and physical fences.

It is certainly true that South Africa is not the American West, and that
the writing of these authors reflects the shift from modern to postmodern.
Yet when we consider Coetzee's novel in light of Leopold's *Almanac*, we
see the same themes of land tenure, displacement, and return played out
in remarkably similar locations. Coetzee himself, in the essay "Farm Novel
and Plaasroman," has identified the *plaasroman*, or agrarian return-to-the-
land novel, as a central preoccupation of Afrikaans fiction and Depression-
era fiction more generally (71), a justification Dirk Penner uses to compare

Steinbeck's *Grapes of Wrath* with Coetzee's novel (Penner 101). Steinbeck's novel, however, diverges from *Michael K* in the latter's invocation of the return: whereas Steinbeck chronicles the setting out for a new Eden in California, Coetzee's protagonist undertakes a journey back home. *Michael K* thus seeks to subvert the narrative by which the colonist creates a sense of belonging to the land, by appropriating what amounts to the narrative arc of Leopold's homecoming and replacing the *Almanac*'s protagonist with a racial outsider.

Perhaps the best way to begin is to ground our analysis of *Michael K* in Coetzee's semi-autobiographical narrative, *Boyhood*, which in many ways sets the scene for the novel's exploration of rural economies and land tenure rights. This is primarily an account of suburban alienation, but the critical location that exists in counterpoise to the suburb is the farm, the place of history, communal and familial wholeness and ecological proximity. The boy "loves every stone of it, every bush, every blade of grass, loves the birds that give its name" (80). Yet the farm is also a place of troubled rights and identity, for the boy is aware that his relations cannot claim the farm exclusively either. The beguiling simplicities and authenticities of farm life are undercut by the painful realization of an irreconcilable outsider status: "As far back as he can remember this love [of the land] has had an edge of pain. He may visit the farm but he will never live there. The farm is not his home; he will never be more than a guest, an uneasy guest" (79). Not only is the boy's claim made tenuous by the uneasy relations with his extended family members who actually inhabit the place, but at a deeper level he must confront the presence of Outa Jaap, the man who was there before his family and who appears to have a deeper claim to knowledge of the landscape.

Belonging becomes a preoccupation for the boy because it cannot be attained: "The secret and sacred word that binds him to the farm is *belong*. Out in the veld by himself he can breathe the word aloud: *I belong on the farm*" (95). The farm does not belong to him, but out in the veld, away from competing human claims, he can almost imagine belonging to the landscape, to the presumably less exclusive ecological community. Coetzee allows only the initial, solitary steps toward belonging to take place here because the Coetzees are "like swallows" (87), transient visitors whose presence is always countered by the permanent, rooted figure of the "coloured man Freek" and Outa Jaap. The solitary experience of belonging is never reconciled with the presence of a community that also belongs to the place, partly because the boy leaves before he can discover the rituals required for this to happen, and more importantly because Coetzee appears to suggest that such rituals do not exist for the white boy confronting the "coloured" community.

While the boy never discovers a way of belonging without honoring prior presences, asking plaintively, "Is there no way of living in the Karoo—the only place in the world where he wants to be—as he wants to live: without belonging to a family" (91), Leopold appears to locate just such an opportunity on his farm. Like the young Coetzee, Leopold is an occasional visitor to his farm, but there is no Outa Jaap in Leopold's *Almanac*, just the unencumbered, abandoned farm that is available for the return journey and the practice of reintegration, a process rendered even less complicated by the absence of a human community that can talk back or make demands. Just as the boy finds a sense of belonging out in the veld, so Leopold can belong in the degraded ecological community of his own farm, because in the absence of a human community, the ecological community becomes more prominent and available, and no communal rituals are necessary to reassert belonging. The boy claims he "wants everything to be as it was in the past" (82), a nostalgia he shares with Leopold's narrator, who also pines for an ecologically diverse, stable, and authentic farm that is coincidentally free of the potentially hostile presence of indigenous people.

Derek Wright's trenchant critique of *Michael K* takes Coetzee to task for presuming to speak, within the conventions of a realist narrative, for those whose experience he cannot presume to know, the "coloured" people of South Africa.[8] *Boyhood* raises the stakes of this accusation still further, because we find the details of that autobiographical narrative transposed not just to the farm as location, or to the history of the family that once farmed it, but to the personal history of K himself, such that K, and the young Visagie whom he encounters on the farm, are expressions of Coetzee's own biography, his own split, ambivalent, native and non-native self. It is hardly surprising, then, that clues to K's ethnicity are hard to come by, consisting only of a checkmark on an identity card, since Coetzee is inhabiting both places simultaneously and drawing them into conflict with each other.

What Wright never states, but what is equally implicit in his argument, is that Coetzee is claiming a partial indigeneity by ascribing to K an ambivalent native identity that denies him what might otherwise be his due: a more stable birthright, a greater sense of communal belonging, a more fulfilling relationship with the ecological system. The physical details of K's engagement with the farm are too similar to those of the boy's encounter with farm life to be accidental, and it is this transposing of memories across the matrices of race and colonization that is both troubling and provocative.[9]

What becomes clear in *Boyhood* is that Coetzee is also transposing personal myths into K's imaginary world, an act of narrative transgression that also allows him to invest himself in the subaltern, indigenous experience.

The restoration narratives of the colonizer often induct a version of indigenous memory into the practice of becoming native, of belonging. This weaving of native story into the narrative of a new presence is central to the legitimacy of bioregional, re-inhabitory practice. What is happening here, however, is the weaving of white memory into fictionalized "coloured" experience, a reversal of sorts that both legitimizes the author's presence in that landscape and undermines it. It represents a presumption that "coloured" experience of the land is akin to white experience when both are seeking the sense of belonging, that the physical markers of belonging—ecology, ruins, the experience of harvest—are universal and therefore potentially transferable.

Coetzee cancels K's bid for communal belonging by separating the young male figure of *Boyhood* from K, transforming K into an Outa Jaap–like man of the earth, and bringing the resulting two characters into conflict with one another over who belongs on the farm. While we remain in K's consciousness, K himself begins to see himself through the eyes of the young Visagie as a primitive figure, closer to the earth of the farm but conversely denied any legal right to reside there. K becomes both the subject, as an extension of the author's fictionalized memories of the farm, and the "coloured" object, and Coetzee refuses to reconcile the two, because the young Visagie also partakes of the mythic material of *Boyhood*. The young Visagie scion has deserted the army and returned to seek refuge on the property he remembers from childhood. It is as if the protagonist of *Boyhood* has grown up to pursue his own return narrative. Which narrative of belonging has primacy? Or is the author, in fact, identifying with both characters, both return narratives? What we are discovering here are the divided loyalties of the mind that is both colonial and postcolonial in its identifications, both native and non-native, legitimized by place of birth and illegitimatized by place of birth.

The denial of mutuality in *Michael K* runs counter to Leopold's narrative and those restoration narratives based upon Leopold's notion of an expanded sense of community and cooperation among species in specific locations.[10] In his midwestern pastoral ideal, Leopold offers the example of humanity and wildlife dwelling harmoniously together within the cyclical and glacially slow evolutions of geologic time. When farmers used the Wisconsin marshes for hay, for example, "man and beast . . . lived on and with each other in mutual toleration," a communal state of affairs that could have continued "forever" (99). Gallagher describes a similar dream of harmony on the South African farm: "The dream of a rural South Africa made up of family farms on which Afrikaner farmers and African laborers live together in paternalistic harmony continues to haunt the South African conscious-ness" (93). The young Visagie offers K this vision of mutually beneficial existence, since for the young deserter, the farm is a forgotten islet of har-mony in a sea of war. Yet K responds that there is "not enough for the both of them" (61). He leaves, and when he returns, the young Visagie is gone, rep-resenting an utter failure of reconciliation and community building. Unlike Wes Jackson and others who seek to reclaim the derelict farm communities of the American West with an ecologically informed gardening that is the antithesis of globalized commerce, Coetzee sets up K's solitary gardening as the contrary practice to communal resistance or reconciliation.

The Taproot of Community

What is missing in both the preceding narratives is a reckoning with the historical roots of localized community. Leopold's ecological narrative re-peatedly swerves away from the implications of native human presence at the restoration site, while *Michael K* destabilizes historical claims to land tenure. Leslie Marmon Silko's *Gardens in the Dunes*, by contrast, suggests that ecological restoration occurs within the context of indigenous history, even in times of cultural suppression and physical displacement. Ecologi-cal practice becomes a ritualized reenactment of communal knowledge that contests or subsumes colonizing claims to the same terrain. Unlike K, who finds his inheritance a jumble of vague memories and missing information, Silko's central figures, two young sisters named Indigo and Sister Salt, are tutored by their grandmother in the ecology of the garden, and this inher-ited knowledge inspires the dreams that sustain them despite displacement. After Grandma Fleet dies, the children know how to continue the harvest.

Their celebration of a harvest meal closely resembles the moment in Coetzee's novel when Michael gets his first taste of the pumpkins he has labeled his children. The sisters also nickname the pumpkins that are like "fat babies that hadn't learned to walk yet" (Silko 56). However, Coetzee invokes the ancestral presence at the restoration site in order to undermine its legitimacy. We can never be sure if K has actually located the place of his mother's birth for his homecoming, and thus while the girls' harvest is a celebration of the next generation's ability to survive, K characterizes the harvest as the symbolic consumption of the next generation. His meal becomes a sacrificial offering to the realization of the self, the feeding of an internal emptiness with the generations to come, a move symbolically akin to the consumption of the cultural capital inherent in seeds. The invocation of an ancestral presence helps the girls to make a claim that neither Leopold nor Coetzee is willing to make—that they belong in their chosen location because of the communal knowledge they have inherited. Michael's "tender cord" is his own creation; the girls' bond to the garden is socially constructed.

The connection between blood and land often devolves into what Gerald Vizenor has called the "blood quantum politics" of exclusion. What we begin to see in Silko's garden, however, and what is most relevant to the practice of restoration, is the beginning of a process of negotiating the terms of cultural survival and interaction. The garden does not exist as an exclusive model for the existence of localized culture, but rather as a refuge for cultural survival in the face of erasure elsewhere. "If anything happens to me," Grandma Fleet warns the children, "you girls stay here. You belong here. Your mama knows she will find you here. Otherwise, how will she ever find you?" (51). Exclusion occurs in the face of disappearance: those in the know will find each other in this place, while those who are attempting to extinguish them will be excluded by their lack of knowledge. However, the garden in the dunes has never been a permanent habitation—it has always been a refuge to weather times of crisis, a home away from home, so knowledge of how to live there is only part of what a Sand Lizard must know to live in the world. As Adamson argues, the garden is only part of a continuum of landscapes necessary for human sustenance, some of them thoroughly humanized, others wild.[11] Building the Sand Lizard community, as opposed to ensuring cultural survival, actually takes place elsewhere, through interactions with other peoples, not isolation. The cause of the girls' departure from the gardens is not their discovery and forced removal by the authorities. They have an overabundance of food to sustain themselves physically in the harsh climate, but the fruit of their labor is not enough. Ostensibly, the girls leave the garden in search of their mother, yet their journey occurs just after Sister Salt's first menstruation, and it is Sister Salt who feels "so lonely for a face besides Indigo's" (59). Their presence in the isolated space is ultimately unsustainable—they will produce no offspring, and the garden will become a prison of the solitary sort Coetzee imagines for K, not a gathering place, if they cannot leave to develop as young women.

Thus the search for other people draws them out into the world, away from the garden, because the garden is separate but not a world of its own. The drama of Silko's novel arises in this tension between experimental motion and protective stasis, the question of whether Indigo will return to the garden and reunite with her family in the physical space they all know and share.

The exotic seeds she collects in the course of her world tour signify the possibility of a dynamic native space that is able to distinguish between healthy terms of trade and exploitation. The seed, the "greatest traveler of them all" (293), becomes the ecological metaphor for cultural survival, locally produced but able to take root in places all over the globe, encapsulating the possibility of future generations to recolonize lost ground, able to survive independently, without intervention, when necessary. This emphasis on the dynamism of the seed is not to suggest that Silko is unaware of its invasive potential or the current anxiety over invasive species. Indeed, as I argue in a forthcoming essay on *Gardens in the Dunes*, Silko uses the seed to highlight the irony of non-native people concerned about the impact of exotic, invasive plants on the landscapes they themselves have invaded. [12] The introduction of non-native plants such as gladioli into the ecologically pristine heart of the desert sanctuary is intended to make the restorationist shudder.

These narratives suggest the need to consider the ecological restoration of landscapes in light of their indigenous cultural history, not just their ecological past. To do so does not necessarily mean constructing a fortress for the expression of nativity but rather to consider the restoration site as part of a mosaic of landscapes, a space in which the terms of power can be negotiated in ways that bring the issues of indigenous displacement and sovereignty into the discussion of goals and methods. One result may be exotic species like gladioli and apricots growing in the midst of native species, as they do in the garden in the dunes, and another may be a more diverse constituency involved in tending the garden. The rituals that evolve in such spaces would undoubtedly be syncretic, not necessarily facsimiles of historic practices but rather explorations of what it means to be indigenous in a contemporary context.

NOTES

1. "The SER International Primer on Ecological Restoration," available at the SER website, http://www.ser.org/content/ecological_restoration_primer.asp.

2. See also Higgs, *Nature by Design*, p. 14, and Jordan, *The Sunflower Forest*, p. 22.

3. Jordan, *The Sunflower Forest*, p. 4.

4. See Benjamin Barber's discussion of Jihad and McWorld as dialectical constructions, one tribal, local, and exclusionary, the other global, diverse, and materialistic, in *Jihad vs. McWorld*.

5. See Higgs, *Nature By Design*, p. 94.

6. Wes Jackson's essay "Matfield Green" describes the "homecomer" as a figure returning to a place-centered, localized experience. "Homecomers," he argues, are searching for a place "to dig in and begin the long search and experiment to become native." See *Rooted in the Land*, pp. 95–103. See also Gregory Cooper's essay "Aldo Leopold and the Values of the Native," in *Rooted in the Land*, pp. 150–60.

7. For a discussion of re-inhabitation, see Gary Snyder's *The Practice of the Wild*.

8. See Derek Wright, "Black Earth, White Myth."

9. Susan Gallagher in *A Story of South Africa* has described the extent to which Coetzee recast the mythic travails of the Boers' struggle for independence into K's own mythic encounters with the camps, the colonial oppressors, and the land.

10. Compare Wendell Berry's Leopold-inspired vision of the farm community in *The Unsettling of America*, Wes Jackson's *Becoming Native to This Place*, and Gregory Cooper in *Rooted in the Land*.

11. Adamson, *American Indian Literature*, p. 183.

12. This essay is forthcoming in a collection of essays on *Gardens in the Dunes* from the University of Pisa Press (Laura Coltelli, ed.).

WORKS CITED

Adamson, Joni. *American Indian Literature, Environmental Justice, and Ecocriticism: The Middle Place*. Tucson: University of Arizona Press, 2001.

Barber, Benjamin. *Jihad vs. McWorld: How Globalism and Tribalism Are Reshaping the World*. New York: Ballantine, 1995.

Berry, Wendell. *The Unsettling of America: Culture and Agriculture*. San Francisco: Sierra Club Books, 1977.

Callicott, J. Baird, ed. *Companion to* A Sand County Almanac: *Interpretive and Critical Essays*. Madison: University of Wisconsin Press, 1987.

Coetzee, J. M. *Boyhood*. New York: Penguin, 1997.

———. "Farm Novel and *Plaasroman*." In *White Writing*, ed. Wes Jackson and William Vitek. New Haven, Conn.: Yale University Press, 1988, pp. 63–81.

———. *Life and Times of Michael K*. New York: Penguin, 1983.

Cooper, Gregory. "Leopold and the Values of the Native." In *Rooted in the Land: Essays on Community and Place*. New Haven, Conn.: Yale University Press, 1996. 150–60.

Gallagher, Susan. *A Story of South Africa: J. M. Coetzee's Fiction in Context*. Cambridge, Mass.: Harvard University Press, 1991.

Higgs, Eric. *Nature by Design: People, Natural Process, and Ecological Restoration*. Cambridge, Mass.: MIT Press, 2003.

Jackson. Wes. *Becoming Native to This Place*. Lexington: University Press of Kentucky, 1994.

Jordan, William, III. *The Sunflower Forest: Ecological Restoration and the New Communion with Nature*. Berkeley: University of California Press, 2003.

Leopold, Aldo. *Aldo Leopold's Southwest*. Ed. David E. Brown and Neil B. Carmony. Albuquerque: University of New Mexico Press, 1990.

———. *For the Health of the Land*. Ed. J. Baird Callicott and Eric T. Fregoyle. Washington, D.C.: Island Press, 1999.

———. *The River of the Mother of God, and Other Essays by Aldo Leopold*. Ed. Susan L. Flader and J. Baird Callicott. Madison: University of Wisconsin Press, 1991.

———. *Round River: From the Journals of Aldo Leopold*. Ed. Luna B. Leopold. New York: Oxford University Press, 1993.

———. *A Sand County Almanac, and Sketches Here and There*. New York: Oxford University Press, 1987.

Penner, Dirk. *Countries of the Mind: The Fiction of J. M. Coetzee*. New York: Westport, 1989.

Silko, Leslie Marmon. *Gardens in the Dunes*. New York: Simon and Schuster, 1999.

Snyder, Gary. *The Practice of the Wild*. New York: North Point, 1990.

Vizenor, Gerald. *Fugitive Poses: Native American Scenes of Absence and Presence*. Lincoln: University of Nebraska Press, 1998.

Wright, Derek. "Black Earth, White Myth: Coetzee's *Michael K*." *Modern Fiction Studies* 38 (1992): 435–44.

AMY M. PATRICK

Apocalyptic or Precautionary?

Revisioning Texts in Environmental Literature

ENVIRONMENTAL APOCALYPTICISM—writing that employs apocalyptic tropes to persuade readers to heed warnings in the face of imminent environmental peril—has been celebrated and criticized since the publication of Rachel Carson's *Silent Spring* (1962). Because public understanding generally equates apocalypse with foreboding doom and gloom, critics have pointed to books like *Silent Spring* as environmentalist hysteria, the products of authors who claim, like Chicken Little, that the sky is falling—or worse, who cry wolf to achieve selfish ends.

Scholars of environmental texts have also commented on environmental apocalypticism. In *The Environmental Imagination* (1995), Lawrence Buell identifies five characteristics of environmental apocalypticism: (1) dramatization of networked relationships; (2) biotic egalitarianism; (3) magnification of scale; (4) conflation of the near and distant; and (5) sense of imminent environmental peril (302–5). He also suggests three things that have specifically characterized this tradition since Carson's *Silent Spring*: "(1) the vision of exploitation leading to 'overshoot' . . . or interference producing irreversible degradation, (2) the vision of a tampered-with nature recoiling against humankind in a kind of return of the repressed, and (3) the loss of all escape routes" (308). Throughout several essays, M. Jimmie Killingsworth and Jacqueline S. Palmer note the propensity for environmental writers to employ apocalyptic tropes in their texts.[1] In fact, the authors contend that the discourse of hysteria provides insight into the ways environmental advocates can encourage social change during periods of environmental crisis ("The Discourse of 'Environmentalist Hysteria'" 37). They go so far as to suggest that "Freud's neurotics anticipate ecological activists in many ways, most notably perhaps in their use of end-of-the-world scenarios, such as we find in the famous prologue to *Silent Spring*, entitled 'A Fable for Tomorrow'" (43). But in their focus on the apocalyptic, neither Buell nor

141

Killingsworth and Palmer do justice to *Silent Spring* and subsequent books
in the tradition.

Environmental Apocalypticism and *Silent Spring*

"A Fable for Tomorrow," *Silent Spring*'s opening chapter, is only two pages,
and while it sets a sobering tone that is threaded throughout the book, Carson acknowledges it immediately as a potential but avoidable future sce-
nario. She goes on to inform the public about the growing evidence against
synthetic chemical pesticides and the lack of evidence that they are not
harmful. Killingsworth and Palmer argue that these "threads of narrative
not anticipated by the 'Fable' get lost in the apocalyptic jumble of the rest"
("*Silent Spring* and Science Fiction" 184). Yet only a few pages after the "Fable," Carson asks: "Have we fallen into a mesmerized state that makes us
accept as inevitable that which is inferior or detrimental, as though having lost the will or the vision to demand that which is good?" (Carson 12).
To this challenge, the answer Carson seeks from readers is a hopeful one:
"No!" While her question resists the pessimistic inevitability of apocalypse
and motivates action toward social change, the complexity of her argument
is often oversimplified. As a result, any optimism has been largely ignored
in the book's reception.

Carson did something important beyond writing a shocking fable: she
empowered her audiences with knowledge to make informed decisions, by
conveying scientific information about the environment and exposing the
uncertainty in which decisions about the environment and human health
are often made. Post-Carson books like Sandra Steingraber's *Living Downstream* (1997) and Edward O. Wilson's *The Future of Life* (2002) do not emphasize irreversible degradation, nature against humankind, or the loss of
alternatives. These books, like *Silent Spring*, may contain apocalyptic characteristics, but it is overly simplistic to focus on this one strategy in the context of what can be understood as a larger precautionary framework.

In a time when environmental interests are increasingly under attack
despite mounting evidence that our health is negatively impacted by con-
taminants in our environment, environmental writers have an obligation
to inform the public, using rhetorical strategies that appeal effectively to
their audiences. Like *Silent Spring*, the post-Carson books mentioned are
meant to help the public make informed decisions about their immediate
interests—their health and the health of their children. In an era when moral

values are at the forefront of public debate, these books appeal to the commonly held value of a high "quality of life" for ourselves and our children.

True, with the end of the Cold War, apocalyptic shock tactics are no longer as effective as they were when *Silent Spring* was published, and it is easy for critics to lump these books together, dismissing them as fanatical. In *Ecospeak: Rhetoric and Environmental Politics in America* (1992), Killingsworth and Palmer critique environmental rhetoric that causes misunderstandings and communication breakdown between opposing views, inhibiting progress on environmental issues. Environmental apocalypticism creates such an ecospeak situation: doomsday warnings are met with skepticism that environmentalists are hysterics crying wolf. Furthermore, the label *environmental apocalypticism* inaccurately reflects the aims of current environmental initiatives and is detrimental to the effectiveness of environmental discourse. By virtue of its negative associations, the label encourages skeptics to discount what they view as fanatical or hysterical rhetoric, thereby justifying the dismissal of all voices associated with the environmental movement. However, rather than typify environmental apocalypticism, *Silent Spring* anticipates the philosophy behind the modern precautionary principle and paves the way for a precautionary tradition in environmental literature.

The Precautionary Principle

Seeking to preserve ecological integrity and human health for future generations, conservation biologists and environmentalists increasingly adopt a long-term perspective in addressing environmental issues. However, because species loss, climate change, and human population density are interrelated, and the system of cause and effect is complex, it is almost impossible to model future consequences of current and past human action with certainty. Consequently, as Bryan G. Norton points out in *The Preservation of Species* (1986), "actions required now to avoid future disasters must be undertaken without sufficient knowledge to make considered choices" (11).

Many conservation biologists, faced with the reality of this uncertainty, advocate that the safest, most economically beneficial way to avoid environmentally related catastrophe is to adopt the precautionary principle and avoid actions that may potentially result in negative consequences to the environment and human health, especially when alternatives exist. The precautionary principle, best articulated in a consensus statement produced at the January 1998 Wingspread conference on implementing the precautionary principle, states:[2]

> When an activity raises threats of harm to human health or the environment, precautionary measures should be taken *even if some cause and effect relationships are not fully established scientifically*. In this context, the proponent of an activity, rather than the public, bears the burden of proof.
>
> The process of applying the Precautionary Principle must be *open, informed and democratic* and must include *potentially affected parties*. It must also involve an examination of the *full range of alternatives*, including no action. (qtd. in Steingraber 284, emphasis mine)

While the precautionary principle is not opposed to all risk taking, it favors safety measures in the face of ignorance, until enough evidence is established to minimize risk adequately (Dobson and Rodriguez 861). Along these lines, Stephen R. Kellert recommends that "inadequate knowledge should not be an excuse for inaction; nor should it be an invitation to act with arrogance as if we know all we need to know. The prudent path will be one of restrained decisiveness, building buffers against the inevitability of surprise and unknowns" (182). However, implementing precautionary and apocalyptic arguments in science can be problematic. The end or even decline of the world via environmental degradation is a diminishing concern to an increasing contingent of skeptics and those who put their faith in technology. Coming from scientists, the admission of uncertainty is often equated with unreliable research, and advocacy from the scientist can thus be construed as bias.

From Environmental Apocalypticism to Precautionary Tales

To date, the literature of environmental apocalypticism has been recognized as the written voice of the environmental movement. In his *Voices in the Wilderness* (1996) chapter on Rachel Carson and *Silent Spring*, Daniel G. Payne examines how *Silent Spring* "became the rhetorical archetype of modern environmental literature, to which the numerous succession of books with titles alluding to environmental Armageddon bears witness" (137). This emphasis on doomsday is counterproductive, and it ignores other aspects of Carson's book that promote dialogue, such as her calls for precaution when effects and consequences are unknown.

Craig Waddell, in his introduction to *And No Birds Sing* (2000), suggests that "rather than generating apocalyptic visions, environmental advocates might more profitably ally their appeals with prevailing concerns, such as human health and economic issues" (9). Placing *Silent Spring* in a precautionary tradition grounds it in current ongoing discourses about environmental policy and public health, making its message more relevant to its modern audience. Recognizing the precautionary rhetoric of *Silent Spring*, as exemplified by Carson's discussion of feasible alternatives to synthetic chemical pesticides, highlights connections to human health and economic issues that might otherwise go underemphasized.

While many have commented on the tradition of environmental apocalypticism in regard to *Silent Spring*, no one has recognized explicitly the tradition of a precautionary approach in her book, and few have examined the post-Carson books in this tradition. While many authors have provided historical and rhetorical reviews of the environmental movement, and some have done so with apocalyptic tropes in mind, no one has explored the employment of precautionary rhetoric as the larger rhetorical frame in which apocalyptic tropes often play a secondary role. From Carson to more recent authors such as Steingraber and Wilson, we see this precautionary grounding emerging with increasing frequency. The term *precautionary*, adopted from public health and environmental policy, more accurately represents the purpose of these books and forces skeptics to engage international discourse centered on a precautionary philosophy.

By engaging human health issues alongside environmental concerns, writers in a precautionary tradition address not only the "land ethic" promoted by Aldo Leopold and others but also more traditionally defined human ethics. Just as traditional cautionary tales or fables, such as Aesop's, have historically conveyed a moral message, precautionary tales also convey an ethical warning. However, whereas most cautionary tales are fictional and address specific moral issues, precautionary tales may employ fiction (as Carson does in her fable) to portray "worst-case" scenarios, but it is in an effort to acknowledge potential yet avoidable consequences for the environment and human health.

These precautionary tales influence emerging texts and global policies. By making the argument that decision making should consider not only scientific evidence and statistical proof but also the weight of evidence and the potential ramifications of uncertainty, Carson and others call for science and public policy to shift strategies, and they make a persuasive case to the public for why what is inconclusive is almost more important than what is statistically proven when it comes to legislation and policy. This is not a change in rhetorical strategy from apocalyptic to precautionary; rather, apocalyptic is subsumed under the larger precautionary frame. Through attempts to empower audiences with knowledge and motivate them to action, Carson and her followers write in the precautionary spirit of foreseeing in order to forestall and should not be noted primarily for using the apocalyptic trope of shocking readers into averting disaster.

Characteristics of Precautionary Tales

The precautionary tales of Carson and others share many of the following seven characteristics: (1) employment of a long-term perspective; (2) adoption of a holistic view of ecosystems; (3) empowerment of the public by communicating information and resources; (4) recognition of the potential for a diminished future; (5) acknowledgement of scientific uncertainty; (6) identification of success stories of precautionary action; and (7) discussion of precautionary strategies and alternatives.

In the spirit of a long-term orientation, recent books in this tradition increasingly reference *Silent Spring* and other seminal environmental works as testimony from the "now-future"—a kind of reverse of the apocalyptic fable. Steingraber's *Living Downstream* references *Silent Spring* throughout its chapters, returning to both the book and Carson's personal life as well as the context in which *Silent Spring* was received. Early in *Living Downstream*, Steingraber reflects, "Reading *Silent Spring* as a member of this generation, across a distance of more than three decades, I gain another view of DDT. What impresses me most is just how much was known about the harmful aspects of this familiar and seemingly harmless substance" (8). One of the best examples of the dialogue between *Silent Spring* and *Living Downstream* centers on Carson's statement: "The public must decide whether it wishes to continue on the present road, and it can do so only when in full possession of the facts. In the words of Jean Rostand, 'The obligation to endure gives us the right to know'" (Carson 13). Steingraber modifies this, saying "with the right to know comes the duty to inquire" (xxii). Later, she elaborates further: "It is time to start pursuing alternative paths. From the right to know and the duty to inquire flows the obligation to act" (117). While Carson met that right to know with her eye-opening book, Steingraber more directly provokes her audience to empower themselves, in essence asking the "potentially affected parties" to participate in an "informed and democratic" process.

Wilson's *The Future of Life* differs from *Living Downstream* in several ways. Wilson does not reference Rachel Carson or *Silent Spring*, and he focuses on biodiversity, only briefly citing pollution as one of the factors "weakening and erasing more species" (50). Yet the rhetorical strategies of Wilson's book share something in common with others in this tradition. Wilson begins his book with a letter, a testimony from the now-future, to another famous environmental advocate of the past: Henry David Thoreau. In closing his letter to Thoreau, Wilson says, "You were the new and we are the old. Can we now be the wiser? For you, here at Walden Pond, the lamentation of the mourning dove and the green frog's *t-r-r-oonk*! across the predawn water were the true reason for saving this place. For us, it is an exact knowledge of what that truth is, all that it implies, and how to employ it to best effect. So, two truths. We will have them both, you and I and all those now and forever to come who accept the stewardship of nature" (xxiv). Here, Wilson acknowledges a shift in focus from aesthetic motivation in the conservation movement to recognition of the importance of ecological integrity to health—the planet's and our own. Through their acts of looking back through time, and by testifying to hopes for a better future, both Steingraber and Wilson defy the pessimism of inevitable apocalypse.

Another significant characteristic of this tradition is the presentation of a holistic view of the connected ecosystem, with humans as tightly interwoven in that web as any other species. For example, *Silent Spring*'s chapter "Earth's Green Mantle" discusses the "intricate web of life whose interwoven strands lead from microbes to man" (69) and the effects disturbance to one species can have on another. Carson reflects, "The earth's vegetation is part of a web of life in which there are intimate and essential relations between plants and the earth, between plants and other plants, between plants and animals. Sometimes we have no choice but to disturb these relationships, but we should do so thoughtfully, with full awareness that what we do may have consequences remote in time and place" (64). To demonstrate readers' intimate connection to distant places, Steingraber muses, "The molecules of water, earth, and air that rearrange themselves to form these beans and kernels are the molecules that eventually become the tissues of our own bodies. You have eaten food that was grown here [in Illinois]. You *are* the food that is grown here" (3). Explaining the global distribution of pesticides, Steingraber later points out that trees and animals of the "pristine" Arctic are now found to contain traces of tropical pesticides

(176–77). In a discussion of the connections between ecosystems, Wilson says: "There is considerable merit in looking at life in this grand holistic manner. Alone among the other solar planets, Earth's physical environment is held by its organisms in a delicate equilibrium utterly different from what would be the case in their absence. There is plenty of evidence that even some individual species have a measurable global impact," such as oceanic phytoplankton, which impact world climate (11). All three scientist-writers emphasize quality of life and human health as bound to these ecosystem relationships.

Just as Carson sought to empower the public with knowledge, these contemporary authors seek to empower the public with an understanding of what is known, what is unknown, what could be, and what can be avoided. Carson's last chapter, "The Other Road," advocates a precautionary view and exhibits hope that an empowered public can make positive changes by exploring alternatives. Carson states: "The choice, after all, is ours to make. If having endured much, we have at last asserted our 'right to know,' and if, knowing, we have concluded that we are being asked to take senseless and frightening risks, then we should no longer accept the counsel of those who tell us that we must fill our world with poisonous chemicals; we should look about and see what other course is open to us" (278). For example, she enthusiastically emphasizes that a "truly extraordinary variety of alternatives to the chemical control of insects is available. Some are already in use and have achieved brilliant success" (277–78). Carson awakens her readers to the existence of a choice, motivating them to ask their own questions about their relationship to the environment and to discover how they can improve their health and the health of the ecosystem.

Also working to empower the public with understanding and provoking people to ask precautionary questions, Steingraber reflects on "the connection between human cancer and environmental contamination. How much evidence do we have for such a link? How should we take action in light of this evidence?" (xv). In the last chapter of Wilson's book, titled "The Solution," he closes with hopefulness: "I hope I have justified the conviction, shared by many thoughtful people from all walks of life, that the problem can be solved. Adequate resources exist. Those who control them have many reasons to achieve that goal, not least their own security. In the end, however, success or failure will come down to an ethical decision, one on which those now living will be defined and judged for all generations to come. I believe we will choose wisely" (189).

Rather than stress the end of the human species, these precautionary tales address what a future with diminished ecological health might look like, and ask if that is the kind of world the reader wants to live in or leave for future generations. In *Silent Spring*, Carson asks: "Who would want to live in a world which is just not quite fatal?" (12). Steingraber observes that many people are now asking "how we can remain alive and secure in an increasingly toxic environment. They ask how we can claim liberty when our own bodies—as well as those of our children—have become repositories for harmful chemicals that others, without our explicit consent, have introduced into the air, food, water, and soil. These are good questions" (xvi–xvii). Wilson's futuristic fable of diminished ecological health, found nearly halfway through *The Future of Life*, begins: "Imagine the natural world a hundred years from now if current environmental trends continue" (75). While human beings still exist, he calls this imagined future century "the Age of Loneliness" for the anticipated loss of biodiversity on Earth. Earlier, in apocalyptic fashion, Wilson had warned, "An Armageddon is approaching at the beginning of the third millennium. But it is not the cosmic war and fiery collapse of mankind foretold in sacred scripture. It is the wreckage of the planet by an exuberantly plentiful and ingenious humanity" (xxiii). Yet he continues in a more optimistic vein: "If the race is won, humanity can emerge in far better condition than when it entered, and with most of the diversity of life still intact. The situation is desperate—but there are encouraging signs that the race can be won" (xxiii). These authors, while using apocalyptic tropes at times, all develop a larger message more reflective of the precautionary principle.

Concerned with public right to know, human health, and the support of a precautionary approach to issues of potential harm, the shapers of this tradition respond to human health concerns that are increasingly recognized as entwined with ecological integrity. Along this continuum we see an increasing integration of science in precautionary tales as well as recognition of scientific uncertainty. In one of Steingraber's many examples, she points out that a "recent assessment of the Illinois environment concluded that chemical contamination 'has become increasingly dispersed and dilute (and thus less visible),' leaving residues that are 'increasingly chemically exotic and whose health effects are not yet clearly understood'" (6). Wilson also acknowledges the complexity and uncertainty of these issues: "A few experts, including the British ecologist Norman Myers, believe the damage to tropical forests has been underestimated by the FAO [Food and Agriculture Organization of the United Nations], with the true figure being closer to 2 percent per year, or the equivalent of all of Florida. On the other hand, recent satellite data support a lower rate that, for South America at least, indicates that the FAO estimates are too high by a factor of as much as two" (60). As a reader, which study do you accept? Showing the scientific uncertainty inherent in examples like these forces the reader to reflect on what the right course of action is in light of this uncertainty, and what risks are worth taking.

While Carson addresses unknown environmental and health consequences for the future and advocates safe solutions, Steingraber and Wilson attest to the accuracy of some of Carson's predictions, yet they also highlight success stories resulting from precautionary action. For example, in discussing the now proven link between cancer and cigarette smoke, Steingraber points out, "For much of my life, I have been protected from a now-proven danger by those who had the courage to act on partial evidence" (xxii). Wilson talks about the case of the Catskill Watershed, which had been polluted due to agricultural runoff and sewage from a growing population. Rather than build a filtration plant, New York City worked to restore the watershed itself, which now ensures clean water, a quality recreational area, and "by its policy of natural water management, the Catskill forest region also secures flood control at very little expense" (108). By restoring the ecosystem, this community may also have secured other unforeseen benefits for the future.

In a continued pattern of explaining what is proven and what is uncertain, Steingraber discusses the purpose of her book and its precautionary philosophy: "I attempt here to bring these two categories of information together—data on environmental contamination and data on cancer incidence—to see what patterns might exist, to identify questions for further inquiry, and to urge precautionary action, even in the face of incomplete answers" (xx). She asks, "At what point does preliminary evidence of harm become definitive evidence of harm? When someone says, 'We were not aware of the dangers of these chemicals back then,' whom do they mean by *we*?" (8–9).

In her final chapter, titled "Ecological Roots," Steingraber discusses the precautionary principle directly. "The principle of the least toxic alternative looks toward the day when the availability of safer choices makes the deliberate and routine release of chemical carcinogens into the environment as unthinkable as the practice of slavery" (271). She ends the afterword with a reprint of the precautionary principle.

Engaging in the characteristic rhetoric of this tradition, Wilson also advocates precaution: "We have been too self-absorbed to foresee the long-term consequences of our actions, and we will suffer a terrible loss unless we shake off our delusions and move quickly to a solution" (xxiv). Calling on the public to engage in acts of precaution, Wilson states: "Although it is possible to predict species extinction for the near future—say, over the next decade or two—such a projection is impossible for the more distant future. The obvious reason is that the trajectory depends on human choice. . . . We know more about the problem now . . . ; it is not too late. We know what to do. Perhaps we will act in time" (101–2).

In their discussions of connectedness, scientific uncertainty, and health, these precautionary tales impress upon us the need to take precautions—in the words of Albert Schweitzer made famous by Carson, to "foresee in order to forestall." These passages are brief examples of characteristics common to precautionary tales, in which the authors synthesize information and attempt to raise public awareness about scientific uncertainty and the complexity of environmental and human health issues in an effort to empower the citizens to act.

Conclusion

Narratives that employ precautionary strategies, including apocalyptic tropes, forecast environmental concerns and problems as worst-case scenarios that deserve attention. These scenarios are not forgone conclusions, however, and they are not intended to be taken as such. Instead, precautionary tales force their opponents to address the fundamental tenets of the precautionary principle: what risks do we agree are worth taking? What alternatives could be explored to avoid unnecessary risk? Do all citizens have access to the information needed to make an informed decision?

For this tradition to continue to be effective, we need a conscious shift in focus from apocalyptic to precautionary in both the literature and the criticism concerning these texts. If ecocritics acknowledge the threads of precautionary rhetoric in environmental literature, calls for precaution will begin to sound more like calls for scientific caution and publicly informed decision making. If scientists employ skepticism, caution, and conservatism in their studies and writing, should the public not also express skepticism and a desire for caution and conservatism in the engagement of activities or employment of agents that are potentially harmful, not only to the environment, but specifically to human health?

An ecocritical recognition of this precautionary tradition is important for at least three reasons. First, by acknowledging a tradition of precautionary writing, we recognize the place of these books in a more extensive global conversation about human interaction with the environment. Because *Silent Spring* became the model in this tradition for later environmental texts and is part of an ongoing conversation about public policy in regard to the environment in the United States, Canada, and the European Union, the threads of apocalyptic and precautionary rhetoric that weave through it from antecedent to descendant texts are crucial to recognize. Second, this orientation joins itself well to issues of concern in environmental justice and policy. Incorporating and recognizing the precautionary strategy brings environmental concerns into the public and urban domain by emphasizing human health and other issues that are pertinent to all rural, urban, and suburban dwellers today. Third, in an increasingly globalized world where environmental problems are often global in scope, it opens the conversation to relevant discussions of non-American environmental issues and literature, such as Ishimure Michiko's *Paradise in the Sea of Sorrow: Our Minamata Disease* (1972).

Rachel Carson came out of a tradition of wildlife conservation, preceded by George Perkins Marsh, Henry David Thoreau, and Aldo Leopold, and added the human health component to her call for environmental protection. *Silent Spring* represents a pivotal point in environmental writing characterized by threads of both apocalyptic and precautionary rhetoric. This tradition continues to evolve, as increasing concern with human health and foresight for the sake of forestalling is evident in the precautionary tales of contemporary writers such as Steingraber and Wilson, who do not cry crisis and end of the world so much as advocate precaution for an uncertain and potentially difficult future.

NOTES

1. In addition to their essays referenced here, see Killingsworth and Palmer's "Millennial Ecology: The Apocalyptic Narrative from *Silent Spring* to Global Warming," in *Green Culture: Environmental Rhetoric in Contemporary America*, ed. Carl G. Herndl and Stuart C. Brown (Madison: University of Wisconsin Press, 1996), 21–45.

2. Wingspread conferences are public-interest conferences sponsored by the Johnson Foundation at their facilities (Wingspread and the Johnson House) in Racine, Wisconsin. These conferences serve to bring together an internationally diverse group of scholars, scientists, policymakers, and laypeople to address issues of public policy. Organizations can propose a conference in the following areas: education, sustainable development and the environment, democracy and community, and family. The Keland Endowment Fund and Racine and southeastern Wisconsin categories are specific to conferences promoting the arts and assisting people with severe disabilities, and sustaining the communities of southeastern Wisconsin, re-

spectively. Organizations involved in these conferences primarily include nonprofits, universities, and public agencies. The conference during which the precautionary principle statement was drafted was themed "Implementing the Precautionary Principle." For more information, including papers presented at the conference, visit www.johnsonfdn.org.

WORKS CITED

Buell, Lawrence. *The Environmental Imagination: Thoreau, Nature Writing, and the Formation of American Culture*. Cambridge, Mass.: Belknap Press–Harvard University Press, 1995.

Carson, Rachel. *Silent Spring*. New York: Houghton Mifflin, 1962.

Dobson, Andrew P., and Jon Paul Rodriguez. "Conservation Biology, Discipline of." In *Encyclopedia of Biodiversity*, ed. Simon Asher Levin. 5 vols. San Diego: Academic Press, 2001. 855–64.

Kellert, Stephen R. *The Value of Life: Biological Diversity and Human Society*. Washington, D.C.: Island Press, 1996.

Killingsworth, M. Jimmie, and Jacqueline S. Palmer. "The Discourse of 'Environmentalist Hysteria.'" In *Landmark Essays on Rhetoric and the Environment*, ed. Craig Waddell. Mahwah, N.J.: Hermagoras Press–Lawrence Erlbaum, 1998. 35–54.

————, eds. *Ecospeak: Rhetoric and Environmental Politics in America*. Carbondale: Southern Illinois University Press, 1992.

————. "*Silent Spring* and Science Fiction: An Essay in the History and Rhetoric of Narrative." In Waddell, *And No Birds Sing*, 174–204.

Norton, Bryan G., ed. Introduction to Part I. *The Preservation of Species: The Value of Biological Diversity*. Princeton: Princeton University Press, 1986. 9–11.

Payne, Daniel G. *Voices in the Wilderness: American Nature Writing and Environmental Politics*. Hanover: University Press of New England, 1996.

Steingraber, Sandra. *Living Downstream*. New York: Random House–Vintage Books, 1998.

Waddell, Craig, ed. *And No Birds Sing*. Carbondale: Southern Illinois University Press, 2000.

————. "The Reception of *Silent Spring*: An Introduction." In Waddell, *And No Birds Sing*, 1–16.

Wilson, Edward O. *The Future of Life*. New York: Random House–Vintage Books, 2002.

Facing the True Costs of Living

Arundhati Roy and Ishimure Michiko
on Dams and Writing

A POPULAR SAYING has it that today we know the price of everything, but the value of nothing. To refine this a little we might say that today we know the price tags of many things, but not the full costs we pay for them, and therefore we do not know their real values. For today it has become difficult for most of us to be sufficiently aware of the full extent of the costs incurred on our immediate lives and on the larger world by the many things we use—be they computers or cars, books or bombs, drugs or dams. Ishimure Michiko from Japan and Arundhati Roy from India, however, are two Asian women writers who are directly facing and writing about the true costs and values of things close to our lives—physically, culturally, environmentally, and spiritually. In this essay I discuss the writing and social-environmental activism of Ishimure and Roy, focusing particularly on their common concern about the effects of dam construction on culture and environment. I relate this concern to their ideas about the power of stories in counteracting the destruction they see occurring and to their views on the interrelationships between fiction, nonfiction, and activism.

There are a number of striking parallels in the life work and art of Ishimure and Roy. Both women have integrally combined social-environmental activism and writing in their lives. Their writings show a particular sensitivity to the fundamental relationships between places and culture. Both have faced considerable literary and social ostracism for their activist involvement and for their writing about it. And both have created new directions for literature that is rooted in the traditions of storytelling and that affirms a belief in the spiritual and redemptive powers of words.

The trajectories of the writing careers of Ishimure and Roy show an inverse symmetry. Ishimure was first recognized for her writing about an environmental pollution issue and for her social activism related to this cause. This writing employed an unconventional mixture of nonfiction reporting, narrative history, autobiography, and social criticism. Later she broadened the focus of her writing to include fiction, poetry, and drama. Roy, in contrast, was first recognized as a novelist but has since been working in social and environmental causes and has been concentrating on nonfiction. Both Ishimure and Roy, however, have successfully woven together the threads of their literary and activist lives to develop a strong body of writing that defies sorting into traditional categories or literary genres.

Ishimure Michiko first became well known in Japan with the publication in 1969 (revised, 1972) of *Paradise in the Sea of Sorrow: Our Minamata Disease* (*Kugai jodo: Waga minamata byo*). This was an artistically courageous book, steeped in Ishimure's equally courageous life of social activism. *Paradise* brought the world's attention to the industrial methyl mercury poisoning incident that occurred in Minamata, Japan. This poisoning was the cause of Minamata Disease, which tragically affected the lives of tens of thousands of victims and continues to be a source of suffering and protest today. Ishimure's book had an effect similar to that of Rachel Carson's *Silent Spring* (1962) in waking up the public to the dangers of environmental poisoning. The impact of Ishimure's writing, like that of Carson, was rooted in the combination of accurate environmental reporting with the highest level of literary expression. Indeed, Ishimure has frequently been referred to as the Rachel Carson of Japan. *Paradise in the Sea of Sorrow* was a genre-defying work, bringing together diverse elements of nonfiction, contemporary reportage, local mythology, and storytelling. In the opening chapter Ishimure speaks directly of her attitude and goals in writing this book:

> As a native of Minamata, I know that the language of the victims of Minamata Disease—both that of the spirits of the dead who are unable to die, and that of the survivors who are little more than living ghosts—represents the pristine form of poetry before our societies were divided into classes. In order to preserve for posterity this language in which the historic significance of the Mercury Poisoning Incident is crudely branded, I must drink an infusion of my animism and "pre-animism" and become a sorceress cursing modern times forever. (60)

Here Ishimure also touches on a central concern underlying all of her writing; the attempt to reawaken the spirit of what she refers to as *kotodama*, the "soul of language," in modern culture. This, she believes, can allow readers to draw on the ancient, mythopoetic powers of words in addressing the problems of the present. In the final chapter of *Paradise*, Ishimure graphically explains her deep commitment to this hope; "I drive the scalpel of thought deep in the flesh of my life. This raw wound will serve as a connecting link between the chains of past and future events" (306).

Ishimure's distinctive style draws on an extremely wide range of literary and cultural sources, stretching from ancient Japanese myths and the traditions of Shinto and Buddhism to the latest problems affecting contemporary society. Her unorthodox writing style has presented significant challenges to the direction of modern Japanese literature. Livia Monnet, the translator of *Paradise*, comments on this challenge: "[It] may be regarded as Ishimure's ambitious attempt to reform the language of contemporary Japanese fiction, which she regards as degraded and unsatisfactory, to create a new literary genre, a mixture of authentic autobiography, fiction, and journalism that seems to point to the literature of the future" (Translator's Introduction v). Upon publication, *Paradise in the Sea of Sorrow* soon earned Ishimure considerable literary acclaim in her country, and it had a far-reaching impact on Japanese environmental consciousness. Monnet further notes:

> It was awarded the Kumamoto Nichinichi Cultural Prize (1969), the Oya Soichi Prize for Non-fictional Literature (1970) and the Republic of the Philippines' Ramon Magsaysay Prize (1973). Ishimure turned down the first two awards, saying that she could not accept any honors as long as the demands of the Minamata Disease victims were ignored. The book's impact was enormous: noted writers and critics referred to it as the most important literary event since the end of World War II; many readers gave up their studies or professions and went to Minamata to help the patients in their struggle for survival. Ishimure's book has also given great impetus to various regional conservationist movements. (Translator's Introduction iv)

After writing *Paradise,* Ishimure went on to expand the Minamata story into a trilogy; the second volume is *Village of the Gods* (*Dai nibu: Kamigami no mura*) and the third is *Fish of Heaven* (*Dai sanbu: Ten no Uo*). Since then she has written several novels, numerous collections of essays and poetry, and Noh drama. In her 2002 Noh play *Shiranui*, Ishimure drew on tales from the ancient world of Japanese myths and wed them to the theme of the contemporary struggle to maintain the health of seas and watersheds. This concern for watersheds and for the people and cultures they support is also the theme of Ishimure's important 1997 novel *Lake of Heaven* (*Tenko*). A recurring message in all her works has been that we need the assistance of an evolving, living tradition of stories if we are to withstand the destructive forces of modernization.

Ishimure's initial success with *Paradise in the Sea of Sorrow*, however, turned out to be somewhat of a mixed blessing for her career, as it led many people—and literary critics in particular—to overidentify her writing and life with her role as an activist and especially with this one book. For some, Ishimure became pigeonholed as "just" a writer-activist, implying that her activism stood in the way of her development as a literary artist. Furthermore, Ishimure has retained a commitment to writing about her local area in the rural south of Japan and has stayed away from the influential literary circles in the big cities. For these reasons, Ishimure's considerable body of fiction has suffered somewhat in gaining its proper literary recognition. In recent years, however, a renewed acclaim for her literary importance has developed (Monnet, Murphy, Fujimoto, Takahashi, Yuki). As evidence of this, in 2002 Ishimure was awarded the prestigious Asahi Prize in Japan, recognizing the full range of her literary and social work. A scholarly seventeen-volume edition of her collected works is now in publication.

ARUNDHATI ROY initially achieved international fame for a novel, her Booker Prize–winning *The God of Small Things* (1997). Since then, however, she has concentrated mainly on nonfiction and social-environmental activism. Like Ishimure, Roy sees no contradiction between writing fiction and nonfiction; rather, she sees the forms as creatively and morally intertwined. Both women see their writing as necessarily linked to involvement in social and environmental causes. Roy's progressive involvement in activism and nonfiction, however, has been to the disappointment and scorn of some critics, who apparently had hoped to see her remain more "pure" as a literary fiction writer. To cite one example of such reaction, Indian columnist Anil Nair charges: "Post-Booker prize, Roy has become a purveyor of pamphlets . . . [including] 'The Greater Common Good,' which excoriates the evil of big dams. . . . It is doubtful if she, in the neophyte's fervor for the Green cause, is aware that in arguing so emotionally and at such length against the pollution of our air, water and soil she is, ironically, polluting her own sources of storytelling" ("The Idea of Apocalypse"). In another example, Ian Buruma writes in the *New Republic:* "Roy has become the perfect Third World voice for anti-American, or anti-Western, or even anti-white, sentiments. Those are sentiments dear to the hearts of intellectuals everywhere, including the United States itself" ("The Anti-American"). Roy's works have also been subject to book burnings and withdrawal from bookstores in India. Thus both Roy and Ishimure have paid a considerable price for their allegedly nonliterary activist involvements and for their writing in genres outside those in which they were initially honored.

Amid such criticism, however, Roy has remained undeterred. On the contrary, she has sharpened her own criticism and has broadened the scale of her literary and social work. Explaining her reaction to the attacks on her nonfiction writing and activism, Roy told one Indian journalist, "Each time I step out, I hear the snicker-snack of knives being sharpened. But that's good. It keeps me sharp" (qtd. in Barsamian). Despite the hostile reception in her own country to her views on topics such as dams, globalization, and nuclear armament, the impact of Roy's writing has been significant and has gained her the respect of many. Sumer Lal, senior editor at the *Hindustan Times*, comments: "The young lady's writing on the Narmada dam has forced the question of the treatment of village people into urban drawing rooms where it might not have been raised. She has married passion and facts and breathed life into a social movement that had given up hope" (qtd. in Marquand). Roy and Ishimure join company with other environmentally conscious writers such as Terry Tempest Williams, Rick Bass, Edward Abbey, and Rachel Carson, who have had to fend off charges of diluting the literary quality of their work by mixing it with activism and nonfiction.

Roy's nonfiction is sharply outspoken and passionate, a quality that may have invited questions as to whether it meets the standards of work written in a cooler scholarly style. This writing, however, is firmly grounded in solid research and presented through the voice of a creative writer who brings the full power of the craft of fiction to all her writing. Thus her writing needs to be judged in the full context of its combined artistic and social contributions. Salman Rushdie remarks in this regard: "Roy combines brilliant reportage with a passionate, no-holds-barred commentary. I salute her courage and skill" (*War Talk* back cover). In her recent nonfiction—*The Cost of Living* (1999), *Power Politics* (2001), and *War Talk* (2003)—Roy has concentrated on the themes of dam construction, nuclear armament, and globalization. This writing shares a level of critical incisiveness with the political writings of Noam Chomsky. Indeed, Chomsky has also highly praised the quality and importance of Roy's work (*War Talk*).

Roy has faced censure not only from the literary community but from the political and legal establishment as well. In 1997 Roy was charged with writing obscenity in *The God of Small Things*. She was eventually acquitted in this case, but in a 2002 contempt of court suit, filed against her for her participation in a protest against dam construction and tried at the Supreme Court of India, she was convicted and sentenced to a night in jail and a fine. Although the court admitted that the original charges were "grossly defective," it described her sentence as "showing the magnanimity of Law, by keeping in mind the respondent is a woman" (Chaudhry). In keeping with her commitment to activist principles, Roy donated her Booker Prize money (about thirty thousand dollars) to a grassroots group working to resist the construction of dams that threaten the homes and livelihoods of tens of millions of Indian people (Barsamian). Roy's action shows a spirit kindred to that of Ishimure's refusal to accept several literary prizes.

Roy's concern for the problem of dams has focused particularly on a mammoth project under construction along the Naramada River in central India. This is a system that, if completed, will include some 3,200 dams, just on this one river. For one of these dams alone—the giant Sardar Sarovar Dam—more than half a million people and their local cultures will be displaced and a vast ecosystem will be submerged. As Roy explains, "more than half of them do not officially qualify as 'project-affected' and are not entitled to rehabilitation. It will submerge thirty-two thousand acres of deciduous forest" (*Power* 72). To fulfill this dam-building agenda, the Indian government has become legally bound to paying the now infamous Enron Corporation thirty billion U.S. dollars—even if the country should ever choose to opt out of completing the project (*Power* 55).

Roy's writing, like Ishimure's, begins at the level of local problems and stories; then it works these elements into larger contexts to show what is happening in the global interplay of culture, economics, politics, and environment. In *The Cost of Living* Roy warns that "the story of the Naramada Valley is nothing less than the story of Modern India" (x). She also explains the logical but normally overlooked link between bombs and dams:

> Day by day, river by river, forest by forest, mountain by mountain, missile by missile, bomb by bomb—almost without knowing it—we are being broken. Big dams are to a nation's "development" what nuclear bombs are to its military arsenal. They're both weapons of mass destruction. . . . They're both malignant indications of a civilization turning upon itself. They represent the severing of the link, not just the link—the *understanding*—between human beings and the planet they live on. They scramble the intelligence that connects eggs to hens, milk to cows, food to forests, water to rivers, air to life, and the earth to human existence. (*Cost* 80–81)

Extending Roy's argument, we might say that the story of dams in India is also the story of much of the rest of the world.

Significantly, Arundhati Roy's concern for the effects of dam construction on communities and environments is also the central theme of Ishimure

Michiko's 1997 novel *Lake of Heaven*. The work is a complex story of stories
that resists any easy attempt at summary, in part because it intricately in-
terweaves so many ancient and modern tales but also because the style in
which these tales are presented resists recounting in a traditional linear time
conception. Frequent flashbacks and superimpositions create a composite,
multidimensional world in which time is better understood as circular in
nature, rather than a forward-pointing, linear progression (Allen, "Multi-
dimensioned World"). *Lake of Heaven* in this respect shows clear similarities with Roy's temporal structuring in her novel *The God of Small Things*.
This, along with the distinctive, genre-merging style of Ishimure's writing,
lies at the heart of her attempt to refashion literature and give rebirth to
the spirit of words. Gary Snyder, commenting on the unorthodox qualities
of Ishimure's work, has described *Lake of Heaven* as "a remarkable text of
mythopoetic quality—with a Noh flavor—that presents much of the ancient
lore of Japan and the lore of the spirit world—and is in a way a kind of
myth-drama, not a novel" (personal correspondence).

As *Lake of Heaven* has not yet been published in English translation, a
brief introduction to the story is in order.[1] The novel centers on the past,
present, and future of a small rural community in the mountains of Kyushu.
At present, this once self-sufficient farming village named Amazoko has
become a degraded resettlement area, left in the wake of the construction
of a large dam that inundated the former village. The dam and the new
reservoir-lake it created have also threatened to seal off the stories, traditions, and dreams that have connected the local people to their village.
Nonetheless, the few, mostly elderly survivors who have not fled to the
cities are struggling to maintain contact with the old village and its spirit.
They still manage to return to Amazoko in their dreams. They enter these
dreams, however, not only when they are asleep but also sometimes during
their waking activities; through participation in stories, songs, dances, and
ceremonies. This sense of participation in a shared "dream time" becomes
a central concern in the novel.

The story juxtaposes the contrasting worldviews of a young Tokyo-bred
grandson named Masahiko and his grandfather, Masahito. When Masahiko
visits his deceased grandfather's dam-displaced village of Amazoko for
the first time, his world is shaken and changed through encountering the
world of nature and the stories and customs of this community. In Tokyo,
Masahiko had been struggling to become a musician and composer but had
reached a creative block. In visiting Amazoko, he comes to realize that his
musical and other problems stem from having lost his ability to listen and
sense authentically. His several months' stay allows him to recover his lost

sense of "true hearing" through listening to the natural sounds of winds, plants, and mountains, along with the human-made sounds of songs and stories. In recovering his senses and becoming a part of this community, Masahiko is able to recover his soul and bring new hope to the community. As the story unfolds, Ishimure makes visible the deep interrelationships between individual, social, and environmental problems. For her the stories, songs, dances, and other creative works of threatened cultures like Amazoko are not mere entertainments but essential keys to ensuring their physical and spiritual survival.

The novel ends with an appropriate lack of resolution regarding the fate of the village, but with a hope that Masahiko and the villagers may be able to preserve the traditions of their community. The clash between the ways of the country and the city is presented not simplistically, as one of good against evil, but as one in which all people—in both urban and rural areas—are inevitably bound together, and one in which all people will have to draw on shared cultural resources if they are to survive.

THE SHARED concern of Ishimure and Roy about the effects of dam construction reflects their shared concern about the effects of modernization and globalization upon culture and environment worldwide. Along with bringing our attention to the tragic results of such modern threats as industrial pollution, nuclear warfare, and globalization, they also encourage a profound and complementary respect for preserving traditional local folkways, stories, and cultures. Both have become social activists by necessity and conscience, yet they see our primary need and hope for resolving such troubles as lying in the basic cultural "medicines" of storytelling and the arts.

At heart, Ishimure and Roy are modern mythmakers. They insist that it is both possible and essential to create new myths through modern forms of storytelling. Indeed, *Lake of Heaven* can be regarded as an extended modern work of mythopoetic storytelling. The following passage gives a good example of the mythopoetic quality in Ishimure's writing. In it the narrator speaks of Masahiko's newly awakened consciousness as he comes to understand the importance of myths, dreams, and community:

> The landscape Masahiko's grandfather had tried to describe to him now began to appear. The place of the wedding of the gods was the lake that lay in the womb of Amazoko Mountain. The villagers paid their respects and offered songs so that the night of the divine wedding would come to pass successfully. . . . .

In his childhood Masahiko had thought of these tales of a far-off forgotten mountain village as merely the fragments of memories of an old man who had been separated from his hometown. . . . Now he had come to realize that in order to see into the world that had been hidden in his grandfather's mind it wasn't necessary to resort to ideas from ethnology, or the recently fashionable ecological theories about saving the earth. All that was needed was to share in the feelings of these elders right here; these people who continued to return to Amazoko in their dreams. (337; translation mine; page reference from Japanese original)

This passage, steeped in the imagination of ancient myths, also contains an embedded modern ecological tale. But this tale is not presented in the scientific, sometimes abstruse language of ecology. Nor are the solutions to the environmental problems he encounters to be found in the usual prescriptions of environmental activities. Rather, the message that Masahiko and we as readers receive is that we need to go back to stories and to community if we are to save ourselves and the land.

Ishimure's belief in the importance of living myth extends to her belief in the necessity of leading lives of shared stories, dreams, and community. She stresses how

Masahiko took great interest in how the shared dreams of the group were steeped in the countless layers of experience, gained over the long passage of time. He recognized that he himself was being reflected in, and taking part in, the movements within dreams in which each person was not merely a single being, but a part of a greater body of the community. (343)

Thus, for Ishimure authentic individual being is incomplete, even inconceivable, without participation in a greater community. Moreover, this community must be widely defined by the entire network of dreams, stories, places, and culture that the community has inherited and to which it must also continually contribute.

THE OTHER essential, interrelated theme underlying all Ishimure's writing is the idea that modern culture, and most of modern writing, has lost a sense of the "true soul of language." This idea has traditionally been expressed in Japanese by the evocative word *kotodama*. *Kotodama* refers to a vital spirit that can be present in words; a spirit that was once at the core of Japanese literature, language, and culture as well as of other world cultures. In the following passage the narrator speaks directly of this idea. In part, the words suggest an elegy, yet they also suggest a hope for a revival through the rebirth of the soul of language:

> Back in the time when the true soul of language still existed, the human voice and the sounds of things must have been bound together far more closely than they are today. They must have existed in a mystical relationship to the structure of the world. Something that has now come to take on an existence similar to that of a musical conductor must have once possessed a far greater power, extending to the farthest reaches of the craggy mountains and to the depths of the swirling high seas. (41)

Ishimure's writing presents a stern warning that modern culture has lost much of its understanding of and connection to the traditional world of "word spirit." But her writing also offers us the hope that we, like Masahiko—a city boy who had been cut off from this world of *kotodama*—may likewise be able to recover and contribute to this sense. And, importantly, she suggests that this recovery may be achieved not only by living in a rural village like Amazoko but also in a modern city.

Ishimure balances her call for a rebirth of the true spirit of language with a beautiful, poetic expression of the fundamental contemporary ecological idea of the interconnectedness of all things, as we see in a final example:

> The rhythms that the mountains exhale with the mists from the inside of the earth's thick strata wait for the unfailing dawning of day while the trees and plants preserve their forms and are elaborately dyed in a multitude of shades of green. And in the flash of the first rays of the light of dawn all the colors of the trees are woven together. Color, like *kotodama*, the spirit of language, is born of such things as the union between the morning light and the grasses, the trees, and the fields and mountains. And in those who can be present in that moment there is joy. The people of Amazoko are characters in such an epic poem that extends back to the reaches of ancient times. (355)

Thus, in *Lake of Heaven* and other writings, Ishimure Michiko offers the hope and registers the plea that we too, living in a threatened society with damaged but recoverable senses, may be able to live within and contribute to such an ongoing epic poem.

ARUNDHATI ROY, in her essay *The Cost of Living*, echoes this hope, mixed with a similar awareness of the difficult realities we face:

> There is beauty yet in this brutal, damaged world of ours. Hidden, fierce, immense. Beauty that is uniquely ours and beauty that we have received with grace from others, enhanced, reinvented, and made our own. We have to seek it out, nurture it, love it. (123)

In weaving together the streams of fiction and nonfiction in their writing, Ishimure and Roy dance a difficult dance between the worlds of art and activism. Amid the criticisms they have received for their unorthodoxy, they have remained firm in their defense of the marriage between art and social action, and of their twisting and reinvention of literary genres. In a 2001 interview, Roy discussed and defended her faith in these principles:

> I don't see a great difference between *The God of Small Things* and my works of nonfiction. As I keep saying, fiction is truth. I think fiction is the truest thing there ever was. My whole effort now is to remove that distinction. The writer is the midwife of understanding. It's very important for me to tell politics like a story, to make it real, to draw a link between a man with his child and what fruit he had in the village he lived in before he was kicked out, and how that relates to Mr. Wolfensohn at the World Bank. That's what I want to do. *The God of Small Things* is a book where you connect the very smallest things to the very biggest: whether it's the dent that a baby spider makes on the surface of water or the quality of the moonlight on a river or how history and politics intrude into your life, your house, your bedroom. (qtd. in Barsamian)

It is the attention to these small things in everyday life, and the ability to connect these things to the larger things happening in the world, and the ability to find new narrative means to revive the mythical imagination, that unite the spirit and writing of Ishimure and Roy.

Roy was once asked by a journalist, "What is the god of small things?" Although writers generally bristle at such explain-it-all sorts of questions, Roy answered this one quite directly:

> To me the god of small things is the inversion of God. God's a big thing and God's in control. The god of small things . . . whether it's the way the children see things or whether it's the insect life in the book, or the fish or the stars— there is a not accepting of what we think of as adult boundaries. This small activity that goes on is the under life of the book. All sorts of boundaries are transgressed upon. At the end of the first chapter I say little events and ordinary things are just smashed and reconstituted, imbued with new meaning to

become the bleached bones of the story. It's a story that examines things very closely but also from a very, very distant point, almost from geological time and you look at it and see a pattern there. (qtd. in Gutheinz)

The "geological time" perspective Roy speaks of connects us with Ishimure's world of *kotodama* and her call for an "epic poem" that "extends back to the reaches of ancient time." Without such a wider, recursive perspective we risk staggering myopically amid the rush of modern society.

Ishimure's "rhythms that the mountains exhale with the mists from the inside of the earth's thick strata," and Roy's "dent that a baby spider makes on the surface of the water, the quality of the moon, the food a child ate before being dislocated by a dam"—these are the intimate, time-reflective observations of the world that are the essence of these two women's stories. And these are the sources of the hope they offer us—if we too can learn to look, listen, and share such small things and then to connect them to the larger things we also must face. Through this awareness we may come to appreciate the true costs, and the true values, of the many things that make up our world.

NOTE

1. This essay incorporates a brief, adapted version of the plot summary of *Lake of Heaven* that appeared in a research report presented to the Japan Ministry of Science and Education: "The Multi-Dimensioned World of Ishimure Michiko's *Lake of Heaven*," in *Kankyo to bungaku: bei-nihon ni okeru ne-cha raitingu no rekishi oyobi riron no kenkyu*, Research report number 122410132 (2003), 227–38.

WORKS CITED

Allen, Bruce. "Arundhati Roy and the Real Costs of Living." *Newsletter of the Association for the Study of Literature and Environment, Japan*, no. 13 (Dec. 10, 2002): 4–7.

———. "The Multi-Dimensioned World of Ishimure Michiko's *Lake of Heaven*." In *Kankyo to bungaku: bei-nihon ni okeru ne-cha raitingu no rekishi oyobi rironn no kenkyu* (English and Japanese versions). Japan Ministry of Science and Education research report no. 122410132, 2003. 227–38. Also in *Ekkyou suru toposu: Kankyou bungaku gakuron josetsu* (in Japanese). Tokyo: Sairyusha, 2004.

Allen, Bruce, and Reiko Akamine. "*Lake of Heaven*" (trans. and introduction to a chapter of Ishimure Michiko's *Tenko*). *Organization and Environment* 11, no. 4 (December 1998): 480–86.

Barsamian, David. Interview with Arundhati Roy, *Progressive*, April 2001, http://www.progressive.org.

Buruma, Ian. "The Anti-American." *New Republic*, April 22, 2002, http://www.the newrepublic.com.

Chaudhry, Lakshmi. "Arundhati Roy Jailed by Indian Supreme Court." AlterNet, March 8, 2002, http://www.alternet.orgstory.html?StoryID=12582.

Fujimoto, Kazuko. "Discrimination and the Perception of Difference." *Concerned Theatre Japan* 2–3 no. 4 (1973): 112–54.

Gutheinz, Emily. "Review of *The God of Small Things*." *WordsWorth Interviews*, June 15, 1997, http://curiousgeorge.wordsworth.com/www/epresent/royint/.

Ikuta, Shogo. "Modern Japanese Nature Writing: An Overview." In *Literature of Nature: An International Sourcebook*, ed. Patrick Murphy. Chicago: Fitzroy Dearborn, 1998. 277–80.

Ishimure, Michiko. *Ishimure Michiko zenshu* (The complete works of Ishimure Michiko; in Japanese). 17 vols. Tokyo: Fujiwara shoten, 2004.

———. *Kugai jodo: Waga minamata byo* (*Paradise in the Sea of Sorrow: Our Minamata Disease*). 1969. Revised ed., Tokyo: Kodansha, 1972.

———. *Lake of Heaven* (*Tenko*). Trans. Bruce Allen. Unpublished manuscript in preparation for publication.

———. *Paradise in the Sea of Sorrow: Our Minamata Disease* (*Kugai jodo: Waga minamata byo*). Trans. with an introduction by Livia Monnet. Kyoto: Yamaguchi Publishing House, 1990. Reprint Ann Arbor: Center for Japanese Studies, University of Michigan, 2003.

———. *Tenko* (Lake of Heaven). Tokyo: Mainichi Shimbun Publishing Company, 1997.

Jana, Reena. Interview with Arundhati Roy. *Salon*, September 30, 1997, http://www.salon.com.

Marquand, Robert. "India's Arundhati Roy: Novelist Turned Social Activist." *Christian Science Monitor*, August 17, 1999.

Monnet, Livia. "In the Beginning Woman Was the Sun: Autobiographies of Modern Japanese Women Writers," pt. 2. In *Japan Forum* 1, no. 2. Oxford: Oxford University Press, 1989. 197–233.

———. "Not Only Minamata: An Approach to Ishimure Michiko's Work." In *European Writing on Japan: Scholarly Views from Eastern and Western Europe*, ed. Ian Nish. Tenterdent, Kent: Paul Norbury Publications, 1988.

———. "Translator's Introduction" to Ishimure Michiko's *Paradise in the Sea of Sorrow: Our Minamata Disease*. Kyoto: Yamaguchi Publishing House, 1990.

Murphy, Patrick. "Ishimure Michiko: The Price of Pollution and the Presence of the Past." In *Farther Afield in the Study of Nature-Oriented Literature*. Charlottesville: University Press of Virginia, 2000. 146–58.

Nair, Anil. "The Idea of Apocalypse." *Rediff*, August 19, 1999, http://www.rediff.com.

Oiwa, Keibo. *Rowing the Eternal Sea: The Story of a Minamata Fisherman*. Narrated by Ogata Masato. Trans. Karen Colligan-Taylor. Lanham: Rowman and Littlefield, 2001.

Roy, Arundhati. *The Cost of Living*. New York: Modern Library, 1999.

————. *The God of Small Things*. New York: Harper Perennial, 1997.

————. *Power Politics*. 2nd ed. Cambridge, Mass.: South End Press, 2001.

————. *War Talk*. Cambridge, Mass.: South End Press, 2003.

Smith, Aileen M. "Why Minamata?" In *Minamata*. Tucson: University of Arizona, Center for Creative Photography, 1981.

Smith, W. Eugene, and Aileen M. Smith. *Minamata*. Tucson: University of Arizona, Center for Creative Photography, 1981.

Snyder, Gary. E-mail communication, June 13, 2003.

Sokol, Kathy Arlen. "Like Sculpting Smoke . . . : Arundhati Roy on Fame, Writing and India." *Kyoto Journal*, no. 38 (1998). 66–73.

Takahashi, Tsutomu, Sadamichi Kato, and Reiko Akamine. "The Conservation Movement and Its Literature in Japan." In *Literature of Nature: An International Sourcebook*, ed. Patrick Murphy. Chicago: Fitzroy Dearborn, 1998. 90–93.

Yuki, Masami Raker. "Eco-rojikaru na disuko-su no ho e: Ishimure Michiko to Teri-Tenpesuto Uiriamsu no kankyou akutibisumu" (Toward an Eco-logical Discourse: Environmental Activism of Michiko Ishimure and Terry Tempest Williams; in Japanese). In *Ekkyou suru toposu: Kankyou bungaku gakuron josetsu*, ed. Noda Kenichi and Masami Yuki. Tokyo: Sairyusha, 2004. 290–93.

ONNO OERLEMANS

Romanticism and the City

Toward a Green Architecture

THIRTY YEARS AGO Raymond Williams pointed to the perceived duality between urban and rural environments as a key aspect of romantic ideology. Surprisingly, while much has been made of the romantic escape to nature, little attention has been paid to the distinctive anti-urbanism in romanticism. I am specifically interested in the collective myth produced through the collaborative poetics of Wordsworth and Coleridge, in which Wordsworth comes substantially to ground his poetic creativity and authority in his childhood exposure to rural/natural landscape, and Coleridge correspondingly is able to find a reason for his self-announced poetic failure in his overfamiliarity with urban landscape.

It is by no means obvious why for Wordsworth and Coleridge natural landscape should have a surfeit of meaning, while urban landscape is essentially meaningless and thus a threat to personal and poetic identity. Indeed, this should strike us as a paradox. Though it is a common metaphor that the natural environment is a "text" designed by God or nature, it is literally true that urban landscape is a human one, designed with deliberation and intent, and so it should be easier to locate meaning in an urban environment than a seemingly natural one. Why then do these poets regard the city as radically other and hostile to the poetic imagination and the country as ultimately sympathetic to imagination, even if it too can be seen as somehow "other"? I want to answer this question by examining the responses of Wordsworth and Coleridge to urban landscape. This anti-urbanism is part of the legacy of romanticism to contemporary environmentalism and ecocriticism, significantly predating the sources identified by Michael Bennett's recent investigation of the subject. My goal in this essay is to sketch some of the causes of this anti-urbanism, and to use romantic writing to suggest a way to a "green" architecture that understands the physical construction of buildings and communities in an environmentalist context.

The romantic myth of the corrosiveness of the urban environment to the imagination has not been carefully examined because it has generally not been taken seriously. Critics have accepted that both Wordsworth's autobiographical narratives about the growth of his imagination (primarily of *The Prelude*) and Coleridge's accounts of his poetic creativity in his early lyrics are self-enabling fictions. Additionally, it has been relatively easy to associate both romantic anti-urbanism and romantic naturalism with an antipathy toward rapid industrialization, and to write off anti-urbanism as a symptom of nostalgia for a simpler rural life. But this view ignores the puzzling ways in which Wordsworth and Coleridge categorized urban and rural landscape. That a specific rural landscape was crucial to Wordsworth's development as a poet is obvious enough. But few would take seriously the proposition that a natural landscape is critical to the development of poetic genius, which is what Wordsworth argues in *The Prelude* and *Home at Grasmere*, and what Coleridge asserts in such lyrics as "The Nightingale" and "Frost at Midnight." Coleridge even argues that an urban environment could impair poetic creativity in general—one of Romanticism's most romantic ideologies. Even Coleridge does not believe it for long; in the *Biographia*, as in "Dejection: An Ode," he points instead to a history of excesses of self-analysis, being too engaged in "metaphysics and in theological controversy" (8) to sustain his faith in the ability of poetic language to reveal and present truth, and nowhere in his voluminous later writings does he return to the idea that contact with urban landscape impairs the imagination.

Yet at least for the time that Coleridge was collaborating closely with Wordsworth, he accepted the notion that engagement with rural landscape promoted a healthy poetic consciousness as well as its seemingly necessary corollary that contact with urban landscape destroyed this. The key idea here is stark and simple and is at the root of romantic anti-urbanism. It is not that there are different kinds of meaning in nature and the city; it is rather that the only source of true meaning, of real insight, must come from the natural world. "Effusion XXXV" thus posits the idea that nature might be "animated" by "one intellectual breeze, / At once the Soul of each, and God of all" (ll. 44–48)—suggesting, as Tim Fulford has argued, that the poet "was portraying the whole of nature as a *literal* emanation of God's plastic power," so that the natural world was understood to be "the embodiment in material mass of his seminal thoughts" (56).

While most of his early lyrics explicitly celebrate nature, and especially childhood contact with nature, as a source of mental well-being and poetic creativity, this argument is made explicit in "Frost at Midnight." In seeking, and explicitly failing to find, a companionable form in the external world, the poet turns to his son, and his fervent belief that Hartley would learn "far other lore, / And in far other scenes!"

> For I was reared
> In the great city, pent 'mid cloisters dim,
> And saw nought lovely but the sky and stars.
> But *thou*, my babe! shalt wander like a breeze
> By lakes and sandy shores, beneath the crags
> Of ancient mountain, and beneath the clouds,
> Which image in their bulk both lakes and shores
> And mountain crags. . . . (ll. 50–57)

Coleridge's account here is not literally true—while he did spend several years at school in London, it is more accurate to say that he was "reared" in the rural setting of Ottery St. Mary. Yet, that the contrast the speaker creates is an exaggeration probably does not matter, since the implicit comparison here is with Wordsworth's childhood, characterized by a continuous and sustaining familiarity with a particular natural landscape that Coleridge imagines Hartley will enjoy. This explanation of his own failure depends both on the sense that there has been a fundamental break in the growth of his own imagination, a break characterized by isolation and intense book-ishness (and thus a turning away from the sustenance of natural landscape), and on the contrast between rural and urban landscape. The argument is that God's eternal presence cannot be read in the forms of the city. The "sky and stars" barely visible "'mid cloisters dim" speak of emptiness rather than the presence that Coleridge projects for his son, one based on a par-ticularized familiarity with the natural world. Like Wordsworth, Hartley shall

> . . . see and hear
> The lovely shapes and sounds intelligible
> Of that eternal language, which thy God
> Utters, who from eternity doth teach
> Himself in all, and all things in himself.
> Great universal Teacher! he shall mould
> Thy spirit, and by giving make it ask. (ll. 58–64)

Hartley's future happiness seems guaranteed not so much by his father's immediate love as by the place to which his father has brought him, and it will be sustained by a perfectly reciprocated inquisitiveness. His imagina-tion will be so connected to a transcendental presence that he will be able to

find meaning even in those forms of the natural world commonly associated
with death, depression, or absence—in winter and night, in snow, frost, and
icicles, and in the "eave-drops fall / Heard only in the trances of the blast"
(ll. 70–71).[1]

Wordsworth's rejection of the city, and his inability to read urban landscape, are as categorical and perplexing as Coleridge's. Though Wordsworth lived briefly in London, his antipathy to the city is striking and
consistent. Indeed, as many readers of *The Prelude* have noted, the poem
presents Wordsworth's sojourn in London as a kind of descent into hell,
a dark night of the soul before he is rejuvenated by his return to the true
home of Grasmere and rural landscape. City landscape and culture are for
Wordsworth a kind of toxic environment for the imagination. It is "the increasing accumulation of men in cities," he argues in the *Preface to Lyrical
Ballads,* that produces the "savage torpor" of the mind that he sought to
combat with his poetry. In *Michael,* Luke simply has to go to the city to
become corrupted, even after receiving a nearly ideal Wordsworthian up-
bringing, suggesting how utterly poisonous the urban environment is even
to healthy transplants. And in the stunning sonnet "Composed on Westminster Bridge," London is rendered beautiful only by a brilliant trick of
the imagination in which city becomes nature, a part of Earth's show, rather
than that of humankind and commerce. Standing at the most famously picturesque stations of the London guidebooks, in the quiet of early morning,
the nature poet is able to imagine London as dead, its "mighty heart . . . lying still." Thus may the city wear the shroud of morning "like a garment,"
the "Ships, towers, domes, theatres and temples" may be thought as lying "Open unto the fields, and to the sky," and the river Blake had called
"chartered" can be thought of as "glid[ing] at his own sweet will." Rather
than reflecting a utopian sacred space, in which "humans live alongside
a diversity of more-than-human others," as Kate Rigby has argued (256),
Wordsworth's sonnet finds London momentarily beautiful only if the poet
evacuates it of human life and meaning, and recreates it as a fantastical
natural landscape.

Jonathan Bate has suggested that Wordsworth is indeed interested in architecture or a built environment, noting that "there are a lot of buildings
in Wordsworth's sonnets. Those he likes best are of an architecture which
is fitting to its environment" (226). *Home at Grasmere* and his *Guide to the
Lakes,* however, suggest that Wordsworth prefers architecture that *hides* in
its environment, working like camouflage to conceal human presence in the
landscape. In the *Guide,* where we can find Wordsworth's closest attempt

at articulating an architectural aesthetic, he states that "the principle that ought to determine the position, apparent size, and architecture of a house [is] that it should be so constructed, and (if large) so much of it hidden, as to admit of its being gently incorporated into the scenery of nature" (120). Like the cottages and hedgerows (and hermits) of "Tintern Abbey," the buildings of the Lake District should for Wordsworth largely disappear into the scenery. Wordsworth argues that in terms of color, size, and outline, buildings should blend into the background to keep the natural beauty of the scenery intact. In *Home at Grasmere*, the poet celebrates that "thy Church and Cottages" are made "of mountain stones" and are "lurking dimly in their shy retreats. . . . / Like separated stars with clouds between" (ll. 121–25). In a city, where there is no nature with which to blend, design would appear to be irrelevant to Wordsworth.

As many critics have noted, Wordsworth's central response to London, in Book VII of *The Prelude*, has largely to do with the fact of its crowds, the relations he thinks exist or fail to exist between people. In the context both of his own writing, in which the effect of the (rural) physical environment on consciousness is paramount, and of writing about urban landscape in the period, in which this relation is also established, the degree to which Wordsworth downplays the physical (as opposed to social) space of the city is indeed surprising. The first detailed description of the city begins with a Miltonic flourish, drawing attention to the arbitrariness of the beginning in a place that cannot be ordered.

> And first, the look and aspect of the place—
> The broad highway appearance, as it strikes
> On strangers of all ages, the quick dance
> Of colours, lights and forms, the Babel din,
> The endless stream of men and moving things,
> From hour to hour the illimitable walk
> Still among streets. . . . (ll. 154–60)

Wordsworth moves quickly from panorama to the dizzying movement both of crowds and of the speaker himself through the city. The physical presence of the city—its buildings, streets, rivers and bridges, its organization—is rapidly obliterated in his lengthy account and becomes increasingly ephemeral. It is as though Wordsworth never found a map to the city. Indeed, as Ross King has persuasively argued, Wordsworth's account of London stresses how its physical reality is reduced to the equivalence of the advertising signs, superficial and floating signifiers with no concrete referents. In rural landscapes, King argues, observers are able to construct panoramas for themselves and thus be a determining force in the creation of a relation or understanding to the landscape. Wordsworth's account of London enacts this sense of dislocation by circling around examples of spectacle—thus the long descriptions of the theater, and the key descriptions of crowds as "A second-sight procession, such as glides / Over still mountains, or appears in dreams" (ll. 602–3), of the blind beggar whose life is reduced to mere text, and of London finally reduced to the spectacle of St. Bartholomew's Fair. The space of the city is converted directly into a network of symbols for a culture that has lost a connection with the physical. In Wordsworth's view of London, all human constructions become equivalent, standing in as self-feeding artifacts, signs detached from the ultimate reality of nature itself.

As several critics have argued, Wordsworth's account of London is important and influential because of the realism and complexity of its impressionism, and its depiction of the alienation and unreality of the city.[2] Yet what does it mean for the city's physical space to fade so completely into the background for Wordsworth, as though London consists of crowds, beggars, and spectacles alone? Why is Wordsworth so dislodged from his normal sensibility, his normal way of seeing the world around him, that he cannot see in the city, as Wollstonecraft, Lamb, Hazlitt, and many others did, a physical environment that expresses "modes of being" and kinds of knowledge not essentially different from those expressed in the country?

It is not simply that the city does not seem like nature. It is also that London's order, design, and art appear groundless, of an utterly different species than that revealed to Wordsworth in the crucial "spot of time" episodes of *The Prelude*. As we have seen with Coleridge, Wordsworth seeks to write poetry, and to create a sense of his own identity, founded on something utterly stable, the first ground, so to speak. The colossal environment of the city shows the degree to which humanity can alter nature, both in terms of the scale of construction and in the pace with which change occurs. The city thus comes to appear to Wordsworth only as upheaval, or an overwriting, rather than as the art he himself produces, which can reveal at every stage his connections to the natural world. Ironically, for a poet dedicated to the power of memory, urban landscape presents too much history, connected to too many people. In contrast, a natural environment, though filled with a deep and largely unknowable history of natural forces, is free enough of human activity to allow the poet to nurture his own memories in its open spaces.

What is perhaps most striking about the antipathy to the city I have sketched here is that it stands in stark contrast to an intensification of interest in urban design in England during the romantic period. A rapid survey shows that urban landscape was indeed a topic of considerable interest to readers of all kinds, and that if anything, it was filled with much more meaning than the kinds of objects or vistas typically represented by the romantic poet. Indeed, it is my sense that the diverse and profound ways in which urban landscape was being *read* during this period show Wordsworth's aversion to urban landscape to be particularly extreme. An extraordinary variety of books of the period in fact aimed to document the physical reality and complexity of cities in general and London in particular, and these texts were themselves a part of a complex history of writing about the urban landscape.[3] Many travelogues, for instance, include extensive and detailed records of city life and cityscapes, as well as the more standard fare of picturesque hills and rural ruins, blurring the seemingly obvious distinctions between the two from the point of view of the picturesque traveler. A large number of travelogues and travel guides appeared during this period specifically on London and its environs (examples of a genre with a long and distinct history), including the popular *Some Account of London* by Thomas Pennant, a yearly guidebook by John Feltham called *The Picture of London*, and C. F. Partington's *Natural History and Views of London and Its Environs*. There is also a relatively distinct genre celebrating what we might call the "architectural picturesque," which, like James Elmes's *Metropolitan Improvements*, provided lessons on architectural history and taste but more often enthusiastically appealed to the obvious awe created by the impressive size and wealth of the city and its grandest buildings, such as Ackermann and Pugin's *Microcosm of London*, Thomas Malton's *A Picturesque Tour through the Cities of London and Westminster*, and John Papworth's *Select Views of London*. These expensively produced texts are characterized by lavish illustrations of exteriors and interiors of famous buildings as well as panoramic views of the city. The writers and artists of these texts clearly understood that the city presented an extraordinary landscape, as appealing to readers as rolling hills and watery horizons, and thus the urban landscape too was worthy of frequent representation and occasional analysis.

While these texts reflect an understanding that cities and cityscapes are obviously different from rural or "natural" landscape, writers of travelogues frequently comment on cities in much the same way as they would on these other landscapes. Cityscapes are recorded in terms of their physical beauty or ugliness, the possibility they presented for picturesque and even sublime views, and for their ability to reflect the stereotyped characteristics of the nation and its people—reflections, that is, of the nature of its specific culture.

Mary Wollstonecraft provides a representative example. In her *Letters Written during a Short Residence,* in which she gives an account of her travels in Scandinavia, she develops an argument about the moral necessity of architectural self-consciousness, taking to task those who imagine "a noble pillar, or arch, unhallowed. . . . . If we wish to render mankind moral from principle, we must, I am persuaded, give a greater scope to the enjoyments of the senses, by blending taste with them" (307–8). That is, people are made better if they can be reminded of the pleasures and rewards of civilization (art, leisure, education, taste), even in the manner in which they recreate and decorate their surroundings. Wollstonecraft frequently employs the term *picturesque* as an architectural category, a characteristic neatness of a general domain, reflecting the consciousness of a person (if she is describing an estate) or a people (if describing a town or city) toward the orderly development of an environment. It can be found, for instance, where "the country is obviously enriched by population" (126)—where, one way or another, there is physical evidence that people are able to construct their environment with an eye to how it will be beheld by others. What is perhaps most interesting about Wollstonecraft's argument is the continuity she sees between urban landscape, characterized for her by the neatness of buildings and the layout of grounds, and the way in which country villages and farmers cultivate their land and preserve (or destroy) forests. For Wollstonecraft, the environment is clearly not starkly divided between urban and rural categories.

What the foregoing survey of writing about urban landscape and architecture shows, in part, is a romantic-period approach to reading constructed environments as revealing meaning on a number of different scales (personal, political, historical, national, and economic) that stands in stark contrast to the "romantic ideology" of Wordsworth and Coleridge, in which these environments become alien, mysterious, other, and dehumanizing. This contrast centers crucially on the manner in which the materiality of the urban landscape—its physical presence—can be conceived of as either continuous with or in stark contrast to human desire. Moreover, this contrast seems to exist more clearly in discussions of urban landscape than in discussions of rural ones, at least in part because the former is more readily associated with artifice and the inorganic, while the landscapes favored by the poets are above all natural, organic, infused with life.

We can gain insight into this contrast by turning briefly to contemporary architectural theory, where there is much debate about the potential "meaning" of buildings in particular and constructed environments in general. Heidegger's writing on dwelling is a frequent source for those critics who see architecture as profoundly meaningful, more than merely a playing with codified signs. Architecture is an appealing topic for Heidegger precisely because it is the most obviously physical or "earth-bound" of the arts, and he wants to show how it is through art that we have necessarily created, and been created by, our world. In a key passage, Heidegger speaks of the mythic significance of the creation of the temple:

> Standing there, the building rests on the rocky ground. This resting of the work draws up out of the rock the mystery of that rock's clumsy yet spontaneous support. Standing there, the building holds its ground against the storm raging above it and so first makes the storm itself manifest in its violence. The luster and gleam of the stone, though itself apparently glowing only by the grace of the sun, yet first brings to light the light of the day, the breadth of the sky, the darkness of the night. The temple's firm towering makes visible the invisible space of air. . . . The temple-work, standing there, opens up a world and at the same time sets this world back again on earth, which itself only thus emerges as native ground. (*Poetry, Language, Thought* 43)

Heidegger is describing an extraordinary act of the imagination that attempts to balance the physical presence of the building with the subjective creativity needed to construct it. Although he writes here of a mythic "ur"-temple, the materiality of the building is a crucial part of the reality he is drawing to our attention. Heidegger's description of the temple presents a fascinating network of perspectives: its very existence depends upon the shaping of the unshaped rock it rests upon; it stands against and is a part of this ground; the storm's ability to do "violence" depends on the stability of the temple, the desires associated with its construction for it to represent permanence and actually to be permanent; as a prominence on the landscape, it becomes the physical object by which we measure other physical qualities of our environment—the light or darkness, or our position on that landscape. The building, Heidegger reveals, marks and informs our world as unmade objects cannot. Buildings do not mark us as aliens within that landscape but reveal us to ourselves as beings who necessarily *make* our world one way or another.

Citing Heidegger, Kenneth Frampton argues that the act of building necessarily causes matter "to come forth for the very first time and to come into the Open of the work's world" (*Studies* 23)—that is, that architecture in essence makes the world human and meaningful, that the reworking of matter into form is a first and powerful way in which consciousness finds and determines its own existence in the physical world. For Frampton or Heidegger this is not a rapacious or imperialistic project (though it can be), but a necessary one. We build to survive, but in building we come to consciousness not just of our ability but also of where and how we exist in the physical world. Similarly, R. D. Dripps argues that in reimaging Vitruvius's myth of the origin of dwelling in his *Ten Books of Architecture,* we can discover that architecture has its roots as the means to the creation of a public space: "dwelling and gathering form a political and architectural bond that . . . defines the essential idea of the public realm" (*First House* 6). Frampton and Dripps, echoing Ruskin's idea of architecture as one of the key "lamps of memory," stress both that architecture is continuous with the creation of urban environments and that architecture is the most immediate way in which culture is made visible to itself.[4]

Yet architecture can of course fail to perform these utopian functions. Perhaps most fundamentally, Heidegger's phenomenological interpretation leaves open the possibility that a building can be regarded as merely a thing, an object with a quality of permanence and silence that speaks of its difference from both organic (natural) life and human subjectivity, not unlike the rocks and stones that embody a fundamental otherness in Wordsworth's poetry. That is, Heidegger's account of "temple-work" presents the ideal effect that buildings can have on our collective experience or within culture. We can easily fail to make similar imaginative associations ourselves in responding to the multitude of buildings we encounter, as Wordsworth seems to in *The Prelude.* This failure is perhaps most likely when we consider buildings not as single isolated objects within an otherwise unconstructed environment but as conglomerations in an urban landscape, where a relation with the seemingly natural seems occluded, and even relations between buildings, or between them and their "environment" (literally, the landscape surrounding them), can seem chaotic or invisible. The urban landscape then fails to cohere, to offer meaning, and buildings come to speak only of their own existence as formed substance. In this view, architecture may be seen to be dominated by the creation of structures that separate and divide, and produce primarily private spaces, in which buildings and structures overwhelm the desire that has produced them. "Then the making and the representing of architecture become separate and disconnected activities. Representation now becomes a substitution or replacement for something not present, and architecture is thought of more as a thing—complete in itself—and therefore closed to further intervention and disclosure" (Dripps 43).

This brings us back to Wordsworth and Coleridge's belief that urban landscape can stifle altogether human desire and imagination, and their larger inability to read or find meaning in these landscapes. For these poets, the actual physical space of the city is corrupting; design and human intention—interaction with the physical world—have become meaningless. The context of the foregoing discussion, I hope, makes this position seem even more extreme, and more interesting. Clearly urban landscape has excited a wide range of responses, from the ability of such landscape to reflect a national culture to the ability of individual buildings to create a sense of awe or to reflect specific relations to the natural world. Regardless of any single individual response, urban landscape in general, and architecture specifically, were found during the romantic period to be full of potential significance. It is important to stress as well that the bulk of responses to the built environment, both then and now, suggest not so much a rupture between rural and urban landscapes as a continuity between them—that clear distinctions are hard to define and possibly unnecessary to make. In other words, thinking about urban landscape has long been a part of, and has even encouraged, the kind of utopian thinking that Coleridge and Wordsworth reserve entirely for natural or seemingly natural environments.

While Wordsworth's writing has been seen as "green" in many respects, his categorical antipathy to the city, mirrored in Coleridge, seems to me deeply problematic in environmental terms. It is founded on a self-defeating notion that humankind at a communal level must always be separate from the natural world and that what we build is always disconnected from both us and nature. When Wordsworth in his poetry describes himself as more or less alone in the natural world, he works in complex and profound ways to counter the metaphysical tenets that consciousness is either easily alienated or connected to the natural world.[5] But in moving from the abstract problem of constructing identity (in nature) to the practical reality of living in the world—which means among other things building in it—the poet's imagination seems stymied. Wordsworth adheres to the belief that in altering nature, we destroy it and disconnect ourselves from it. And yet, of course, like all living beings, we must alter nature in order to exist in it, as he grudgingly allows in the *Guide*. William Cronon's analysis of the problematics of an absolute divide between natural and altered landscapes is relevant here. Unless we "embrace the full continuum of a natural landscape that is also cultural, in which the city, the suburb, the pastoral, and the wild each has its proper place," he argues, we must conclude that virtually all of the places we inhabit are abominations ("Trouble with Wilderness" 89). We need to find ways to accommodate and understand the ways we inhabit the world, to recognize that the places in which we live can also be constructed in ways varyingly healthy or unhealthy, beautiful or ugly, sustainable or destructive.

Obviously, cities consist of more than just architecture and relations to building and nature. They are about large and rapidly moving economies, centers of culture and power and commerce. But just as a house is a profound expression of its residents' relation to the earth, so too are cities the expression of a society's relation to the world. We have seen this idea reflected in the romantic period already in Wollstonecraft, and it is an obvious tenet of much travel writing about cities and of the guides to architecture in London. We can see this idea as well in the poetry of Blake, the most urban poet of the period, to whom I now turn as a way of concluding. The poem "London" presents a complex dystopian theme by showing that the city's landscape profoundly reflects the character of the society that has created it and affects those who live within it—an idea crucial to any notion of a green architecture. The poem's dramatic action involves the speaker directed by the layout and organization of city streets, and resisting that order in the act of wandering. He is, in a sense, a tourist, seemingly going nowhere in particular, and taking careful note of his surroundings, which include both the city's population and its physical environment. The poem insists on the necessary relation between consciousness and landscape. In the first stanza the environment, characterized by "charter'd streets" and the "charter'd Thames," is implicitly connected to the "Marks of weakness, marks of woe" that the speaker sees and hears in the people he meets. Chartering is a political and economic act—a granting of privilege—and London and many businesses were chartered in this way. Chartering establishes an institution, including a city, and the most palpable way in which chartering is evidenced is in the construction of buildings, the organization of streets. Thus chartering is at the core of the building of cities. Even residential structures are involved in this process; real estate was (and is) an intensely speculative market, and housing for the poor, as for the rich, produces profits for the builders and speculators and eventually for the aristocratic landowners who lease the land, and whose original ownership is also chartered. That the

Thames is chartered too points to how dramatic and complete this process is—a conversion of the natural landscape into clear and material forms of power. The effects of this external organization are seen in the people who occupy and are occupied by this power, who reveal their "marks of weakness, marks of woe." For Blake the overwhelming and immediate presence of the city's constructed landscape is an instrument of power, part of what produces and maintains the "mind-forg'd manacles."

The third stanza too emphasizes the connection between power and buildings. It is in part the physical manifestations of the institution of the Church, through its massive presence in the form of chapels, steeples, cathedrals, and the like that gives the Church its authority and through which it can be seen to condone the status quo. The fact that every guidebook on London celebrates the great churches as a way of pointing to the general wealth, power, and prestige of the city makes this association very clear. So too, it is the ability of the institution of the state to construct palaces that marks its ability to conscript the hapless soldier.[6] Yet the poem clearly allows for, and invites, resistance to these massive forms of power. The speaker marks his own resistance through his wandering, showing that he is not imprisoned by the grid of streets and buildings, and by his very recognition of the effect of building. (In contrast, Wordsworth's wandering in Book VII emphasizes his sense of being overwhelmed by the chaos of the city.) And in "London," resistance is made palpable in the idea that the misery of the chimney sweeper and the soldier could "mark" or violate the buildings associated with power. The church, blackened by pollution (literally figuring the corruption of the city at large), is "appalled" or made white by the chimney sweeper's cry, and the presumably pristine walls of the palace are marked by the blood of those forced to fight for it. These acts of resistance are of course imaginative, but they evince the will to see through and transform the constructed environment.

What is perhaps most interesting about Blake's interpretation of the city is that it goes so much against the grain of writing about architecture and urban landscape in that period, even as it contains within it the seeds of a utopian conception of architecture. The guidebooks and picturesque tours of the city all celebrate the buildings that represent obvious forms of power and prestige. Moreover, as noted earlier, they complain, generally, about the apparent lack of order in the city, the seemingly random process of development and sprawl producing an ugliness that was considered a sign of the failure of government and business to produce a clear physical manifestation of their worth. Blake's brief poem, on the other hand, shows how the physical landscape reflects the system, or complex of systems, that has produced it and the misery that infects both the landscape and its inhabitants.

Seeing the physical design of cities and buildings as necessarily ideological, which Blake does in "London," is a fundamental first step in any green architecture. This is, indeed, what turns the city into a text, an artifact or set of artifacts that can be written and rewritten. A green architecture would not only emphasize sustainability, preservation of natural resources, and the effects of our development on other species; it would also take into account economic and political relations between peoples and their constructed landscapes, and thus too the mental and physical health of the people who live within a particular designed space. These aspects of design require that both the designer and the occupant realize and reimagine connections to the natural world. Blake, finally, comes close to envisioning this kind of utopianism in his poem *Jerusalem*, in which a personified London states that "My Streets are my Ideas of Imagination. . . . / My Houses are Thoughts" (plate 40: 31, 33). Moreover, in the poem Los builds Golgonooza, with a new kind of construction and design:

> The stones are pity, and the bricks, well wrought affections:
> Enameld with love & kindness, & the tiles engraven gold,
> Labour of merciful hands: the beams & rafters are forgiveness:
> The mortar & cement of the work, tears of honesty: the nails,
> And the screws & iron braces, are well wrought blandishments,
> And well contrived words, firm fixing, never forgotten,
> Always comforting the remembrance: the floors, humility,
> The cielings, devotion: the hearths, thanksgiving:
> Prepare the furniture O Lambeth in the pitying looms!
> The curtains, woven tears & sights, wrought into lovely forms
> For comfort. (plate 12: 30–40)

This is not yet green architecture either, of course, but although Blake's poem is utopian, abstract, and heavily symbolic, it is telling and characteristic that he represents both the process of radical imaginative change and its effect through a transformation of the physical space of the city. A truly green architecture, in romanticism, occurs only in an imaginary space between Blake's concrete imagining and reading of the city, his sense of human nature and culture being part of a larger natural order, and Wordsworth's particularized understanding of how imagination is nurtured by its connection to physical things.

NOTES

1. This understanding of the effect of urban landscape is suggested briefly too in "This Lime-Tree Bower My Prison," in which the narrator enables his own ability to posit meaning in the natural world by imagining Charles Lamb's having "pined / And hungered after Nature, many a year, / In the great City pent."

2. See especially Heffernan, J. Johnston, Lindenberger, and Sharpe.

3. See, for instance, Roberts, "London Here and Now."

4. As contemporary architect Adam Caruso writes, "In the same way as in art and literature, but in a less easily ignored way, architecture contributes to our collective memory" ("Tyranny of the New" 25).

5. See chapter 1 of my book *Romanticism and the Materiality of Nature*.

6. As Lewis Mumford argues in *The City in History*, "In the citadel the new mark of the city is obvious: a change of scale, deliberately meant to awe and overpower the beholder. Though the mass of inhabitants might be poorly fed and overworked, no expense was spared to create temples and palaces whose sheer bulk and upward thrust would dominate the rest of the city. . . . What we now call 'monumental architecture' is first of all the expression of power, and that power exhibits itself in the assemblage of costly building materials and of all the resources of art, as well as in a command of all manner of sacred adjuncts" (65).

WORKS CITED

Ackermann, R., and A. G. Pugin. *Microcosm of London*. 3 vols. London: 1808–11.

Bate, Jonathan. *The Song of the Earth*. Cambridge, Mass.: Harvard University Press, 2000.

Bennett, Michael. "From Wide Open Spaces to Metropolitan Places: The Challenge to Ecocriticism." *Interdisciplinary Studies in Literature and Environment* 8 (Winter 2001): 31–52.

Blake, William. *Blake's Poetry and Designs*. Ed. Mary Lynn Johnson and John E. Grant. New York: W. W. Norton, 1979.

Buell, Lawrence. *Writing for an Endangered World: Literature, Culture, and Environment in the U.S. and Beyond*. Cambridge, Mass.: Belknap Press, 2001.

Caruso, Adam. "The Tyranny of the New." *Blueprint* 150 (May 1998): 24–25.

Coleridge, Samuel Taylor. *Samuel Taylor Coleridge*. Ed. H. J. Jackson. New York: Oxford University Press. 1985.

Cronon, William. "The Trouble with Wilderness; or Getting Back to the Wrong Nature." In *Uncommon Ground: Rethinking the Human Place in Nature*, ed. William Cronon. New York: W. W. Norton, 1996. 69–90.

Dripps, R. D. *The First House: Myth, Paradigm, and the Task of Architecture*. Cambridge, Mass.: MIT Press, 1997.

Elmes, James. *Metropolitan Improvements of London in the Nineteenth Century*. London: Jones and Company, 1828.

Feltham, John. *The Picture of London for 1804* . . . . London: Lewis and Company, 1804.

Frampton, Kenneth. *Studies in Tectonic Culture: The Poetics of Construction in Nineteenth and Twentieth Century Architecture*. Cambridge, Mass.: MIT Press, 1995.

Fulford, Tim. *Coleridge's Figurative Language*. New York: St. Martin's, 1991.

Glen, Heather. "The Poet in Society: Blake and Wordsworth on London." *Literature and History* 3 (1976): 2–28.

Hazlitt, William. *Notes of a Journey through France and Italy. The Complete Works of William Hazlitt*. Vol. 10. Ed. P. P. Howe. New York: AMS Press, 1967.

Heffernan, James. "Wordsworth's London: The Imperial Monster." *Studies in Romanticism* 37 (Fall 1998): 421–43.

Heidegger, Martin. *Poetry, Language, Thought*. Trans. Albert Hofstadter. New York: Harper and Row. 1971.

Johnston, John H. *The Poet and the City: A Study in Urban Perspectives*. Athens: University of Georgia Press, 1984.

Johnston, Kenneth. *The Hidden Wordsworth: Poet, Lover, Rebel, Spy*. New York: W. W. Norton, 1998.

King, Ross. "Wordsworth, Panoramas, and the Prospect of London." *Studies in Romanticism* 32 (Spring 1993): 57–73.

Lindenberger, Herbert. *On Wordsworth's "Prelude."* Princeton: Princeton University Press, 1963.

Malton, Thomas. *A Picturesque Tour through the Cities of London and Westminster*. London: T. Malton, 1792.

Mumford, Lewis. *The City in History: Its Origins, Its Transformations, and Its Prospects*. New York: Harcourt Brace Jovanovich, 1961.

Oerlemans, Onno. *Romanticism and the Materiality of Nature*. Toronto: University of Toronto Press, 2002.

Papworth, John. *Select Views of London*. London: J. Ackermann, 1816.

Partington, C. F. *Natural History and Views of London and Its Environs*. 2 vols. London: Black and Armstrong, 1837.

Pennant, Thomas. *Some Account of London*. 5th ed. London: J. Faulder, 1813.

Pugin, A. G. *Contrasts, or A Parallel between the Noble Edifices of the Middle Ages, and Similar Buildings of the Present Day*. 1836. Reprint New York: Humanities Press, 1973.

———. *Principles of Pointed or Christian Architecture*. 1841. Reprint New York: St. Martin's Press, 1973.

Rigby, Kate. *Topographies of the Sacred: The Poetics of Place in European Romanticism*. Charlottesville: University of Virginia Press, 2004.

Roberts, Gary. "London Here and Now: Walking, Streets, and Urban Environments in English Poetry from Donne to Gay." In *The Nature of Cities: Ecocriticism and Urban Environments*, ed. Michael Bennett and David W. Teague. Tucson: University of Arizona Press, 1999. 33–54.

Scruton, Robert. *The Aesthetics of Architecture*. London: Methuen, 1979.

Sharpe, William Chapman. *Unreal Cities: Urban Figuration in Wordsworth, Baudelaire, Whitman, Eliot and Williams*. Baltimore: Johns Hopkins University Press, 1990.

Williams, Raymond. *The Country and the City*. London: Chatto and Windus, 1973.

Wollstonecraft, Mary. *Letters Written during a Short Residence*. Ed. Carol H. Poston. Lincoln: University of Nebraska Press, 1976.

Wordsworth, William. *The Illustrated Wordsworth's Guide to the Lakes*. Ed. Peter Bicknell. New York: Congdon and Weed, 1984.

———. *The Prelude*. Ed. Jonathan Wordsworth, M. H. Abrams, and Stephen Gill. New York: W. W. Norton, 1979.

———. *William Wordsworth: The Poems*. 2 vols. Ed. John O. Hayden. New Haven: Yale University Press, 1981.

Annie Dillard and the *Book of Job*

Notes toward a Postnatural Ecocriticism

IN THE *Book of Job*, delivering his climactic speech out of the whirlwind, God humbles Job with a series of acute reminders of the limitations of mere humanity while extolling his own status as the divine creator and sustainer of nature. That status appears to be a matter of both power and knowledge. "Where were you," God demands of Job,

> when I founded the earth?
> Tell me, if you know so much . . .
> Who shut the sea within doors . . .
> Saying, "Thus far come, but no more,
> Here your wild waves halt"? . . .
> Have you entered the springs of the sea,
> Walked in the recesses of the deep? . . .
> Do you know the birth season of the ibex,
> Do you watch the calving of the hind,
> Do you count the months they fulfill,
> Mark the time they give birth? (Pope 247–48, 257)

As anyone familiar with the *Book of Job* can attest, it is a great speech, filled with some of the world's oldest and most vivid nature writing and posing a series of theologically acute questions well calculated to awe Job into silence.

Those questions were meant to be understood rhetorically, but a contemporary reader might be forgiven for responding to them literally—by noting, for example, that we *have* "walked in the recesses of the deep."[1] In fact it has been more than forty years since divers first explored the Marianas Trench, reaching a depth of more than thirty-five thousand feet ("Depths"). A contemporary reader might note in addition that we *do* "know the birth season of the ibex" and "watch the calving of the hind." I did not have to leave my desk to learn that *Capra nubiana*, the species of ibex most likely referred to by the Job writer, is a crepuscular ungulate, feeding mainly on shrubs, herbs, grass, and lichens; that adult specimens typically weigh between 25 and 70 kilograms and stand from 65 to 75 centimeters at the shoulder; that their body length varies from 105 to 125 centimeters and their tail length from 15 to 20 centimeters; that the horns are semicircular, growing up to 120 centimeters long on males (35 centimeters on females) and sporting 24–36 knobs along the outer curve; that they live in single-sex herds; that they reach sexual maturity at two to three years; that mating occurs during the fall, generally in October; that their gestation period is five months, after which the females give birth to one or two young; and that the kids are weaned after three months but continue for three years to live with the maternal herd (Pope 259; "Nubian"). About the hind, *Capreolus dama*, we know even more: it is a medium-sized deer, typically standing 91–97 centimeters high at the shoulder, and so on. The "months they fulfill"—the hind's gestation period—is seven and a half months, and "the time they give birth" is April through June ("Deer").

To respond thus literally to God's questions is clearly to read the *Book of Job* quite differently than did the book's ancient audience—to read it, in fact, in a way not *possible* for that audience. It is not merely that we moderns know more than the ancients about nature, but that, because we read at this particular historical moment, we behold nature in a particular way: as the object of the sort of panoptic gaze that for the ancient reader was the sole prerogative of God. Our perspective has been decisively shaped by *global biosurveillance*, a term I use to denote the vast and growing complex of activities that enable us, first, to understand living nature as a biological whole—as the biosphere—and second, to strip it of layer after layer of what used to be spoken of as its "mystery" (and thereby render it increasingly amenable to human ends). Global biosurveillance produces these effects in ways so numerous and varied that I can only begin to list them here: by monitoring the temperature and chemical composition of the atmosphere; by tracking the temperature of the oceans and the circulation of marine nutrients; by recording the movements of migratory wildlife as animals and birds distribute themselves across an international system of flyways and refuges; by "mapping" the genomes of a variety of species; and by deploying any of a rapidly proliferating number of other techniques for rendering nature increasingly transparent.

Global biosurveillance is the totality of that "modern biological vision," to borrow the words of the entomologist and sociobiologist E. O. Wilson, that "sweeps from microseconds to millions of years and from micrometers to the biosphere." It includes the gathering of biospheric data about the past and present—everything from the excavations of paleobiologists to the up-to-the-minute virus tracking of the Centers for Disease Control to the Audubon Society's annual bird counts to the satellites that monitor the movements of radio-collared animals. And while ultimately "it is merely ordinary vision expanded by the electron microscope, earth-scan satellite, and other prosthetic devices" (44), it depends for its functioning on an institutional foundation that not only underwrites its activities but also effectively organizes and disseminates the data it generates (as is done, for example, by universities, government agencies, and institutions like the Smithsonian). Also necessary are conceptual frameworks adequate to the task of inscribing and synthesizing such masses of data (for example, the increasingly sophisticated computer models of evolutionary biology, atmospheric science, population ecology, epidemiology, and genomics).

Ubiquitous as it now is, global biosurveillance is only one of a number of other scientific, technological, and philosophical developments that are radically revising our understanding of nature, problematizing the previously straightforward vocabulary of environmentalism, multiplying the threats to which environmentalism must respond, and thereby commanding our attention as ecocritics. Some of these developments, like the following, are by now quite familiar:

The deconstruction of nature, which understands "nature" and "wilderness" as discursive constructs ineluctably shaped by the desires of the cultures that deploy them, and thus unavailable as guarantors of stable meaning.

Postmodern ecology, which stresses the nonlinearity and instability of natural ecosystems, rejects the earlier notion of an orderly "natural succession" culminating in a stable "climax community," and thus precludes any resort to "natural" baselines in guiding efforts to "restore" disturbed ecosystems to their "original" state.

Cyborgism, the creation of technological bodies that destabilize the nature-culture binary and any number of other once "natural" categories.

Gene splicing, which allows the creation of genetically modified organisms (such as the OncoMouse, Starlink corn, and AquAdvantage salmon). Such genetically altered life forms comprise an artificial flora and fauna, the genes of which are almost certain to escape into wild populations, threatening the genetic integrity and stability of the biosphere itself.

Equally important, but currently almost entirely absent from ecocritical discourse, are a number of other concepts that have the potential not only to scramble further a variety of deep-seated assumptions about nature but also to create wholly artificial forms of life, significantly furthering the transition to a genuinely "postnatural" world:

> *Radical materiality*, the idea that phenomena like life and consciousness are material "all the way down," fully explicable without recourse to mystifying concepts like "soul" or "spirit."

> *The information model* of life, which holds that life's "essence" or *élan vital* is information. In carbon-based life, this information is encoded in DNA, but it could conceivably be encoded in other substrates as well, so that, for example, silicone-based life forms could exist in the virtual environment of a computer network.

> *Emergence*, the idea that life, consciousness, and intelligent behavior are epi-phenomena that emerge spontaneously out of recursive nonlinear systems governed by comparatively simple rules.

Taken together, these postnatural developments have the potential to implicate the biosphere so completely in human affairs that at some not-too-distant point it might make more sense to think of it as a *technosphere*: a "world designed by people" (Clark).[2]

THE UNDERSTANDING of global biosurveillance as a relatively new and widely institutionalized nexus of knowledge and power owes much, of course, to Michel Foucault, who was famously uninterested in nature and nature writing. His concern rather was to understand the role of surveillance and panopticism in disciplining human subjects in social institutions such as the prison, clinic, and school. How, then, might terms like *panopticism* and *surveillance* figure in an analysis of nature writing? In *Discipline and Punish*, Foucault noted that Jeremy Bentham's famed Panopticon may have been inspired not by any attempt to monitor the social realm but by an attempt to render transparent a representation of the natural realm—by the royal menagerie at Versailles, redesigned in the 1660s by the architect Louis Le Vaux in a way that made the zoo's specimens completely and continuously observable. "By Bentham's time," writes Foucault,

> this menagerie had disappeared. But one finds in the programme of the Panopticon a similar concern with individualizing observation, with characteriza-

tion and classification, with the analytical arrangement of space. The Panopticon is a royal menagerie; the animal is replaced by man, individual distribution by specific grouping and the king by the machinery of furtive power. With this exception, the Panopticon also does the work of a naturalist.[3]

Here I want to reverse Foucault's formulation by restoring "the animal" to its original place in the Panopticon, and then explore how biosurveillance— as just one element of the larger, ongoing historical shift to the postnatural— is altering fundamental aspects of our relationship to nature. In changing how we see nature, global biosurveillance also changes the political and imaginative uses to which we put it, the ways we write about it, and the ways we read what others have written about it.

Consider this passage from the "Bernhardsdorp" chapter of Wilson's *Biophilia*, in which he describes a moment in the rain forest when he is able to slip into the alert, observant mode he calls "the naturalist's trance":

> In a twist my mind came free and I was aware of the hard workings of the natural world beyond the periphery of ordinary attention, where passions lose their meaning and history is in another dimension, without people, and great events pass without record or judgment. I was a transient of no consequence in this familiar yet deeply alien world that I had come to love. . . . The effect was strangely calming. (7)

Readers will immediately recognize here the language of a very old desire—the postlapsarian yearning to escape from human history, to effect a "calming" retreat into a "familiar yet deeply alien world," one "without people," without "consequence," and prior to "record or judgment." This desire is expressed but not, of course, in any way effected; Wilson is as thoroughly immersed in history as he is in nature; he would not be in the rain forest at all were it not for the historical development of global biosurveillance, whose agenda he is there to serve. Wilson's participation in the historically specific activities of his time brings him into close contact with nature (both by bringing him to the rain forest in the first place and by increasing his understanding of it to a level impossible for the Job author to imagine). At the same time, he describes that participation using the ancient discourse of the Fall, invoking the figure of prelapsarian nature as the site of an escape, however momentary, from the very history that has brought him into such intimate contact with it.

Like the Job writer, Wilson here expounds a theme that can properly be termed biblical. But unlike the Job writer, he is not a member of an ancient

Israelite society but a contemporary western scientist. Two decidedly different perspectives are thus brought into dialogue, and a writer more attuned
to the literary possibilities of irony and paradox might have sensed, and
then chosen to thematize and explore, the tensions inherent in such a situation. Thoreau noted these tensions in *Walden*:

> At the same time that we are earnest to explore and learn all things, we require
> that all things be mysterious and unexplorable, that land and sea be infinitely
> wild, unsurveyed and unfathomed by us because unfathomable. (575)

But Wilson declines the invitation to irony, choosing instead to suggest that
ancient desires and modern technologies of seeing are perfectly compati-
ble—one is tempted to say *consilient*—because biosurveillance is ultimately
not historical at all: "the naturalist's vision is only a specialized product" of
a universal "biophilic instinct." Again subtly alluding to—but now substantially revising—the story of the Fall, Wilson goes on to assert that knowledge does not really alienate us from nature: "Humanity is exalted not because we are so far above other living creatures, but because knowing them
well elevates the very concept of life" (22). Yet "the very concept of life" is
precisely what postnaturality is now calling into question.

WILSON'S REFUSAL to acknowledge and exploit the ironies of his historical situation could not be more different than Annie Dillard's treatment of
biosurveillance in *Pilgrim at Tinker Creek* (1974). Trained in theology rather
than biology, with a fine writerly appreciation of dialogical tension and the
true Christian's fearlessness in the face of paradox, she is far readier than
Wilson to exploit the literary opportunities created by the historical specificity of her mode of seeing. Instead of trying to resolve or explain away
the conflict that biosurveillance was already rendering acute by the time of
Pilgrim (1974), she thematizes it—in ways I wish now to explore.

   Pilgrim at Tinker Creek is as heavily indebted to the *Book of Job* as the "Bernhardsdorp" chapter of *Biophilia* is to the *Book of Genesis*. The first of its many
biblical allusions is in fact a quote from *Job*, and much of its subsequent language and imagery are recognizably Jobean. We hear echoes of the book, for
example, in Dillard's fondness for the word "swaddling," in her description
of the earth passing through its seasons "like a leviathan breathing" (75),
and in her set pieces about the intricacies of the longleaf pine (130) and the
mouth parts of the dragonfly (136), both of which echo *Job*'s descriptions
of Behemoth and Leviathan and make a very *Job*-like theological point. In
addition, *Pilgrim* is, like *Job*, a work of natural theology. It sees nature as
revelation and claims to find in that revelation a number of "evidences,"

as William Paley famously called them, of the attributes of the deity—in
Pilgrim's case, that God has a "manic exuberance" (234) and a "generous
spirit" (135); that he "loves pizazz" (137); that he creates "with a spendthrift
genius and an extravagance of care" (127); that the creation is "not in any
real sense necessary" to him (129); that he will "stop at nothing" and "is apt
to create *anything*" (135, emphasis in original); and my favorite, that he is "a
deranged manic-depressive with limitless capital" (65). *Pilgrim*'s narrator
makes her theological project explicit when she writes that she is "coming
around to fish as spirit" and "Christ as fish" (185–86). When she glimpses
the muskrat, her biblical language suggests that she is actually seeing not
nature but God: "and there it came, swimming right toward me. Knock;
seek; ask" (192).

Dillard is writing nearly two centuries after Paley, however, and the observations upon which she bases her natural theology are not merely those
of an armchair theologian but rather those of a diligent student of global
biosurveillance:

> I have at the moment a situation which allows me to devote considerable
> hunks of time to seeing what I can see, and trying to piece it together. . . .
> I've read books. I've gathered statistics feverishly: The average temperature
> of our planet is 57 degrees Fahrenheit. Of the 29 percent of all land that is above
> water, over a third is given to grazing. The average size of all living animals,
> including man, is almost that of a housefly. The earth is mostly granite, which
> in turn is mostly oxygen. (128)

Here are several telltale symptoms of global biosurveillance, most notably
the obsessive accumulation of biospheric data and the effort to construct
intellectual frameworks "to piece it together." The goal of all this activity is
nothing less than a complete transparency, a panoptic view of nature that,
to repeat Wilson's words, "sweeps from microseconds to millions of years
and from micrometers to the biosphere." Writes Dillard:

> I want to have things as multiply and intricately as possible present and visible
> in my mind. Then I might be able to sit on the hill by the burnt books where the
> starlings fly over and see not only the starlings, the grass field, the quarried
> rock, the viney woods, Hollins Pond, and the mountains beyond, but also, and
> simultaneously, feathers' barbs, springtails in the soil, chloroplasts streaming,
> rotifers pulsing, and the shape of the air in the pines. (137–38)

Such exuberant panopticism cannot help but disrupt *Pilgrim*'s natural theology. After all, what makes the muskrat and the fish such great stand-ins

for God—the reason the narrator's infrequent sightings of them can be presented as epiphanies—is their hiddenness and mystery, the very things annihilated by her postnatural habits of seeing. Anyone who has read both Paley's *Natural Theology* and Charles Darwin's *Origin of Species* will understand the problem; while reading the *Origin* one cannot help but feel sorry for Paley as one after another his purportedly incontrovertible "evidences" of a supernatural designer are convincingly explained in purely naturalistic terms by Darwin, who has the advantage of a more truly global knowledge of nature as well as a superior framework for synthesizing that knowledge. From the standpoint of the natural theologian, it is possible to know too much about nature. To the extent that natural theology was predicated on close observation of nature, it always contained the seeds of its own destruction.

Pilgrim at Tinker Creek thematizes this latent problem at length, perhaps nowhere more obviously than in the chapter titled "Stalking," where the book's narrator hones her ability to spy on even the most secretive of animals. In doing so her hope is to find God, but what really happens is that she becomes a minor functionary of the Global Biosurveillance Regime, doing her bit to render nature's remaining opacities transparent and thereby destroying the very basis of her natural-theological project. In the case of the muskrat, for example, the narrator at first goes to considerable lengths to portray her quarry much as the *Job* writer portrayed the ibex and the hind—as a part of the creation swaddled in mystery, a secret, whose stubborn impenetrability can point up God's omniscience by contrasting it to the limits of merely human knowledge. Practice, however, makes perfect, and the narrator-cum-stalker soon becomes competent enough to bring even the muskrat under the glare of biosurveillance. She reenvisions *Pilgrim*'s muskrats much as I did *Job*'s ibex, replacing the elevated rhetoric of mystery and epiphany with the mundane language of the familiar:

> [A] female might have as many as five litters a year, and each litter contains six or seven or more muskrats. The nest is high and dry under the bank; only the entrance is under water, by several feet. . . . The very young have a risky life . . . even snakes and raccoons eat them. . . . The newborns hanging on their mother's teats may drop off if the mother has to make a sudden dive into the water, and sometimes these drown. (193–94)

Augmenting her personal observation with the mountain of information accumulated through generations of increasingly intensive biosurveillance and now readily available in her local library, the narrator knows too much about the muskrat for it to perform theologically as it might have for an earlier writer like Paley (much less the *Job* author). Despite her desire to experience the muskrat sighting as an epiphany, she is too deeply implicated in postnaturality to sustain a *Job*-like sense of the mystery of nature.

Pilgrim's narrator sees nature panoptically and thus is herself postnatural, yet the theological project in which she is engaged was born of an earlier and incompatible discursive regime. *Pilgrim* is thus most sensibly read not ahistorically, on the narrator's own terms, as a lively reinscription of the timeless story of the pilgrim seeking God in the mystery of creation, but ironically, as the story of a historically situated figure struggling to conduct her spiritual quest in a fundamentally changed world that renders the effort problematic, if not completely self-defeating. To do so is in fact to read *Pilgrim* much as alert readers have long read *Job*. Several critics have noted *Job*'s dramatic irony and stressed how profoundly that irony complicates the book's interpretation. In its theologically scandalous opening verses, God places Job at the mercy of Satan, a fact revealed to readers but not to Job, thus giving us a privileged position from which to watch Job struggle to find some semblance of moral order in a universe whose essential amorality is pointedly withheld from him. Even the voice in the whirlwind declines to reveal to him the cause of his suffering; his situation remains much darker than his limited knowledge permits him even to imagine. *Pilgrim* can be read similarly, as a book in which, from a position informed by a critical awareness of postnaturality—of how, in this case, global biosurveillance both deepens and compromises our relation to nature—we watch the narrator struggle hopelessly to satisfy her anachronistic spiritual longing.

Such readings situate both *Job* and *Pilgrim* in a history of changing material relations to nature. The key ironies enlivening these works arise from dual perspectives rooted not only in the texts themselves but in their contexts; they are artifacts of historically specific changes and the effects those changes have upon readers. The *Book of Job* is believed to have been redacted during a time of fundamental transition, when the old and rather simple pieties of the biblical Wisdom tradition were becoming harder to square with the moral complexities of an increasingly urban Middle Eastern society. And its ancient audience read it in light of a key assumption about nature: that nature could serve human ends by revealing an intelligible moral order. Today this assumption has been replaced by an equally anthropocentric but otherwise wholly different assumption: that nature comprises "a set of regularities potentially knowable and masterable by humans" (Connolly 197). *Pilgrim at Tinker Creek* is just as profoundly situated, at a time when the old verities of nature, despite the brief recrudescence they enjoyed in the 1960s and '70s, had become acutely incompatible with a world whose technologies of seeing were transforming the very idea of nature—and thus transforming as well the ways in which nature writing might be read.

NOTES

1. In *The Comforting Whirlwind: God, Job, and the Scale of Creation*, Bill McKibben anticipates part of this essay's argument, calling the Voice out of the Whirlwind speech "the first piece of modern nature writing" (57) and noting how modern readers might be tempted to respond to it from a perspective similar to that which I am terming "postnatural." Contemporary readers, writes McKibben, might respond to God's flaunting of his knowledge and power with a sarcastic hubris of their own: "Screw off, Grandpop—we do all that stuff now, and more. We set the boundaries of the forests—no more beech trees in the lower forty-eight. That coral you're always talking about—we got rid of that. Behemoth? Leviathan? Give me a break—we're building them twice as big now" (80). McKibben raises this possibility, however, not to explore its literary-critical implications but merely to condemn it. His Christian-ecocentric reading of *Job* prefers to see the text's "first meaning" didactically, as a reminder "that we are a part of the whole order of creation—simply a part" (37), and eco-poetically, as providing a biblical "argument for deep [ecological] change that summons the majesty of the wisdom literature" (x).

2. See Clark, *From Biosphere to Technosphere*. One indication of the increasing purchase of technospheric thinking is the appearance of academic programs in "earth systems engineering," the goal of which is "better understanding of the challenges posed by complex, nonlinear systems of global importance—notably environmental systems—and development of tools that respond effectively to those challenges" (National Academies). See also the website of the University of Colorado's Earth Systems Engineering Initiative (University of Colorado). For an introduction to the discursive construction of nature, see the essays in William Cronon's *Uncommon Ground*. The classic introduction to postmodern ecology is Daniel Botkin, *Discordant Harmonies*. Jeremy Rifkin's *Biotech Century* provides a good (if polemical) overview of genetic engineering issues. Accessible coverage of the nascent field of artificial life is provided by Steven Levy, *Artificial Life*, and Mark Ward, *Virtual Organisms*. For a thorough discussion of the theory and importance of emergent phenomena, see Steven Johnson's *Emergence*.

3. Foucault 203. See also Loisel 106–22.

WORKS CITED

Botkin, Daniel B. *Discordant Harmonies: A New Ecology for the Twenty-First Century*. New York: Oxford University Press, 1990.

Clark, Stephen R. L. *From Biosphere to Technosphere*. http://www.abdn.ac.uk/philos ophy/endsandmeans/vol5no2/clark.shtml.

Connolly, William E. "Voices from the Whirlwind." In *In the Nature of Things: Language, Politics, and the Environment*, ed. Jane Bennett and William Chaloupka. Minneapolis: University of Minnesota Press, 1993. 197–225.

Cronon, William. *Uncommon Ground: Toward Reinventing Nature.* New York: W. W. Norton, 1996.

"Deer." *The International Standard Bible Encyclopedia.* http://www.searchgodsword .org/enc/isb/view.cgi?number=T2606.

"Depths of Discovery." http://www.ocean.udel.edu/extreme2002/tools/discovery .html.

Dillard, Annie. *Pilgrim at Tinker Creek.* New York: Harper and Row, 1985. (1974)

Foucault, Michel. *Discipline and Punish: The Birth of the Prison.* New York: Random House, 1979.

Johnson, Steven. *Emergence: The Connected Lives of Ants, Brains, Cities, and Software.* New York: Touchstone, 2002.

Levy, Steven. *Artificial Life: A Report from the Frontier Where Computers Meet Biology.* New York: Vintage, 1992.

Loisel, Gustave. *Histoire des ménageries de l'antiquité a nos jours*, vol 2: *Temps modernes.* Paris: Octave, 1912.

McKibben, Bill. *The Comforting Whirlwind: God, Job, and the Scale of Creation.* Grand Rapids, Mich.: Eerdmans, 1994.

The National Academies. NAE Annual Fund: Earth Systems Engineering. http:// www7.nationalacademies.org/giving/Earth_Systems_Engineering.html.

"Nubian Ibex: *Capra nubiana.*" *Ultimate Ungulate.* http://www.ultimateungulate .com/ibexnubian.html.

Paley, William. *Natural Theology: or, Evidences of the Existence and Attributes of the Deity, Collected from the Appearances of Nature.* 1802. Reprint, Houston: St. Thomas Press, 1972.

Pope, Marvin H. *The Anchor Bible: Job.* Garden City, N.Y.: Doubleday, 1965.

Rifkin, Jeremy. *The Biotech Century: Harnessing the Gene and Remaking the World.* New York: Jeremy P. Tarcher, 1998.

Thoreau, Henry David. *A Week on the Concord and Merrimack Rivers; Walden, or, Life in the Woods; The Maine Woods; Cape Cod.* Ed. Robert F. Sayre. 1854. Reprint, New York: Library of America, 1989.

University of Colorado. *University of Colorado's Earth Systems Engineering Initiative.* http://civil.colorado.edu/ese/.

Ward, Mark. *Virtual Organisms: The Startling World of Artificial Life.* New York: St. Martin's, 2000.

Wilson, Edward O. *Biophilia.* Cambridge: Harvard University Press, 1984.

Contact! Contact!

Interdisciplinary Connections

Seeking Common Ground

Integrating the Sciences and the Humanities

MY SITUATION reminds me of Emerson's opening words at his first London lecture, in 1848.[1] Emerson had been attending scientific lectures in London and Paris, "and, in listening to Richard Owen's masterly enumeration of the parts and laws of the human body, or Michael Faraday's explanation of magnetic powers," he "could not help admiring the irresponsible security and happiness of the attitude of the naturalist, sure of admiration for his facts, sure of their sufficiency. They ought to interest you: if they do not, the fault lies with you" (*Later Lectures* 1:137). Emerson quite envies the scientists—compared with them, what has *he* to offer? He will, he decides, borrow some of their power, and make a similar enumeration "of the laws and powers of the Intellect," for are not here, also, "facts in a Natural History," "objects of science," to be numbered and recorded like stamens and vertebrae? Thus Emerson outlines his own project of consilience. Yet he does foresee a problem: the laws and powers of the mind have "a stupendous peculiarity, of being at once observers and observed, so that it is difficult to hold them fast as objects of examination, or hinder them from turning the professor out of his chair." Thus such a study "intoxicates all who approach it"—including Emerson himself, who vows nevertheless to pursue his analysis despite such difficulties and to attain for the laws of the mind the same accuracy as the laws of "chemistry, anatomy, astronomy, geometry, intellect, morals, and social life:—laws of the world" (1:137).

Yet being Emerson, and just a humanist after all, he declares not "laws" but observations and experiences, claiming for himself merely a Baconian empiricism of the personal, and attempting, finally, only "some sketches or studies" for a picture, or representation, of a Natural History of the Intellect—for what else, he asks, can a simple observer do? It seems a terrible come-down, from a Theory of Everything to just a few sketches.

Emerson's problem is one I share: that is, by virtue of being human, we are grounded. We have a viewpoint, but it is necessarily only one viewpoint;

and alas, no one way of looking at the universe can coordinate multiple observations. As Thoreau said, the universe is always wider than our views of it. If we knew all the laws of nature, we would need only one fact to infer everything; but we are limited to those instances that we, the observers, can detect. It is like viewing a mountain: "The particular laws are as our points of view, as, to the traveller, a mountain outline varies with every step, and it has an infinite number of profiles, though absolutely but one form. Even when cleft or bored through it is not comprehended in its completeness" (*Walden* 290–91). The mountain is real, whole, and one, but our view of it is necessarily partial. Insofar as each discipline is founded on a single mode of vision, then no one discipline can cash out the entire universe: not literature, for all its scope and beauty; not science, for all its range and power.

Thoreau called this the "intentionality of the eye." Late in life he observed that "It requires a different intention of the eye in the same locality to see different plants, as, for example, *Juncaceae* and *Gramineae* even; *i.e.*, I find that when I am looking for the former, I do not see the latter in their midst. How much more, then, it requires different intentions of the eye and of the mind to attend to different departments of knowledge! How differently the poet and the naturalist look at objects!" (*Journal* 11:153). Following Thoreau, I would suggest that each discipline carries with it a different intentionality of the eye, and becomes, by virtue of that intention, a powerful tool or mode of vision that sees what it chooses to see extraordinarily well but is necessarily and systematically blind to everything else. "A man sees only what concerns him," ruminates Thoreau; "A botanist absorbed in the pursuit of grasses does not distinguish the grandest pasture oaks. He as it were tramples down oaks unwittingly in his walk" (11:153).

Thoreau worried that this meant it was "impossible for the same person to see things from the poet's point of view and that of the man of science" (*Journal* 4:356). If true, this does not bode well for our present project, although as a sign of hope I would offer Thoreau himself, who sought to entrain his vision in multiple directions—poetry, science, politics—so that he, though a single observer still, could nevertheless move across disciplinary boundaries. Both Emerson and Thoreau, as I have written at length elsewhere, found themselves in the nineteenth century in a world where a common intellectual culture was fragmenting into disciplines and professions with their own rules and vocabulary. In the twentieth century C. P. Snow designated the deepest division with the phrase "the Two Cultures," meaning science and the humanities, and the twenty-first century continues to labor under this split vision, even as the conditions that surround us—that constitute our environment—make the mutual alienation of the humanities and sciences increasingly dangerous.

We do have before us one particularly eloquent and passionate proposal for their reunion, in the "consilience" of Edward O. Wilson. No one has written more beautifully than he of the loss we face, of the approaching ruin of the natural world, which as Wilson writes in his recent letter to Thoreau is "everywhere disappearing before our eyes—cut to pieces, mowed down, plowed under, gobbled up, replaced by human artifacts" (*Future* xxii). Wilson concludes that the two truths of poetry and science—the truth of "the green frog's *t-r-r-oonk!* across the pre-dawn water" and our knowledge of what that truth is, what it implies, and how it can be employed—are both necessary to lead us to a future stewardship, rather than destruction, of nature.

Yet Wilson's proposal of consilience has not been taken up by the majority of my colleagues in literature. I would like to suggest why and propose a slightly different version, also borrowed from the nineteenth century but only now, I believe, coming into being. My guiding star for this vision is "Cosmos," a term adopted by Alexander von Humboldt to name his own ideal, the ideal that inspired Emerson, Thoreau, and Darwin, all three, and that should inspire us today.

Before I go there I must, with all due respect, indicate why so many of my colleagues in the humanities have turned away from Wilson's proposal for consilience. First, let me note what it is, precisely, that they are refusing. In his book *Consilience*, Wilson asserts that "the cutting edge of science is reductionism, the breaking apart of nature into its natural constituents" (54). Reductionism is the instrument the scientist uses, as a surgeon his scalpel, to carve the otherwise impenetrable complexity of nature into its "elemental units," which will then be reintegrated into a new whole. This is the weaker form of reductionism; the stronger form is "to fold the laws and principles of each level of organization into those at more general, hence more fundamental levels" (55). The name for the strongest form of reductionism is "total consilience, which holds that nature is organized by simple universal laws of physics to which all other laws and principles can eventually be reduced" (55). Or, as Wilson summarizes in the opening of his final chapter, "The central idea of the consilience world view is that all tangible phenomena, from the birth of stars to the workings of social institutions, are based on material processes that are ultimately reducible, however long and tortuous the sequences, to the laws of physics" (266).

Wilson, in short, offers a reductionism that collapses all the workings of the humanities and social sciences to the fundamental laws of science, ultimately of physics. It is a sublime view, offered with all the confidence of the scientist "sure of admiration for his facts, sure of their sufficiency" (Emerson, *Later Lectures* 1:137). Emerson himself was attracted to such a view, for he believed the moral and natural worlds were bound into one by the laws of nature, and he looked forward to the day when the multitude of those laws would converge on the few, and, ultimately, the one, such that "the whole of [nature's] laws may be written on the thumbnail, or the signet of a ring" (Emerson, *Collected Works* 3:105). The allure of this ring of power is, I believe, the keystone of Emerson's own worldview—it is a profound metaphysical commitment. Yet note that the first step in making that commitment is to remove science out of culture into the realm of transcendence, to agree that the worldview of science does, in fact, cash out the entire universe. This makes science not one discipline among many, one mode of vision among others—one more way of looking at the mountain—but ultimately the only discipline that really matters. Thus all other cultural forms—that is, all *merely* cultural forms—can be reduced into versions of itself, epiphenomenal to those underlying and all-commanding laws of physics.

This is what worries my literary colleagues, for what becomes of literature in this view? Wilson, too, seems seduced by the ring of power when he offers the testable scientific hypothesis that "even the greatest works of art might be understood fundamentally with knowledge of the biologically evolved epigenetic rules that guided them" (*Consilience* 213, 229). In his view, the role of the arts "is the transmission of the intricate details of human experience by artifice to intensify aesthetic and emotional response. Works of art communicate feeling directly from mind to mind, with no intent to explain why the impact occurs. In this defining quality, the arts are the antithesis of science" (218). Literature is about feeling, science is about knowing—this brings back the old Victorian opposition between facts and feeling; on the one hand, the mushy Romantic poet, and on the other, Dickens's fearsome Mr. Gradgrind. In this view literature is indeed the antithesis of science, and literature cannot be independent and equal, for it is not a way of knowing but of expressing, and what it expresses are the emotions engendered by our biology and hence explainable by the knowing scientist.

For myself, while I agree that the arts transmit the "intimate details of human experience," I might put the case slightly differently. Literature is the site where society plays out the "paradoxes and disjunctures," in Andrew McMurry's words, of its various subsystems: science, economics, politics, religion. As a site on which a particular experience is played out, literature cannot be reduced or abstracted without destroying the intricate interrelationships that make it literature—interrelationships between words, histories, writer, and reader, for starters. Literature does not just communicate feeling. It is itself a form of knowledge, a form that can subsist nowhere else but at the site where it is created. One can, of course, extract *Moby Dick* or paraphrase *Walden*, but then one would have Cliff Notes, not a work of literature. The contrast, in brief, is this: the knowledge of science is distilled, abstracted, reduced, in order to be highly mobile, to travel from the laboratory or field to the wider society, across continents and centuries, the way a mathematical formula can be abstracted and applied anywhere, infinitely. By contrast, the knowledge of literature cannot be mobilized; it is inseparable from experience, dependent on direct participation. Even translating a poem from one language into another changes the experience of that poem irrevocably.

Wilson also suggests that literature is a natural, intuitive expression, which reminds me of Walt Whitman sounding his marvelous barbaric yawp. Yet if literature were expressive in this sense one would simply appreciate it rather as I appreciate the songs of wood thrushes, which I do not judge critically; nor do I fault catbirds and cardinals as less adequate aesthetically. Wendell Berry remarks of the chickadee that it "is not constructed to exemplify the principles of its anatomy or the laws of aerodynamics" (*Life* 113). Similarly, *Walden* was not constructed to exemplify American individualism, nor to outline the ten steps to transcendence, nor to provide a taxonomy of New England's ecosystems, although a reader can learn much about all three from it, and more besides. Furthermore, when one takes up a pencil, pen, or word processor to respond to Thoreau, or to one's own Walden, one is now working in a new environment partly constructed by one's reading of *Walden*. Writing becomes a process of thought about a complex world that now includes *Walden*, the book, plus a whole literary tradition, plus whatever one understands of the realms of history, economics, politics, and so forth, plus Walden Pond itself, the endangered woods around it, and now Wilson's letter to Thoreau in the context of a possible twenty-first-century environmental Armageddon. Henry Thoreau's *Walden* thus becomes the beating heart of a vast, interlinked vascular system, which continues to pulse with life exactly as long as *Walden* finds readers—for this, like any book, exists only as it is being read, thought, discussed, reread.

I would say, then, that to "reduce" literature is to destroy it, at least *as* literature. Wilson's hypothesis might make interesting sociology, but it will

have little to say to departments of English, and these are precisely the people we most need to reach. I would rather see us turn down a road that
would allow literature to exist as literature, not as an exemplification of the
laws of nature; a road down which poets and scientists can travel amiably,
partners arm in arm, each set confident in their own self-sufficiency but also
aware that should they part company, they will lose not just one eye of two
but an entire dimension of sight.

To find that road, we need first to return to Emerson's insight that all
our observational systems include the observer. By means of this sideways
step outside itself, a system of knowledge can recover the knowledge of
itself *as* a system—become self-conscious, know itself as powerful in one
dimension, blind to other dimensions. Thoreau struggled to articulate this
insight, which he saw as the key to knowledge:

> I think that the man of science makes this mistake, and the mass of mankind
> along with him: that you should coolly give your chief attention to the phe-
> nomenon which excites you as something independent on you, and not as it
> is related to you. The important fact is its effect on me . . . The philosopher
> for whom rainbows, etc., can be explained away never saw them. With regard
> to such objects, I find that it is not they themselves (with which the men of
> science deal) that concern me; the point of interest is somewhere *between* me
> and them (*i.e.* the objects). (*Journal* 10:164–65)

Elsewhere Thoreau clarifies the stakes: "There is no such thing as pure *objective* observation. Your observation, to be interesting, *i.e.* to be significant,
must be *subjective*. The sum of what the writer of whatever class has to report is simply some human experience, whether he be poet or philosopher
or man of science. The man of most science is the man most alive, whose life
is the greatest event" (*Journal* 6: 236–37). Herein lay Thoreau's most telling
critique of science: that it too often forgets its grounding in human experience, in our relationship with what we see: that what we see comes into
being *as we see it*. To Thoreau, therefore, all knowledge is what I have called
"relational knowledge," not of subject against object but of the new whole
that subject and object make together.

Thoreau's basis for this insight was consilience—not Wilson's version
of 1998 but the original consilience proposed in 1840 by William Whewell,
the British philosopher and historian of science. According to Whewell,
consilience occurs when "an Induction, obtained from one class of facts,
coincides with an Induction, obtained from another different class. This
Consilience is a test of the truth of the Theory in which it occurs" (Wilson,
Consilience 8). Given, that is, a "theory" or mode of vision (recall Darwin

marveling at how anyone could fail to see that only in the light of some theory does any fact have any significance), that theory is validated when it brings together two disparate facts that "leap together" to form a new, coherent truth. As Whewell emphasizes, this is a profoundly creative process: "The facts are not only brought together, but seen in a new point of view. A new mental element is *superinduced*," or in other words, this "leap" is not made independently of the mind but by a creative act of the mind, a creative act that results in "a new conception, a principle of connexion and unity" (*Theory* 139, 163). In 1995 I suggested that Thoreau modeled consilience in just this way: "Thoreau's act of consilience seeks to give voice to all the participating agents, not by blending them together but by giving each a distinct hearing in a medium of sustained attention. In consiliating literature and science, Thoreau tried to enable and enact both, as real knowledge situated in, not beyond, the world" (*Seeing* 11–12).

The advantage for humanists of Whewell's original version of consilience is that it is not reductive but additive. When Whewell visualizes the progress of scientific knowledge, his metaphor is not mathematical but geographic. Two separate inductions that coincide are said to "converge" into a "collection of one truth from many things": "By this means the streams of knowledge from various classes of facts will constantly run together into a smaller and smaller number of channels; like the confluent rivulets of a great river, coming together from many sources, uniting their ramifications so as to form larger branches, these again uniting in a single truth" (*Theory* 162–63). Elsewhere Whewell states that "the Table of the progress of science would thus resemble the Map of a River, in which the waters from separate sources unite and make rivulets, which again meet with rivulets from other fountains, and thus go on forming by their junction trunks of a higher and higher order" (*Selected* 8).

Imagining knowledge as a system of rivers or watersheds allows us to see simultaneously, as Whewell stresses, both general truths and the particular truths from which they were derived. This "map" of the advance of knowledge turns time into space, allowing all history to appear at once, encouraging the explorer to navigate upstream or downstream at will. In this vision, every stage in the development of a science retains its separate identity: earlier truths are taken up and included in later doctrines, but nothing "reduces" to anything else. That is, points downstream are not reductive but "confluent," as a stream does not "reduce" to a river nor a branch to a trunk; generalizations contain the particulars of which they are composed and will themselves, through a similar process of alliance, become components of "higher" or "larger" generalizations still farther downstream.

Thus Whewell's unity is composed of a stacking series of holons, or organizational levels composed of wholes that are themselves parts to higher
wholes. Rather than an iron-bound causal sequence, Whewell constructs a
connective network that may be either causal *or* historical, and indeed, in
his vision, a network that unfolds historically across time. He thus leaves
open the possibility of plural knowledges and of emergent properties; his
geographical metaphor is undisturbed by the failure of simple components
to predict complex behaviors.

This leads me to my final step upstream and my concluding figure, Cosmos, itself a spatial image of the entire historical universe. The concept of
Cosmos was popularized in Thoreau's heyday by Alexander von Humboldt's multivolume blockbuster work of popular science, titled *Cosmos*.
Humboldt chose his title carefully, for he hoped to revive in modern sensi-
bilities the ancient Greek concept of the universe as an ordered and beautiful whole. His leading assertion was that nature does exist wholly independent of us, but the Cosmos does not—for the vision of nature as an ordered
and beautiful whole is a human achievement, an achievement just as much
part of the Cosmos as the most distant stellar nebulae or the lichens on a
nearby rock. Humboldt, who in some accounts was the founder of modern
science, seemed incapable of thinking dualistically. While as a scientist he
could perfectly well objectify matter as separate from the human mind, he
also believed that our only understanding of matter is through mind; as
Whewell said, we know facts only by thinking about them. Knowledge, including scientific knowledge, lies not in the separation of object and subject
but in their convergence. Nature, while a product of laws, cannot be reduced to those laws, for as nature unfolds (or as Humboldt's close student
Darwin would say, evolves), it does so in a historical process, a sequence
of causal events that is not deterministic because it is open to the accidents
of contingency, variation, and chance that cannot be predicted. One cannot,
therefore, sit in a London lecture hall and pronounce on the basis of elegant
physical laws what the animals and plants of the Americas are like. There is
simply no telling. One must pick oneself up, go there, and look, fully educated in the laws of the Cosmos but wholly open to the empirical surprises
of the local. For the Cosmos exists nowhere else but in the local, and the
local becomes meaningful to us as we see in it the realization of the Cosmos
in this place, at this time, unique in itself yet infinitely connected in all its
relations with all other places, all other times.

Humboldt prided himself on the depth and rigor of his empirical research and saw himself as the exponent of a kind of historical and geo-

graphic science quite different from the deductive science practiced by so many of his colleagues, yet equally valid, equally consilient—as Darwin, the greatest of Humboldt's followers and a master of consilience, would demonstrate. Because mind was intrinsic to science, Humboldt devoted the second volume of *Cosmos* to the history of the *idea* of Cosmos, including landscape art, gardening, poetry, and science, from the ancient Greeks and Romans and peoples of India and Arabia through Columbus and Galileo to Goethe and the latest understanding of the shape of the earth. Cosmos is the ultimate consilience, and one sees the power and beauty of Humboldt's ideas in the generation of thinkers and writers he inspired, a generation that included Whewell, Darwin, Emerson, Thoreau, and Whitman. Wilson suggests that "the love of complexity without reduction makes art, the love of complexity with reductionism makes science" (*Consilience* 54). Those of us who love both complexity and science can take heart: as I hope I have shown, there is a way to reweave mind and nature, biology and culture, science and humanity in a nonreductive consilience that sacrifices neither complexity nor truth.

Today, the word *Cosmos* has reverted to the lesser meaning that Humboldt resisted: the stars beyond us, the universe apart from the world, as if when we turn our telescopes to the stars we could put the earth behind us. And when we turn our technologies to earthly nature, we still would turn our backs to the role of the mind and the agency of language, as if we could put our humanity behind us as well. A lifetime in science taught Humboldt that there could be no true progress until the reciprocal halves of the Cosmos—nature and culture, inductive reason and imaginative vision, science and the arts—were conceived together as one integrated whole. In the grand earthscape of the Cosmos, I hope that Wilson and I, that the sciences and the humanities, can indeed find common ground on which to link arm and arm and go forward, for the task ahead of us will need all of our vision, all of our voices, all of our truths.

NOTE

1. This paper was originally delivered as part of a plenary session on "Seeking Common Ground: A Dialogue on Integrating the Sciences and Humanities," with Edward O. Wilson, at the Fifth Biennial Conference of the Association for the Study of Literature and Environment, held June 3–7, 2003.

WORKS CITED

Berry, Wendell. *Life Is a Miracle: An Essay against Modern Superstition*. Washington, D.C.: Counterpoint, 2000.

Emerson, Ralph Waldo. *The Collected Works of Ralph Waldo Emerson*. Ed. Alfred B. Ferguson et al., 6 vols. to date. Cambridge: Harvard University Press, 1971–.

———. *The Later Lectures of Ralph Waldo Emerson, 1843–1871*. Ed. Ronald A. Bosco and Joel Myerson. 2 vols. Athens: University of Georgia Press, 2001.

McMurry, Andrew. *Environmental Renaissance: Emerson, Thoreau, and the Systems of Nature*. Athens: University of Georgia Press, 2003.

Thoreau, Henry David. *The Journal of Henry David Thoreau*. Ed. Bradford Torrey and Francis Allen. 14 vols. Boston: Houghton Mifflin, 1906; New York: Dover, 1962.

———. *Walden*. Ed. J. Lyndon Shanley. Princeton: Princeton University Press, 1973.

———. *The Writings of Henry David Thoreau: Journal*. Ed. John D. Broderick et al. 7 vols. to date. Princeton: Princeton University Press, 1981–.

Walls, Laura Dassow. *Emerson's Life in Science: The Culture of Truth*. Ithaca: Cornell University Press, 2003.

———. *Seeing New Worlds: Henry David Thoreau and Nineteenth-Century Natural Science*. Madison: University of Wisconsin Press, 1995.

Whewell, William. *Selected Writings on the History of Science*. Ed. Yehuda Elkana. Chicago: University of Chicago Press, 1984.

———. *Theory of Scientific Method*. Ed. Robert E. Butts. Indianapolis: Hackett, 1989.

Wilson, Edward O. *Consilience: The Unity of Knowledge*. New York: Alfred A. Knopf, 1998.

———. *The Future of Life*. New York: Alfred A. Knopf, 2002.

Mindless Fools and Leaves That Run

Subjectivity, Politics, and Myth
in Scientific Nomenclature

OFF THE SHORES of eastern Hawaii at a place called Laupahoehoe, brown birds swoop and wheel just out of reach of the waves, turning and spinning in the summer sun. These birds are called brown noddies, their Greco-Latin binomial *Anous stolidus* meaning "mindless fool." As I watch their grace and skill, I wonder why science has applied a demeaning label to birds that wrest their living from a treacherous ocean. To Hawaiian fishermen, these birds provided valuable assistance in locating fish, for people knew that the *noio* (Hawaiian name for noddy) would gather above schools of skipjack and bonito, to snap up the small fishes fleeing these larger predators (Kamakau 72). In fact, a Hawaiian proverb that speaks of the noddy treading the billows of the distant sea is understood as "an expression of admiration for a person outstanding in wisdom and skill," according to Mary Kawena Pukui, a noted scholar of Hawaiian language and culture (Pukui 92).

The brown noddy commonly lives to an age of twenty-five to thirty years, raising many chicks (Shallenberger 10). Anything that survives that long cannot be entirely stupid. My first thought was that the name stems from a subjective interpretation of the way the bird moves, but further research indicates that the name was suggested by mariners, who noted that the noddy had little fear of humans and was easily caught (Jobling). When I indicated to one scientist that this designation revealed a limited and crude perspective on the part of the namers, his reply was that the generic and specific combination was a "useful description of the bird." Although he may have intended this to mean that binomials in general are useful, it seemed to me a perverse defense of a boorish designation.

Linnaeus can be credited with this particular binomial, and with setting up the system that allows scientists the world over to communicate in a *lingua franca*, avoiding the confusion that can result from common names and a variety of languages. While I do not dispute the value of this system,

I believe it is important to recognize that our culture's acceptance of science as an objective process may cause us to miss subjective ways in which science is constructed. My aim is to promote deeper conversations among humanists and scientists, to encourage an honest examination of the terms in which we frame our inquiries. If we are to converse productively with one another across disciplines, we must become aware of unintended resonances our words may carry to someone in a different field. In this article, I discuss what some scientific classifications convey to a person with a background in classical languages.

The impetus for the article arose from questions I had about certain scientific names, followed by a realization that acts of naming always involve an agenda, whether of humor, possession, displacement, or the urge to make order and sense. This last provides the common and reasonable justification for taxonomic practice, but I have discovered a number of examples in which scientific names seem to undercut reason and order. I explore several instances in which Latinized binomials present a barrier to understanding, contrasting these with imaginative names that provide various perspectives on an organism. By focusing on some of the associations with the names, I hope to show the value of an interdisciplinary approach to this situation.[1]

The codes that govern taxonomy and nomenclature are complex, with copious sections on homonyms, anagrams, paratypes, and holotypes but little on the ethics of choosing a name. One is in a hierarchical world here, with only eighteen members on the Board of the International Code of Zoological Nomenclature, to be drawn from the ranks of eminent academics throughout the world. The board periodically solicits suggestions for revising the code, but in the words of the secretary for the last set of revisions, Philip Tubbs, "the publicity was muted" ("International Code of Zoological Nomenclature"). Most of the revisions aim at resolving duplication problems or incorrect species identification, and the principle of priority is championed as taking precedence over issues of appropriateness. For example, chapter 4, article 18 of the International Code of Zoological Nomenclature states: "The availability of a name is not affected by inappropriateness or tautology," and it gives examples of names like *polyodon* (many-toothed) or *albus* (white) that "are not to be rejected because of a claim that they denote a character or distribution not possessed by the taxon in question" ("International Code of Zoological Nomenclature"). The principle of priority as given in the code states that the valid name of a taxon is the oldest available name, which should be used to promote stability and universality of name and to prevent taxonomic confusion (chapter 6). This begs the question of the confusion that arises when the binomial assigned to an organism fails to represent its characteristics accurately. Books that frame rules for naming specimens promote the idea that it is an orderly, objective, and straightforward process. For example, Chamberlin's *Entomological Nomenclature* sets forth an explanation of the aims and principles of zoologists. Item 1 states: "We are not satisfied to stop at mere naming of the object, but wish to classify each particular species by placing it in its proper niche, which should, insofar as we are able to judge, show its relationship to others of its kind in the animal or plant world" (Chamberlin 1).

This statement raises the question how a name based on Greek mythology or ancient Roman politics can show the relationship of an organism to others of its kind in the animal world. As an example of Roman politics, we find *Popilia japonica*, designating a familiar garden pest, the Japanese beetle (Scarborough 107). The genus name *Popilia* originates from a violent Roman clan, some of whose members were responsible for assassinating the orator Marcus Tullius Cicero, others for hounding the followers of the murdered statesman Tiberius Gracchus. The beetle appears to have been given this designation by an entomologist named Newman who was active in the 1830s and '40s. To date I have found little information about this scientist, specifically what was in his mind when he chose the name. Beetles and other insects sport an amazing array of classical connections, ranging from Sisyphus to Avernus, Mopsus, Proserpina, and in the case of a butterfly commonly called the Shy Yellow or Caribbean Dainty White, *Eurema messalina*, another curious reference from Roman politics. Messalina was the promiscuous and devious wife of the Emperor Claudius. She manipulated the emperor into executing men who rejected her advances and then made a secret marriage to a man with whom she plotted to replace Claudius as emperor, until the plot was detected, resulting in her own execution (Durant 272–73). What relationship all this has to the butterfly continues to elude me.

One authority on tropical fish asserts that "if one wants to communicate precisely about plants or animals, scientific names have no substitute" (Hoover 11). But what, precisely, do some of these names communicate? To find out, consider what beings you believe the following binomials describe. First, consider *Anelpistus americanus*, "the helpless American." This designation could apply to many humans in a variety of circumstances but happens to refer to yet another type of beetle. Another binomial that conjures a host of possibilities is *Venus mercenaria*, "the goddess of love working for pay."

This one, named by Linnaeus, designates the quahog or littleneck clam.

Linnaeus's reason for the species name is that the shells of these clams were often made into wampum and used for barter by Native Americans. The Venus part may be a joke, since clams are not legendary for beauty, or it may be an allusion to Botticelli's Venus or to a female body part, but it does raise questions about the objectivity that scientists claim as the basis for the names they devise. We must ask why organisms receive labels that tell so little about their appearance, behavior, or relationship to other organisms but reveal instead the eccentricities of the nomenclator.

Recently, in an attempt to test just how much nomenclature matters to scientists, I asked a marine biologist what came to mind when she heard the genus name Palinurus. Looking puzzled, she asked me to spell it, which I did. She then said that she had no associations with that name. Upon hearing that it was the genus designation for the spiny lobster, she attempted to correct me, insisting that had I only said "Panilurus," she would have known immediately what I meant. Having seen this spelling in several local fish guides, I gently informed her that it was a misprint. She insisted that the spelling with which she was familiar was in fact correct and implied that I, the nonscientist, must be mistaken. When I asked whether she knew the myth attached to Palinurus, she walked away.

Although names for lobsters exist in both classical Latin and ancient Greek (for example, *Astacus* and *Cammarus*, and even one called *Justitia longimanus*, which might be translated as "justice with a long reach"), and are used in scientific binomials for other types of lobster, this name has no connection with those words but instead seems to originate in book 5 of Vergil's *Aeneid*. Palinurus was the pilot of Aeneas's ship; he was overwhelmed by Somnus, the god of sleep, and was swept overboard as the ship made its way toward Sicily. In one of the more poignant and lyrical passages in the *Aeneid*, Vergil describes Palinurus's resistance to sleep and his struggle to keep hold of the tiller, which goes overboard with him.

Why would an eighteenth-century scientist choose this name for a lobster? One possibility lies in the discussion between Aeneas and the ghost of Palinurus, whom he encounters in the underworld in book 6. When Aeneas expresses his surprise that Palinurus did not survive the fall and make it to shore, Palinurus indicates that he did indeed try to land but was stoned by savages, who mistook him for a prize and ran him through with a spear as he was scrambling up a cliff. The scientist who chose this name may have noticed lobsters clinging to bits of wood, as Palinurus clung to the tiller; or the name may refer to the inaccessibility of the meat—the natives who stoned and speared him may have thought they were getting a prize, but he proved hard to crack and yielded no treasure. Spiny lobsters do present sharper difficulties and slimmer rewards for the diner than does the Maine lobster, which has large meaty claws that are lacking in the spiny lobster.

Yet another basis for the lobster's name may be its extraordinary navigational ability. Recent research has determined that Caribbean spiny lobsters practice true navigation; that is, when moved from a home area, they return to it by the most direct route, even when their eyes are covered (Boles and Lohmann 61). Did Fabricus, the scientist who gave the spiny lobster its mytho-scientific name, choose to link it with Aeneas's helmsman because he knew something about its ability? Or should we choose another explanation: that the name originates from the Greek words *palin ourein*, meaning "to urinate again," perhaps signifying that the lobster squirted someone twice. Further research indicates that in addition to *Palinurus*, some lobsters *are* designated *Panulirus* (Cobb and Phillips). *Panuliros* does not occur in classical Greek or in Latin comparable to this, but the word could be coined from *panu*, meaning "completely" and *liros*, meaning "shameless." An ancient Greek word that looks more logical does exist: *paliouros*, for a plant known as Christ thorn or jujube (Liddell and Scott). Its bristly appearance indicates that it might be the word that was intended for the spiny lobster. Because *Palinurus* was familiar to me, I assumed that it was the correct designation and that there must be a connection between lobster and helmsman, but the more I read about scientific nomenclature, the more I realize how many slips have occurred and been allowed to stand under the principle of priority.

Pondering the marine scientist's reaction and the various inconclusive trails I had followed, I began to question the significance of the cultural relics that lurk behind so many scientific names. Obviously they are of little consequence to the advancement of science; mostly, it appears, they present obstacles to learning—just long, difficult names for which most have little or no frame of reference. But the fact remains that these are lost stories; they emerged from imaginative links that earlier scientists saw between their ideas about a particular organism and the world of the ancient Greeks and Romans. What I find here is not so much an occasion for examining the place of science in ecocriticism as a query about the place of literature in science. Does it matter that scientists do not know what these words mean? I think it does, because language used consciously exerts power, whereas language that is garbled, referencing something of which the speaker is ignorant, erodes understanding and erases a context that has been shared for centuries. The lack of grounding in Latin and mythology is one symptom of the drive to specialize, but in fairness, I must note that although I studied the *Aeneid* in Latin on several occasions, none of my classics professors ever mentioned the possible connection of Palinurus with a lobster.

Given that common names can be numerous and confusing, and may offer little significant information about an organism, the need for an international system of names is obvious, but I believe it is important to ask what is lost when an organism bears a name from the world of Greek myth instead of a local name that may reflect something about the behavior, medicinal properties, or cultural uses of an organism. For example, a fish found in the Hawaiian Islands bears the Hawaiian name *hina lea 'aki lolo*. The first part of the name seems to mean "tumbling wave," perhaps a reference to where the fish is found; the second part means "brain-biting," because the fish was used as a cure for headaches (Hoover 151). This might be valuable information for someone stranded far from a source of aspirin but is unavailable from the Latinized name, *Coris gaimard*, or the English name, yellow-tail coris. The word *coris* is from the Greek for bedbug, perhaps from markings that look like bedbugs. *Coris* is also found in the word *coriander*—the name of this common herb also being derived from bedbugs because the seeds looked and smelled like them. The second part of the fish's Latin name, *gaimard*, commemorates a French officer who visited the Hawaiian Islands in 1819 and collected the fish, but it gives no information about the fish itself. Another coris, the yellow-striped (*Coris flavovittata*), is called *hilu*, meaning "well-behaved" in Hawaiian, because pregnant women who ate this fish believed that it would help them bear quiet and refined children (Hoover 150). Given the emerging understanding of how prenatal nutrition can influence a developing fetus, this belief seems worth investigating, but the connection may be as inaccessible to the average Hawaiian as the stories behind scientific names are to many scientists.

Cultural practices may also be conveyed by local names, as in the case of the flagtail, called in Hawaiian *aholehole*, which means "to strip away," referring to the way that the fish was prepared—by grasping the dorsal fin with one's teeth and pulling the flesh out. The name has a dual significance in that the fish was used in ceremonies to strip away evil spirits (Hoover 60). Neither the English nor the Latinized names give this information. The Latin *Kuhlia sandvicensis* tells for whom it was named, a scientist named Kuhl, and where it is found, in the Sandwich or Hawaiian islands, but nothing about other context or associations. Someone may object that a name cannot be expected to tell us everything relevant about an entity. In answer to that, I would like the name to tell us more about that entity than about the person who collected it. To insist that an organism be labeled in a way privileging the scientist's designation over local knowledge evolved over centuries of experience with an organism is questionable and might be construed as arrogant. In many cases, organisms were collected with gun or dynamite and named only after they had deteriorated on the long ocean voyage to London or other centers of scientific inquiry, so the person who chose the name may never have seen the organism alive in its own environment. Perhaps that practice explains why numerous organisms are named after monsters and other creatures of myth, as many specimens must have been unrecognizable by the time they reached the namer.

The artificiality of names arrived at in this manner is troubling enough, but Jamaica Kincaid addresses an even more problematic dimension to naming in *My Garden (Book)*, a collection of thoughts on plants and colonization. Reflecting on the way plants in her native Antigua and the land itself were renamed by explorers and colonists, she asserts: "This naming of things is so crucial to possession—a spiritual padlock with the key thrown away—that it is a murder, an erasing and it is not surprising that when people have felt themselves prey to it (conquest), among their first acts of liberation is to change their names (Rhodesia to Zimbabwe, LeRoi Jones to Amiri Baraka)" (122).

Her comment on the difference between common and scientific names bears out what I have said about the loss of local knowledge: "These plants had two names; they had a common name, that is a name assigned to them by people for whom these plants have value, and then they had a proper name or a Latin name, assigned to them by an agreed upon group of botanists" (161). Like the explorers, she says, the scientists "emptied the worlds of things animal, vegetable and mineral of their names and replaced these names with names pleasing to them, these names are pleasing to them because they are reasonable; reason is a pleasure to them" (161).

As I have shown, some Latinized names are not based on reason. Kincaid notes that the act of renaming imposes on organisms a whole new set of narratives (165), and this is what I find problematic in nomenclature; it plops us into a fantasy landscape where a jellyfish (*Clytia languidum* or drowsy Clytie) is named for a Greek nymph who was transformed into a flower, an albatross is named for a Greek warrior whose horses ate human flesh (*Diomedea immutabilis*, the changeless Diomedes), and a peculiar-looking bird called a guan is named after Odysseus' long-suffering wife Penelope

(Isaak). We are stranded amid a blitz of narratives here, and the stories are all interesting—but apparently irrelevant to those closely involved with the entities.

Another side to Jamaica Kincaid's concern about the privileging of scientific over local names is provided by sociolinguist Suzanne Romaine and anthropologist Daniel Nettle, who in their book on the extinction of the world's indigenous languages, *Vanishing Voices*, have cited a large body of traditional knowledge that gives valuable information on maintaining biodiversity in complex ecological systems. They suggest that this knowledge is too often overlooked because "what goes by the name of modern science is still based largely on the worldview of Europeans and their languages. . . . most scientific research is still done by scientists from the world's industrialized countries who are interested primarily in First World problems. . . . Our examples of naming fish and of fishing practices in the Pacific islands show how native perceptions and detailed knowledge of the environment have been encoded in patterns of . . . fishing practices and technology. When these words are lost, it becomes increasingly difficult even to frame problems and solve them in any but the dominant culture's terms and scientific classification schemes, which are not always adequate to the task" (77). As Romaine and Nettle document throughout their book, the disappearance of indigenous languages has implications for the health of the entire planet, not just for that of the culture that is lost.

Despite the drawbacks of some Latin binomials, I am not arguing that the whole system be overhauled but simply that people become more informed about what the names actually signify. Some Latin names offer humor, poetry, and even wisdom if we learn what they mean and what the connections are. For example, the deadly bushmaster snake bears the ominous name of *Lachesis muta*, the "silent fate." One of the most elaborate instances of a name taken from mythology is Linnaeus's christening the bog rosemary Andromeda, after the maiden who was tied to a cliff as sacrifice to a sea monster. He develops the comparison as follows: "Slender, kneeling with fettered feet, she lies surrounded by water, imprisoned to a rock, exposed to horrible dragons (amphibia); sadly she bows her face toward the ground and stretches heavenwards her innocent arms (twigs) . . . until the longed-for Perseus (midsummer sun) defeats the brute and rescues her from the water, no longer a virgin, but a happy mother who lifts her head toward the Highest" (Gourlie 62–63).

This excursus into myth gives us an idea of what lies behind the choices that Linnaeus and other scientists have made and of how much we miss when we do not know the stories. A botanist familiar with this story has an anthropomorphic association that some may frown upon as "unscientific" but that others could argue offers a different way of seeing the plant. My favorite candidate for a name that encourages a new way of seeing is the family name Phyllodromiidae, "leaves that run," designating a group of cockroaches (Scarborough 88).

Ursula LeGuin has written a short story called "She Unnames Them," which offers a feminist perspective on the issue of names. In this tale, Eve undoes Adam's work by letting the animals give back the names he assigned them so that they are free of labels and of the separation that those labels caused. Eve notes the result when she gives back her own name: "I had only just then realized how difficult it would be to explain myself. I could not chatter away as I used to do, taking it all for granted. My words must now be as slow, as new, as single, as tentative as the steps I took going down the path away from the house, between the dark-branched, tall dancers motionless against the winter shining" (*Buffalo Gals* 196).

In other words, when we relinquish hierarchy in language, we can step into poetry, and we may see and express new things about ourselves and the world around us. In the words of Walker Percy in his excellent essay "The Loss of the Creature," we can salvage the creatures from the packaging (Percy 63). We are all aware of how insulting and denigrating labels make it easier for people to abuse a race or an individual; it is important that we teach ourselves and our students to interrogate labels like "mindless fool" in the case of the brown noddy, so that any encounters we have with the actual bird are not prejudiced by inaccurate assumptions based on its name. We can hope that as scientists continue to revise their practices for naming, their choices will reflect an organism's place in its world. By working more closely with indigenous peoples in choosing names, scientists can salvage local knowledge instead bypassing it in favor of connections to remote worlds.

Those familiar with the history of science will remember that the way knowledge has been constructed has made scientists and philosophers nervous over many centuries. An early example is Chinese sage Hsun Tzu, who wrote on the rectification of names, indicating that unauthorized names cause doubt and confusion (Chai 266). Another is Francis Bacon, who reminds us that "human understanding is like an uneven mirror that cannot reflect truly the rays from objects, but distorts and corrupts the nature of things by mingling its own nature with [them]" (Bacon 54). He goes on to observe:

For speech is the means of association among men; but words are applied according to common understanding. And in consequence, a wrong and inappropriate application of words obstructs the mind to a remarkable extent. Nor
do the definitions or explanations with which learned men have sometimes
been accustomed to defend and vindicate themselves in any way remedy the
situation. Indeed, words plainly do violence to the understanding and throw
everything into confusion and lead men into innumerable empty controver-
sies and fictions. (55)

I close with an example of how we can encourage our students to clear
their minds of obstructions that the words of others may cause and to reclaim their own power to name. This exercise, based upon a U.S. Department of Agriculture class field trip to a farm in Virginia, could be modified
for various levels and disciplines. We had been studying Native American
uses of plants and were invited to range over this farm and find a plant that
we could name based on something that we noticed about it. The results
created giddy delight as people came back having learned and seen new
things about common plants. One brought jewel-weed, which she chris-
tened "moon-in-the-water," for the way that translucent orbs ran over the
backs of its leaves. Another tasted yarrow and renamed it "numb-tongue."
One man found some algae and dubbed it "koolmuc" for its soothing properties when applied to hot skin. We learned to experience the world in a
new way that day and found that our names revealed possibilities that the
conventional names did not. Whether we teach biology, Latin, composition,
or environmental studies, taking some time to let our students explore the
making of names can foster keener observation and may perhaps lead to
some new discoveries. Teaching the stories behind the names may also save
students and professors from being swamped by a torrent of unfamiliar
words. At least they can be encouraged to consider why there is a salaman-
der bearing the name *Oedipus rex* and a clam named *Pandora* (Isaak). As
students learn taxonomy, perhaps one lesson that needs to come through
clearly is that scientific objectivity is in many instances itself a myth. The
taxonomists may insist that a name is only a name, but they should not be
allowed to monopolize the process, especially after what they have done to
the brown noddy.

NOTE
    1. For additional perspectives on taxonomy and nomenclature, I particularly
recommend works by Saner, Conniff, Simpson, Gould, Hearne, and Mayr among

the works cited. I wish to acknowledge the assistance of Cheryl Berg and Yvonne Ypshishige, who collaborated with me in tracking down taxonomic particulars; Suzanne Romaine, who clarified issues surrounding the use of indigenous names; and Will Howarth for a conversation at the 1997 NEH summer institute on the environmental imagination, which prompted me to pursue this topic.

WORKS CITED

Bacon, Francis. *Novum Organum with Other Parts of the Great Instauration*. Trans. Peter Urbach and John Gibson. Chicago: Open Court, 1994.

Boles, Larry, and Kenneth J. Lohmann. "True Navigation and Magnetic Maps in Spiny Lobsters." *Nature* 421 (January 2003): 60–63.

Brown, Roland Wilbur. *Composition of Scientific Words*. Washington, D.C.: Smithsonian, 2000.

Chai, Ch'u. *The Sacred Books of Confucius*. New York: Universal Books, 1965.

Chamberlin, W. J. *Entomological Nomenclature and Literature*. Westport: Greenwood, 1952.

Cobb, J. Stanley, and Bruce F. Phillips. *The Biology and Management of Lobsters*. New York: Academic Press, 1980.

Conniff, Richard. "What's in a Name?" *Smithsonian* 27, no. 9 (1996): 66–70.

Durant, Will. *Caesar and Christ*. New York: Simon and Schuster, 1944.

Gould, Stephen Jay. *Bully for Brontosaurus: Reflections in Natural History*. New York: Norton, 1991.

Gourlie, Norah. *The Prince of Botanists, Carl Linnaeus*. London: Witherby, 1953.

Hearne, Vicki. *Adam's Task: Calling Animals by Name*. New York: Alfred A. Knopf, 1986.

Hoover, John P. *Hawaii's Fishes: A Guide for Snorkelers, Divers and Aquarists*. Honolulu: Mutual Publishing, 1993.

"International Code of Zoological Nomenclature." http://zeus.ruca.ua.ac.be/Evolutionary Biology/coll/doc/iczn4txt.htm.

Isaak, Mark. "Curiosities of Biological Nomenclature." http://home.earthlink.net/~misaak/taxonomy/taxrefs.htm.

Jobling, J. A. *A Dictionary of Scientific Bird Names*. Oxford: Oxford University Press, 1995.

Kamakau, Samuel Manaiakalani. *The Works of the People of Old*. Trans. Mary Kawena Pukui. Honolulu: Bishop Museum Press, 1976.

Kincaid, Jamaica. *My Garden (Book)*. New York: Farrar, 1999.

Koerner, Lisbet. *Linnaeus: Nature and Nation*. Cambridge, Mass.: Harvard University Press, 1999.

LeGuin, Ursula. "She Unnames Them." In *Buffalo Gals*. New York: NAL, 1990.

Lewis, C., and C. Short. *A New Latin Dictionary*. New York: Harper, 1894.

Liddell, H. G., and R. Scott. *A Greek-English Lexicon*. Oxford: Clarendon, 1968.

Maro, P. Vergilius. *Opera*. Oxford: Clarendon, 1969.

Mayr, Ernst. *Toward a New Philosophy of Biology: Observations of an Evolutionist*. Cambridge, Mass.: Harvard University Press, 1988.

Nettle, Daniel, and Suzanne Romaine. *Vanishing Voices: The Extinction of the World's Languages*. Oxford: Oxford University Press, 2000.

Percy, Walker. *The Message in the Bottle*. New York: Farrar, Straus and Giroux, 1954.

Pukui, Mary Kawena. *'Olelo No'eao: Hawaiian Proverbs and Poetical Sayings*. Honolulu: Bishop Museum Press, 1983.

Saner, Reg. *The Four-Cornered Falcon: Essays on the Interior West and the Natural Scene*. Baltimore: Johns Hopkins University Press, 1993.

Scarborough, John. *Medical Technologies: Classical Origins*. Norman: University of Oklahoma Press, 1992.

Shallenberger, Robert. *Hawaii's Birds*. Honolulu: Hawaii Audubon Society, 1981.

Simpson, Sherry. *The Way Winter Comes*. Seattle: Sasquatch Books, 1998.

MICHAEL P. COHEN

Reading after Darwin

A Prospectus

THIS PROSPECTUS is part of a larger project I have modestly named "Evolutionary Theory: Ecological Theory: Literary Theory." After reading Gould's *The Structure of Evolutionary Theory*, I wondered: (1) Why don't we call ourselves "evocritics," taking Darwin as our methodological source? (2) Why shouldn't we rigorously integrate the theoretical methodology of biological science into our studies? (3) For instance, if the idea of limited global resources is central to modern environmentalism, it is also rooted in evolutionary theory, from Malthus onward. Like biologists, ecocritics have adopted an idea at the root of evolutionary thinking, formative of the creative forces and constraints that shape life: limited local and global resources. Environmentalists and ecocritics have inherited evolutionary theory and embedded it in our own ideology: this act, conscious and unconscious, calls for critical scrutiny. Ecocritical theory must examine and explore its grounds in evolutionary theory if we hope to understand our own methods.

In this essay I attempt only to juggle some aspects of literary and evolutionary theory and to ramify the following questions:

Is an evolutionary narrative treatable as a text? How are evolutionary narratives read and written?

How do evolutionary narratives intersect evolutionary theory? To what kind of critiques are these narratives subject?

Can we profitably apply literary methods to evolutionary narrative, evolutionary theory, and scientific critique?

Can scientists and humanists share their concerns about evolutionary narratives?

What is the value of evolutionary narrative, as historical narrative?

As anyone can see, this is a simple and straightforward task. "Well, sir," as the fat man put it in *The Maltese Falcon*, "here's to plain speaking and clear understanding."

There has been widespread use of literary tools to discuss evolutionary narrative, using Darwin's *Origin of Species* as a master narrative and tracing the results, especially in the plot structures and languages of American and British fiction (G. L. Levine, *Darwin and the Novelists* and *Dying to Know*; Beer, *Arguing with the Past* and *Darwin's Plots*; Carroll, *Evolution and Literary Theory*). Typically, as Greg Myers shows in *Writing Biology*, these studies are "tracing influence in only one direction—from science to literary texts." He notes that "very rarely do literary critics use their skills to help us understand science" (10). My project shares with Myers's the aim of reversing the process.

In addition, philosophers and evolutionary scientists themselves have discussed the literary structures and values of evolutionary narratives (Dennett, *Darwin's Dangerous Idea*; Dennett, *Consciousness Explained*; Gould, *The Structure of Evolutionary Theory*, *Wonderful Life*, and *Full House*; Levine, *Realism and Representation*).

My purpose is *not* to show that evolution has become a master narrative, or to list the kinds of narrative, or to explore the influence of evolutionary master narratives on literature, generally. It is to consider how evolutionary theory—especially since the rise of the "Modern Synthesis" in the 1930s and 1940s, and including the rise of the genome after the discovery of the structure of DNA in 1953—has led to a set of narrative shapes within a group of largely but not exclusively scientific writers. These writers not only influence our cultural perceptions of the so-called environment, but they have also predicted the possible shapes of our own future roles within it.

Certain writers—especially R. Dawkins, S. J. Gould, R. Lewontin, E. O. Wilson, and B. Goodwin—have not only produced their own evolutionary narratives but have critiqued those of their colleagues (Goodwin; Hull and Ruse; Levins; Lewontin; Lewontin, Rose, and Kamin; Morris; Ruse; Sterelny; Wilson).

To be categorical, these authors are the most influential "nature writers" of our era. Some of them are philosophers, some literary critics, some historians of science, and most are scientists. If one is interested in what Natures those nature writers give us and in what literary shapes, one must not use literary theory alone to investigate these issues but must consider that writers like Dawkins, Gould, Keller, Kitcher, Dennett, Lewontin, Richards, and Maynard Smith are themselves evolutionary theorists as well as nature writers: they offer their own critiques of the evolutionary narrative (Keller and Lloyd; Kitcher, *Vaulting Ambition* and *The Advancement of Sci-*

ence; Richards; Maynard Smith, *Did Darwin Get It Right?* and *Evolution and the Theory of Games*).

These writers are often interested in critiquing the narratives about natural processes told by the general public and especially by environmentalists. We also have our own literary and sociological critiques of them (Wilson, Segerstrale). David Robertson has put the relationship this way in his privately published *Ecohuman's Four Square Deck*: "What constrains artist and scientist alike is an imperative to tell the truth. One asks, 'what tropes must I find to tell the truth.' The other asks, 'What equations must I solve to tell the truth.' " A reciprocal critical relation between the two is worth pursuing. As ecocriticism, such a project requires engaging in this reciprocal and probably recursive thinking and goes well beyond the idea that ecocritics should use scientists as authorities; we must critique the methods and conclusions of scientists, in their various guises as professionals, as popularizers, as critics of one another's work; and we may also expect them to perform these tasks for us.

This may be the very task that philosopher Holmes Rolston III attempts in a recent work. In order to accomplish this aim, he has to read against the grain of evolutionary biology, and reinterpret key terms, like *selfish* as used by Dawkins. His reinterpretation is problematic, not only because he runs against the methods of evolutionary theorists by mixing levels of selection but also because he emphasizes the ecosystem as context and *adaptation* as an ecological term. It is hard to know what kind of hearing he will get as a result, but his effort is interesting.

Several major cautions are necessary here. The "sociobiology debate," which continues to this day, has aroused considerable fear and distrust of the meddling of the humanists in politics of the scientific community. If I were to follow Greg Myers, and quote D. R. Cocker, a biologist speaking of the writing of biology, then the results might not be salubrious. Here is Crocker: "I suspect the authors let their genuine feelings spill out into their nature books and that academic pressure to be objective simultaneously encourages them to dissemble. My bet is that the popular informs the academic rather than the other way around" (Crocker, qtd. in Myers 190). If future processes of critique follow the pattern of the sociobiology debate, as Myers suggests, then it will be unending and unproductive (215, 236).

Recursion is a mathematical metaphor (and as Steve Gould, bless his heart, might say, a double play as well, from Hofstadter to Dennett, to Chance).

re•cur•sive *adj.*

1. repeating itself, either indefinitely or until a specified point is reached

2. involving the repeated application of a function to its own values

re•cur•sion *n.*

1. the return of something, often repeatedly

2. the use of repeated steps, each based on the result of the one before, to define a function or calculate a number

3. a routine's calling of itself in order to repeat a process in computing

With art we might say:

self-ref•er•en•tial *adj.*
used to describe an art form that employs references to the art itself or to personal experience or character

But the term *self-referential* lacks the dynamic of recursion: does art lack the methodological aspect of scientific thought?

BECAUSE EVOLUTIONARY theory includes the thinking subject, *us*, as part of its inquiry, the immediate value to *us* may be that through recursion and self-referentiality, it confuses and clarifies—therefore complicates—categories that have been used too facilely by some humanists, of nature and culture, objective and subjective, inside and outside, and even what environment, species, and organisms are. What happens to theory then, in evolution, ecology, literature?

What Is Theory as Reading and Writing?

Thomas McGlaughlin answers, in the introduction to *Critical Terms for Literary Study*: "By 'literary theory' I mean the debate over the nature and function of reading and writing that has followed on the heels of structuralist linguistics and cultural analysis" (Lentricchia and McLaughlin 1). As he goes on to point out, this debate occurs because of "a shared commitment to understanding how language and other systems of signs provide frameworks which determine how we read, and more generally, how we make sense of experience, construct our own identity, produce meaning in the world."

Douglas Futuyma in *Evolutionary Biology* indicates that theory in science entails writing "a mature, coherent body of interconnected statements, based on reasoning and evidence, that explains a variety of observations" (11). "Because a theory is a complex of statements, it usually does not stand or fall on the basis of a single critical text (as simple hypotheses often do)." Therefore, "evolution is a scientific fact. But it is explained by evolutionary theory" (11).

Gould speaks of theory as an "organizing concept," a kind of grounds of investigation (*Structure of Evolutionary Theory* 37). Such a concept is complex, as Futuyma has indicated, and for Gould can be visualized as having roots and branches. "The central trunk (the theory of natural selection) cannot be severed, or the creature (the theory) dies" (18). But Gould speaks of Darwinian Logic as including linked branching conceptions of Agency, Efficacy, and Scope (15, 16). When an evolutionist theorizes, the process of reading and writing might include pruning and gardening the Darwinian tree (19).

Some people do not like theory, of course; Knapp and Michaels in "Against Theory" argue from an antagonistic definition of theory, as "the attempt to govern interpretations of particular texts by appealing to an account of interpretation in general" (Leitch 2460). By this criterion, theory is "any attempt to guide or regulate critical practice by general principles standing outside or above human interests, beliefs, practices" (2460). Such an approach has been taken toward evolutionary theory and Darwinism, but not profitably.

Perhaps it is best to ask not what theory is but what theory does. One answer in the *Norton Anthology of Theory and Criticism* is that theory *frames* study: "Theory raises and answers questions about a broad array of fundamental issues." It also "opens literary and cultural studies to neighboring disciplines," and since everyone has a theory, they must be "examined, debated, and tested" (Leitch 28).

Testing is done by the method of critique. The *Norton Anthology of Theory and Criticism* explains that "critique presupposes a hidden set of questionable or dangerous premises and values undergirding a complex document" and that "critique calls for a critic at once suspicious and ethical, committed to a set of values different from, or directly opposed to, those expressed in the text" (2). I could go on for some time about critique and whether the critic is inside or outside the frame.

Gillian Beer places us all inside the frame: "Precisely because we live in a culture dominated by evolutionary ideas, it is difficult for us to recognize their imaginative power in our daily readings of the world. We need to do so" (*Darwin's Plots* 5). There are many evolutionary ideas and often they do not agree. Evolutionary theory, like literary theory, is contested terrain, contested from within and from without: contested by groups of experts and by members of the public, which is why there are science wars and culture wars, as we have come to call them. Examining, testing, and debating: are these the same processes in these different wars? Part of an answer may come from asking about the way humanists, scientists, and general publics read. One thing we might cautiously claim: humanists and scientists use methods closer to each other's than they might like to think. For instance, Beer writes: "Because of its preoccupation with time and change, evolutionary theory has inherent affinities with the problems and processes of narrative" (7).

What if we consider, provisionally, that evolutionary theory is a way of reading biology historically? With Darwinian logic, of course. "Reading," as Beer argues, "is an essentially question-raising procedure" (6). What questions, and how are they raised differently by scientists and literary folk?

Also, such thinking about reciprocal relations between humanistic and scientific methods of reading and critiquing allow one to ask about the process we sometimes call "interdisciplinary." The tree scientist Ronald M. Lanner once told me he preferred the term *multidisciplinary*, because *interdisciplinary* suggested a process of falling through the cracks. But *multidisciplinary* can suggest a too-simple additive process.

The point of interdisciplinary work might be that it is collaborative, that it is dialogical and not monological, that it breaks down hierarchies and structures of authority, that it avoids the pitfall of hero worship ("great scientific genius") and iconography (personalities; great media stars).

I dream of an interdisciplinarity as a "between" not a "falling through," as a real discourse between good-willed people of various disciplines. This means that there is no place for the "Strong Programme" in a discussion of the social construction of science—that claims both "true" and "false" scientific theories are caused by social factors or conditions, including cultural context and self-interest. Nor is there room for the kind of antihumanism we find in such polemics as *Higher Superstition* (Gross and Levitt).

One might even name these kinds of reciprocal activities of critique and dialogue true consilience, because they put nature and nurture, nature and culture, wilderness and civilization, in our dialogue but not in the polemical (warlike) or hierarchical or reductive fashion that seems evident in the writings of Pinker, Wilson, Gould (*The Hedgehog*), and others.

The truth *is* the dialogue; because the most important problem we may have to solve is how to work together during times of crisis.

Beginning Again: Reading and Writing after Darwin

Michael Ruse has written:

> The fact that we are contingent end-products of a natural process of evolution,
> rather than the special creation of a good God, in his own image, has to be just
> about the most profound thing we humans have discovered about ourselves.
> (*Taking Darwin Seriously* i)

It is not quite so simple for most of us. I, for instance, never thought God
made me and was taught this lesson young, within my immediate family,
the earliest and smallest unit of my culture, and have been trying ever since
to understand what it means, discussing it, and expressing my own sense
of the human place in the world in light of this "discovery." Certainly there
was no talk of God when I studied physical chemistry and geochemistry at
UCLA in the 1960s. Darwinism affects every story I tell about myself and
other living things. It colors my whole world, and especially it shapes my
conscious and unconscious use of language.

To speak globally, evolution has become a creation or emergence story:
as we continue to read and write the story of evolution, many of us are
consciously Darwinian. This means that the structures of this story's many
variants, as told and heard, reveal the cultural predispositions of our times.
Those who study literature are interested in how those stories are written.

I might use Italo Calvino to explore the writing of evolutionary stories,
because of his elaborate experiments in what I call "as-if fictions" in such
works as *Cosmicomics*. Calvino wrote in that book:

> When you're young, all evolution lies before you, every road is open to you,
> and at the same time you can enjoy the fact of being there. . . . If you compare
> yourself with the limitations that came afterwards, if you think of how having
> one form excludes other forms, of the monotonous routine where you finally
> feel trapped, well, I don't mind saying life was beautiful in those days. (131)

Sure: the diversification of life looks quite different when seen from its beginnings than from its ends. Possibility and limitation war, largely, in the
perspective of the beholder, and their magnitudes in our minds are shaped
particularly by the beholder's position in time and in history. This is also a
major bone of contention among evolutionary theorists (see Janet Radcliffe
Richards).

In the aftermath of the 1970s, Donald Worster can call it "The Dismal Science" and speak of Darwin's writing making "the natural world a far more

troubled, unhappy place than before" (*Nature's Economy* 114). The natural
world as charnel house, in plot, symmetry, and theme. Of course, texts lead
to texts: after Darwin, nature red in tooth and claw, and all that. Remarkably,
humans continue to imagine themselves at the end of a history that leads
to their present condition. In this humans have not changed over the ages.
Natural history leads to us. It is a habit of mind.

One reads at the beginning of the new millennium:

> One of the charms of coming with a Darwinian eye to the study of organisms
> is recognizing the mixture they display of *astonishing adaptive sophistication
> and botched improvisation*. . . . what increasingly impressed biologists was the
> extent to which organisms turned out—despite being miracles of coordination
> and functioning—to be *riddled with absurdities that no self-respecting designer
> would have allowed as far as their drawing board*. (Richards 1, italics mine)

This method of reading the past from the present is named, by some, reverse
engineering.

As Calvino understood, such reading is framed: "It is the frame that
marks the boundary between the picture and what is outside. It allows the
picture to exist, isolating it from the rest; but at the same time, it recalls—and
somehow stands for—everything that remains out of the picture" (*Under the
Jaguar Sun* 86).

Of course we want an explanation for these botched improvisations, the
absurdities that riddle the world and riddle us in it. We want to solve the
riddle. We want to understand the past of our inquiries, reach into the past
of our present selves and into the presence of past selves within us, and
trace the genealogy of life. What walks upon two legs at noon? It makes one
dizzy, and one must sit down, or at least slouch a little. In what direction
do we slouch? We subject ourselves to lectures, and exhortations, to the
knowledge of others, to the authority of others. What do they promise?

At the bottom of all this talk that washes over us is rocky ground, shifting all the time, creating paradoxes, internal and external, endless. Control $\Longleftrightarrow$ Lack of Control. The purpose of knowing is to control ourselves,
our destiny, our lives, the way we love and reproduce, and how we cherish
our world—if we are willing to get that corny. But the very law we found
is no law, gives no principle of order, is ad hoc. And yet we suppose that if
we know the historical roots of our *condition*—why did those hunters and
gatherers come to think that way?—we will control our *conditions*.

Surely the story of evolutionary theory is the story of finding a story and
telling it and not forgetting it, while it continues to change. Meanwhile, the

danger of forgetting frames the story to be remembered. In this, our generation's evolutionary story is framed similarly to the story of *The Odyssey*. As Calvino has noted:

> What Ulysses saves from the power of the lotus, from Circe's drugs, and from the Sirens' song, is not just the past or the future. Memory truly counts—for an individual, a society, a culture—only if it holds together the imprint of the past and the plan for the future, if it allows one to do things without forgetting what one wanted to do, and to become without ceasing to be, to be without ceasing to become. (*Why Read the Classics* 32)

We should not be diverted when these complicated evolutionary stories appear as simplifications in the pages of stupid newspapers, on corrupt public radio reports, and as bestsellers by arrogant if slovenly academics. But we must ask: How has it happened that the role of this storyteller for evolution has been relegated to those who understand so little about the way stories function in human affairs? And how is it that the modes of storytelling have changed so little among humanists and scientists after Darwin?

Writing after Darwin

It is recursive, of course. The evolutionary psychologists and cognitive scientists who are experts in verbal and nonverbal language, who wish to write the structure of our human brains—they desire to describe the history of the very tools that allow them to describe. Why do so many write so conventionally and how can the knowers know themselves, if they do not understand the story as story and its transformations? (Why has Chomsky refused to be part of the projects of the prominent evolutionary psychologists Cosmodes and Toobey and Pinker?)

A simple answer is that scientists desire to write their theory under control and in a rational mode. "Be the thing that you are not, and control it." Yet there is often a scientist to treat the writing of another scientist as a text. In *How the Leopard Changed Its Spots*, Brian Goodwin provides the following structural analysis of the Dawkins teleology in *The Selfish Gene*:

> (1) Organisms are constructed by groups of genes, whose goal is to leave more copies of themselves; (2) this gives rise to the metaphor of the hereditary material being basically selfish; (3) this intrinsically selfish quality of the hereditary material is reflected in competitive interactions between organisms, which

result in survival of fitter variants generated by the more successful genes. (4) Then you get the point that organisms are constantly trying to get better, fitter, and—in a mathematical, geometrical metaphor—always trying to climb peaks in fitness landscapes.

The most interesting point emerged at the end of *The Selfish Gene*, where Richard said that human beings, alone amongst all the species, can escape from their selfish inheritance and become genuinely altruistic, through educational effort. I suddenly realized that this set of four points was a transformation of four very familiar principles of Christian fundamentalism, which go like this; (1) Humanity is born in sin; (2) we have a selfish inheritance; (3) humanity is therefore condemned to a life of conflict and perpetual toil; (4) but there is salvation (Goodwin 30, 31).

How can our experience be Darwinian, or Dawkinsian, or Dennettian, or Gouldian, except that we share, or resist, the covert structures of thinking about the nature of nature and human nature too? Some scientists might say that this is just about style. But it is about a good deal more; it is about the degree of success or failure of the Darwinian revolution. What if reading and writing after Darwin were actually unchanged?

WE ARE THE actualizing animal: we tell the stories.

Evolution, as if Textual Narrative

Evolution is narrative because it is dynamic. The narrative is conceived as continuous (Dennett's algorithms) or discontinuous (Gould's punctuations). The narrative is a linguistic structure and therefore metaphorical because incompletely known. As Evelyn Fox Keller writes, "The core of my argument is that much of the theoretical work involved in constructing explanations of development from genetic data is linguistic—that it depends on productive use of the cognitive tensions generated by multiple meanings, by ambiguity, and, more generally, by the introduction of novel metaphors" (Keller 117). The narrative has actors and those acted upon, and yet it has a missing subject (Myers). Narrative is an action, though not with an end. Environment is an actor: it is plotted or plotless, it has structure, but it is open-ended and hypothetical, without teleology (G. L. Levine, *Darwin and the Novelists*).

An ecocritic's job includes decoding and encoding. Understanding the evolutionary narrative has included decoding of natural history by scientists, encoding by scientists in narratives, decoding of narratives by readers, and encoding by nonscientific writers whose narratives derive from scientific "knowledge." In popular narratives, these encoding and decoding processes have a range of rigor from Dawkins and Gould to what Kitcher calls "pop sociobiology," Thornhill and Palmer's infamous *A Natural History of Rape*, and the evolutionary psychologists.

One can have fun decoding pop sociobiology, as Louis Menand does with Pinker in the *New Yorker* ("Jesus wept," Menand writes, after attempting to summarize Pinker's knowledge of aesthetics, and before attempting to correct Pinker's slovenly reading, quoting, and understanding of literary texts). But it is too easy and too silly to make fun of the ignorance of scientists, just as it would be ridiculous for a literary critic to read like them. For instance, I hope you would laugh if I offered at this point "a sociobiological reading of 'To His Coy Mistress.'"

The central and most recursive question is this: What aspects of the story or narrative that causes people to remember and pass on information and methods of thinking about evolutionary theory are necessary to human survival and survival of the biological systems of the earth? If storytelling itself has been an adaptive trait, in emergence and creation stories of the past, or the narratives that allow islanders to navigate the open seas, then is the evolutionary narrative (scientific, popular, or vulgar) also a mechanism for survival? We need to know something about this before we invest blindly in Darwinian derivatives.

WORKS CITED

Beer, Gillian. *Arguing with the Past: Essays in Narrative from Woolf to Sidney*. London: Routledge, 1989.

———. *Darwin's Plots: Evolutionary Narrative in Darwin, George Eliot, and Nineteenth-Century Fiction*. London: Routledge and Kegan Paul, 1983.

Calvino, Italo. *Cosmicomics*. Trans. William Weaver. New York: Harcourt, Brace and World, 1968.

———. *Under the Jaguar Sun*. Trans. William Weaver. 1st ed. San Diego: Harcourt Brace Jovanovich, 1988.

———. *Why Read the Classics?* Trans. Martin Mclaughlin. New York: Pantheon, 1999.

Carroll, Joseph. *Evolution and Literary Theory*. Columbia: University of Missouri Press, 1995.

Dawkins, Richard. *The Selfish Gene*. Oxford: Oxford University Press, 1976.

Dennett, Daniel Clement. *Consciousness Explained*. Illus. Paul Weiner. Boston: Little, Brown, 1991.

———. *Darwin's Dangerous Idea: Evolution and the Meanings of Life*. New York: Simon and Schuster, 1995.

Futuyma, Douglas J. *Evolutionary Biology*. 2nd ed. Sunderland, Mass: Sinauer Associates, 1986.

Goodwin, Brian C. *How the Leopard Changed Its Spots: The Evolution of Complexity*. New York: Scribner's, 1994.

Gould, Stephen Jay. *Full House: The Spread of Excellence from Plato to Darwin*. New York: Harmony, 1996.

———. *The Hedgehog, the Fox, and the Magister's Pox: Mending the Gap between Science and the Humanities*. New York: Harmony, 2003.

———. *The Structure of Evolutionary Theory*. Cambridge, Mass.: Belknap Press of Harvard University Press, 2002.

———. *Wonderful Life: The Burgess Shale and the Nature of History*. New York: Norton, 1989.

Gross, Paul R., and Norman Levitt. *Higher Superstition: The Academic Left and Its Quarrels with Science*. Baltimore: Johns Hopkins University Press, 1994.

Harpham, Geoffrey Galt. "Ethics." *Critical Terms for Literary Study*. Ed. Frank Lentricchia and Thomas McLaughlin. Chicago: University of Chicago Press, 1996. 387–405.

Hull, David L., and Michael Ruse, eds. *The Philosophy of Biology*. Oxford; New York: Oxford University Press, 1998.

Keller, Evelyn Fox. *Making Sense of Life: Explaining Biological Development with Models, Metaphors, and Machines*. Cambridge, Mass.: Harvard University Press, 2002.

Keller, Evelyn Fox, and Elisabeth Anne Lloyd, eds. *Keywords in Evolutionary Biology*. Cambridge, Mass.: Harvard University Press, 1992.

Kitcher, Philip. *The Advancement of Science: Science without Legend, Objectivity without Illusions*. New York: Oxford University Press, 1993.

———. *The Lives to Come: The Genetic Revolution and Human Possibilities*. New York: Simon and Schuster, 1996.

———. *Vaulting Ambition: Sociobiology and the Quest for Human Nature*. Cambridge, Mass.: MIT Press, 1985.

Leitch, Vincent B., ed. *The Norton Anthology of Theory and Criticism*. New York: Norton, 2001.

Lentricchia, Frank, and Thomas McLaughlin, eds. *Critical Terms for Literary Study*. Chicago: University of Chicago Press, 1996.

Levine, George Lewis. *Darwin and the Novelists: Patterns of Science in Victorian Fiction*. Cambridge, Mass.: Harvard University Press, 1988.

———. *Dying to Know: Scientific Epistemology and Narrative in Victorian England*. Chicago: University of Chicago Press, 2002.

Levine, George Lewis, ed. *Realism and Representation: Essays on the Problem of Realism in Relation to Science, Literature, and Culture*. Madison: University of Wisconsin Press, 1993.

Levins, Richard, and Richard Lewontin. *The Dialectical Biologist*. Cambridge, Mass.: Harvard University Press, 1985.

Lewontin, Richard C. *The Triple Helix: Gene, Organism, and Environment*. Cambridge, Mass.: Harvard University Press, 2000.

Lewontin, Richard C., Steven Rose, and Leon J. Kamin, ed. *Not in Our Genes: Biology, Ideology, and Human Nature*. New York: Pantheon, 1984.

Love, Glen A. *Practical Ecocriticism: Literature, Biology, and the Environment*. Charlottesville: University of Virginia Press, 2003.

Maynard Smith, John. *Did Darwin Get It Right? Essays on Games, Sex, and Evolution*. New York: Chapman and Hall, 1989.

————. *Evolution and the Theory of Games*. New York: Cambridge University Press, 1982.

Menand, Louis. "What Comes Naturally: Does Evolution Explain Who We Are?" *New Yorker,* November 25, 2002, 96–101.

Morris, Richard. *The Evolutionists: The Struggle for Darwin's Soul*. New York: W. H. Freeman, 2001.

Myers, Greg. *Writing Biology: Texts in the Social Construction of Scientific Knowledge*. Madison: University of Wisconsin Press, 1990.

Pinker, Steven. *The Blank Slate: The Modern Denial of Human Nature*. New York: Viking, 2002.

Richards, Janet Radcliffe. *Human Nature after Darwin: A Philosophical Introduction*. London; New York: Routledge, 2000.

Rolston, Holmes. *Genes, Genesis, and God: Values and Their Origins in Natural and Human History*. Cambridge, U.K.: Cambridge University Press, 1999.

Ruse, Michael. *The Evolution Wars: A Guide to the Debates*. Foreword by Edward O. Wilson. Santa Barbara, Calif.: ABC-CLIO, 2000.

————. *Taking Darwin Seriously: A Naturalistic Approach to Philosophy*. Amherst, N.Y.: Prometheus, 1998.

Segerstrale, Ullica Christina Olofsdotter. *Defenders of the Truth: The Battle for Science in the Sociobiology Debate and Beyond*. Oxford: Oxford University Press, 2000.

Sterelny, Kim. *Dawkins vs. Gould: Survival of the Fittest*. Cambridge, U.K.: Icon Books, 2001.

Thornhill, Randy, and Craig T. Palmer. *A Natural History of Rape: Biological Bases of Sexual Coercion*. Cambridge, Mass.: MIT Press, 2000.

Wilson, Edward O. *Consilience: The Unity of Knowledge*. New York: Knopf, 1998.

————. *On Human Nature*. Cambridge, Mass.: Harvard University Press, 1978.

Worster, Donald. *Nature's Economy: The Roots of Ecology*. San Francisco: Sierra Club Books, 1977.

TINA GIANQUITTO

Of Spiders, Ants, and Carnivorous Plants

Domesticity and Darwin in Mary
Treat's *Home Studies in Nature*

MARY TREAT (1830–93), the prolific naturalist of the New Jersey pine barrens, saw the world around her small Vineland home as a rich field of inquiry for scientific investigation. "To the lover, especially of birds, insects, and plants," she writes in the preface to *Home Studies in Nature* (1885), "the smallest area around a well-chosen home will furnish sufficient material to satisfy all thirst of knowledge through the longest life" (6). The diverse collection of essays gathered in *Home Studies* reveals Treat as an equal opportunity naturalist who bonds with all of the organisms that come under her purview, from birds and bees to spiders, wasps, and ants. Observing wild animals allows Treat to "domesticate" them, to bring them in and make them into participating members of an expanded household, a household defined by reciprocal relationships. Treat embraces this model of cohabitation with the birds, insects, and plants that populate her home-laboratory. Her observations take the form of carefully crafted, objective, and regulated experiments, and her essays resemble narrative laboratory reports that successfully engage both the armchair naturalist and the trained botanist. In these essays, Treat openly acknowledges that she is a participating member of a famous and controversial circle of professional scientists that includes Charles Darwin and Asa Gray, and she warns the unsuspecting reader that she writes for a professional audience first and a popular one only second.

Treat was more than just one of Darwin's occasional correspondents; she was one of the few women writers of the time to advocate a sophisticated brand of Darwinian evolution, and she embraced a model of the natural world that focused on the scientific not the moral connections in nature. The lavishly illustrated essays in *Home Studies in Nature* are cannily organized to ease the reader into what will at times be a disturbingly up-close view of the natural world. In the opening section on birds, Treat tells her readers how to become "good" observers of nature. She outlines the bias

234

around which she organizes her observations—specifically that of seeing the natural world as a web of distinct yet interrelated communities. In the next section, "Habits of Insects," readers learn how they can apply these observational techniques in controlled experiments on the crawling and flying creatures around them. The daily life of the insect world that Treat illuminates for her readers is a peaceful, familial one in which spiders, ants, and wasps build nests in which to bear and rear their young. It is also a vicious, violent one full of war, danger, and death. Other sections demonstrate Treat's skills as a leading plant scientist who produced better results from her observations than either Asa Gray or Charles Darwin.

Treat's willingness to interact with nature in a systematic manner, the investigation of nature based on scientific as opposed to moral principles, and the author's active participation in a community of professional scientists distinguish her from other women writing about nature in the nineteenth century. This essay investigates how Mary Treat bridged the gap between the constraints of a domestic ideology that limited a woman's pursuit of scientific knowledge and her own desire (and economic need) to present herself to the public as a skilled and original scientist. Specifically, I examine how Treat *saw* the world around her. She adapted to the demands of her environment and produced popular nature books and articles that described the natural world according to the terms Darwin lays out in *On the Origin of Species* (1859) and *Descent of Man* (1871). At the same time, she interrogates, as Darwin did, the role of perception in scientific investigation.

It would be hard to overstate the impact of *Origin of Species* and *Descent of Man* on the understanding and representation of nature in the late nineteenth century. While evolutionary ideas had been circulating around the culture for a while before Darwin published his account of natural selection and species adaptation, he was the first to use the tools that earlier writers so value—accurate observation coupled with precise description—to sever the ideological links between theology and nature. These writers acknowledged the pressures that scientific discoveries made on these links, but before Darwin, they successfully navigated the uneasy truce between science and sentiment by using scientific texts, such as Humboldt's *Cosmos*, that were sympathetic to their view of nature.

Darwin's explication of the mechanisms of evolution informs Treat's writings in a manner that is different from the way Linnaeus's botany or Humboldt's natural philosophy structure the works of earlier women writers of nature. For these writers, science is specifically a *structure*; it provides a system by which individual elements in nature—a plant, a tree, a bird—are assigned fixed meanings. For Treat, these fixed links are gone, and science can no longer be considered a secure framework upon which to hang her sundry views on nature. Instead, Treat actively constructs her own definition of home under the new paradigm of a nature "red in tooth and claw." Although there was little consensus among scientists and writers as to how to organize the natural world in the face of Darwin's conclusions, the methods and principles of Darwinian thought provided Treat with a vocabulary, and she relied upon it to explain very specifically what was occurring around her.

THE RELATIONSHIP between domesticity and the space of investigation—the "Home" in *Home Studies in Nature*—is a key aspect of Treat's work, even though she did not easily fit into the role of either a domestic woman or a professional scientist. Two quotations, one from the nineteenth-century historian John Harshberger, and one from the naturalist Charles Darwin, illustrate this contradiction as they present to the public two very different portraits of Mary Treat and her work. Harshberger writes:

> [Mary Treat's] most prominent characteristic is a modesty so shrinking as to make any public recognition of her services painful to her, while her joyous enthusiasms for her life-work is so great and so contagious that her home is always the center of attraction . . . and where she dispenses the bounty of her gifts and attainments with a modest lavishness and an unwearied patience, which appears to be to their own reward. (Harshberger, *Botanists of Philadelphia* 298–99)

Darwin describes Treat differently in his seminal work on flesh-eating plants, *Insectivorous Plants*. He writes: "Mrs. Treat of New Jersey has been more successful than any other observer, and has often witnessed in the case of *Utricularia clandestina* the whole process. . . . [Her] excellent observations have already been largely quoted" (281).

As these competing descriptions indicate, Treat embodies what Margaret Rossiter identifies as the "contradiction" of the woman scientist who is caught between the "two almost mutually exclusive stereotypes" of "woman" and "scientist." Harshberger's description controls Treat; it places her firmly inside the domestic realm and narrowly circumscribes her by emphasizing her overtly feminine and therefore lovable characteristics: she is modest, delicate, emotional, noncompetitive, and nurturing (Rossiter xv). In this rendering, Treat's active qualities as an accomplished botanist, entomologist, and ornithologist are removed, and she becomes merely a passive reader of the book of nature, a teacher only and not even a professional one at that. Darwin's account moves in the opposite direction. It takes Treat out of the home, privileges her skill as a professional person, and places her in a dialogue with a circle of established scientists. At the same time, this description suggests that Treat conforms to the stereotype of the scientist that Rossiter identifies as "rigorous, rational, impersonal, masculine, competitive, and unemotional" (xv). Which description fits Mary Treat? Can she be both the domestic lady and the accomplished scientist?

At first glance, Treat also seems to want to present an image of herself as the modest domestic lady. Like so many other women writers in the nineteenth century, she opens the preface to her collection with the promise to her audience that she had initially intended to keep her nature observations to herself: "Many years ago, when I began my studies in Nature's open book, I had no thought of ever giving them to the public." But the similarities between Treat and the shy, retired, domestic woman sharing her thoughts by the fireside end shortly after this conventional line. The author takes firm control of the narrative she is about to present to her audience and boldly proclaims that during her "studies in Nature's open book" she found "so many things new to me, and some new to science, that [her] correspondents, especially those engaged in similar pursuits, urged [her] to publish the result of these observations."

Treat uses the preface to authorize herself by providing a record of her publishing history: "Some of [her articles] were printed in scientific journals, but as the interest deepened, the wish came to tell a greater number of readers what I saw around me, and I therefore sent notes of my investigations to some of our popular periodicals, mostly to *Harper's Magazine*, and this volume is composed mainly of these papers" (5). Treat had been alerting readers to the results of her plant studies for some time—her interest in publishing appears to have begun as early as 1864, when she contributed grass specimens to an article in the *Horticulturist*. By the late 1860s she was publishing the results of original research in respected scientific journals, and her work had attracted the attention of American's leading entomologists, Benjamin Walsh and Charles Riley, who nominated Treat for membership in the American Association for the Advancement of Science in 1870. Treat's publishing career spanned an astonishing forty-six years, during which time she wrote six books and over one hundred articles on topics as diverse as white grub fungus and pine barren vines.[1]

Treat's presentation of herself and her work in these prefatory remarks mirrors the seeming contradiction uncovered in the quotations already discussed. She confirms her position as a domestic woman performing role-appropriate observations of the familiar birds and flowers in her proximate world, while simultaneously presenting herself as an accomplished scientist involved in a range of scientific investigations. The opening line of the first essay of the collection "Our Familiar Birds" subtly reveals the balancing act that Treat performs as domestic woman and professional scientist. She writes: "During the past summer my time and attention have been devoted almost exclusively to the birds which nested around the house" (15). Even though Treat's studies take up all her time, she reassures her audience that she has stayed well within her domestic bounds while conducting the investigations she mentions in the preface, and she welcomes these lay readers into her home by giving them a detailed description of the place: "The house is situated on the main avenue, near the business part of the village, and is surrounded by a thick grove of native oak and other trees. Back of the grove is a fruit orchard, extending to the next street" (15). Treat's home represents the domestic ideal of the nineteenth century—a place marked by its perfect fusion of outside and inside, industry and sanctuary, home and nature. Nature has been tamed, and she encourages her readers to tour the grounds with her, as she identifies with charming assurance the variety, habits, and nest patterns of the many birds that call her orchard home.

By defining the physical parameters of her field of inquiry as "the grounds connected with the cottage where [she] reside[s]," Treat aligns herself squarely with amateur nature enthusiasts and consciously sets herself apart from the "expert naturalists" who feel the need to venture into grand landscapes in order to claim discoveries of natural events (207). And as the title of the collection—*Home Studies in Nature*—indicates, Treat is keenly interested in studying the *home in nature*; she wants to know how insects and animals build their homes and structure their communities. As her descriptions of bird families indicate, many of her investigations (and the conclusions she draws) are firmly in line with a conventional domestic ideology that places the female—whether human or nonhuman—in the domestic space. Moreover, as a woman writing within the confines of this domestic ideology, she respects the *physical* limitations placed on her investigations and confines her studies to the area around her home in Vineland.

While Treat might accept these restraints, they do not limit her research, and she constructs a domestic space that conforms to her role as a practicing scientist. She likewise encourages her readers to do the same by suggesting that the materials to construct a home laboratory are close at hand. Even though she rarely ventures far from her yard, under her skillful eye (and by her concerted efforts at importing species), Treat turns this apparently safe area into a foreign land populated by the mysterious creatures whose habits she wishes to learn. In order to accomplish this transformation, Treat transforms her house and yard into an active laboratory. Her world is one of fluid borders between outside and inside—birds nest in the eaves of her porch, "pet ants" live in jars in her study, burrowing spiders inhabit her backyard "arachnidan menagerie," and carnivorous plants ingest their prey in her living room.

The contradictions that Treat attempts to overcome in her studies are revealed throughout her work. For instance, in an essay entitled "Ground Spiders" she offers descriptions and illustrations of the "Insect Menagerie" that she constructs in her backyard. The reader is first introduced to the idea of Treat's outdoor spider observatory by an illustration that shows the author seated comfortably under the shade of a tree, near the center of a circular hedge. In the illustration the hedge appears to be low and the circle small, relative to the seated figure, and the world outside the circle is vague and ill defined; this outside space appears as an unknown—outside the reach, ken, or even interest of the woman seated within the circle. The space within, on the other hand, is clearly presented—small glasslike objects dot the ground and a pedestaled basin sits opposite the tree. The image is placid, calm; the seated woman is protected from the world outside the hedge. Her head is down, her hands are on her lap, and she appears to be resting. From this picture, it is easy to read Treat's insistence that home and garden are arenas for nature study as both ready acceptance and vocal support for a conventional understanding of a woman's place in the home, as several critics have done.[2]

Even so, the gentle reader might become quite disconcerted upon reading Treat's description of the space, which qualifies the information conveyed first in the illustration. The hedge of arborvitae is not low, nor is the circle small—at fifteen feet in height and a hundred and fifty feet in circumference, the space is large enough to shut the willing scientist away completely from the space outside it. The vaguely defined world outside the circle (home, family, society) in the illustration is a space the solitary woman within the circle chooses not to know about. The "drooping branches" of the maple tree in the center hide nests of both playful birds and murderous wasps, while the small objects dotting the ground are glass covers protecting the burrows of the giant, hairy "burrowing spiders, whose habits [she] wishes to study" (113–14). The scientist-author's "retreat" is pleasant in a conventional way—complete with ornamental plants and chirping, splashing birds. Yet even the birds are valued for more than their aesthetic appeal; their actions provide a useful service and help maintain the ideal habitat for the "large number of burrowing spiders" she has "brought together" in this space. In her description of this space, Treat indicates the multiple roles she plays—she is both the scientist who conducts experiments on the creatures around her and the protective mother who creates a home and protects her charges.

The interplay of illustration and description reinforces the contradictory position of the woman scientist previously discussed and indicates just how far the author is from the ideal domestic lady whom Harshberger describes. It is true that in the investigations on ground spiders, for instance, Treat often resorts to traditional metaphors of home and family to describe the domestic behavior of her subjects. In one striking example, she describes how a spider mother picks up some of her children and "holds them straight in front of her . . . perhaps giving them a homily on manners" (105). At the same time, she does not hesitate to describe in graphic terms how a spider kills its prey: "The spider would get astride [the moth], and hold its wings down with her legs, and pierce it with her mandibles until it was dead" (96). Treat gleans no moral lesson from these examples, the spider mother only "perhaps" giving her children a homily on manners. Nor does she use these instances to instruct readers on their own behavior. She simply lets the act stand for itself. In this, Treat distinguishes herself from the domestic woman looking for connections between the human, the natural, and the divine home.

If Treat found herself in a difficult position as a woman and a scientist, she does not address this in her writings. Instead, she shows readers how she relentlessly pursues knowledge. Her dedication to science places her outside what was considered acceptable for women in the late nineteenth century, yet she was clearly skilled at her chosen work. She is well aware of, and perhaps quietly bristles at, the limits of her position—expert naturalists, she writes in a later essay, are able to "take a wide range, not *being obliged* to settle down and stay in one spot" (207, emphasis added). As Margaret Rossiter observes, the assumption of the mantle of the scientist particularly disturbed both men and women in this period. While male scientists decried the impending feminization of science by the attempts of women to break into their professional ranks, women, even those who had fought long and hard for higher education in the sciences, saw these scientific women as defeminized and as a threat to the home (Rossiter xvii).

The point of scientific instruction, according to influential educators like

Almira Phelps and Emma Willard, was to produce an informed, moral, scientific, and self-sacrificing mother. Treat, born in New York in 1830, would have imbibed a healthy dose of this ideology in her early scientific education as she attended school when Phelps's scientific textbooks dominated science curricula at girls' academies. Nevertheless, few of these women, Phelps included, seem to have been able to live up to that ideal themselves. Treat is no exception. She seems to have started her married life happily, in a productive working relationship with her husband, Dr. Joseph Burrel Treat; the two investigated growing fruit trees on their modest property in Vineland and contributed notes and articles on the insects that attacked those trees to entomological magazines in the late 1860s (Creese 4). Joseph, however, grew bored with the limited round of life in Vineland and moved to New York City around 1870, leaving Mary to continue her studies in Vineland. The two became increasingly estranged, and Joseph conducted his various affairs in New York until he died in 1879.

Treat's personal reaction to her husband's departure is unknown; perhaps, if her publishing record is any indication, she found consolation for her domestic woes in her scientific investigation, as she published an array of articles in the years immediately following Joseph's departure from Vineland. On the other hand, perhaps his presence in the years before that hindered her devotion to her studies, and she was free to devote herself to them only once he was gone. In any event, the details of Treat's home life are almost unimportant, as she was clearly part of a new generation of educated women who separated traditional domestic roles from the pursuit of scientific investigation.

Treat, then, is not the shrinkingly modest woman that the historian John Harshberger describes. Although she often couches her criticisms of other scientists in appropriately self-effacing terms, Treat rightfully and repeatedly claims her status as a renowned botanist and entomologist. And while her published writings show the author crafting a public persona as a conventionally domestic woman, her extensive correspondence with British and American botanists, entomologists, and naturalists demonstrates her conception of herself as a scientist. Treat's personal correspondence consists almost exclusively of letters from prominent botanists and entomologists such as Forel, Mayr, Gray, Walsh, Riley, Sargent, and Watson. Darwin and Treat wrote a total of fourteen letters to each other between 1871 and 1876 (Darwin wrote five of these). In these letters, Darwin asks Treat to supply him with a variety of information and directs her to perform (or repeat) specific experiments on the fly-catching activities of several carnivorous plant species as well as those on the relation of the sex of a butterfly to the nutrition of the larvae.[3] Darwin also encourages Treat about her work, asks to see her published and soon-to-be-published pieces, acknowledges her superior powers of observation in his own published work (see *Insectivorous Plants*), and discusses with her the reception of his theories in America.

Despite her cordial relationships with these leading scientists, Treat openly argues with them in her published works and uses their letters to prove her superior powers of observation. In one instance, she writes of Darwin's faulty observations on the valve of the plant *Utricularia*: "Even here Mr. Darwin's argument would hardly hold good" (*Home Studies* 161). She ends the article with an excerpt of Darwin's reply to her: "In a letter bearing the date June 1, 1875, Mr. Darwin says: 'I have read your article with great interest. It certainly appears the valve was sensitive . . . but I cannot understand why I could never, with all my pains, excite any movement. It is pretty clear I am wrong about the head acting like a wedge'" (162).

Regardless of Treat's difficult position vis-à-vis the home, bird and insect constructions of a domestic space *do* occupy the central organizational position in Treat's *Home Studies in Nature*, but this is not simply because the home remains the only interesting and acceptable topic for a woman writing about nature. Instead, Treat's interest in how animals construct their homes has more to do with her participation in a larger discussion of the connections between human and nonhuman animals initiated by Darwin in *On the Origin of Species*, *The Descent of Man*, and *The Expression of the Emotions in Man and the Animals* (1872). In order to understand how far Treat is from women writing earlier in the century, it is essential to understand what "home" means to Treat.

In *Home Studies in Nature*, she repeatedly describes her attempts to "domesticate" animals and insects, to accommodate them to her presence so that they would act as though she were not watching them. The description and illustration of the menagerie, for instance, graphically represent to the reader how Treat envisioned the task of domesticating animals to her presence. She acknowledges that animals possess an acute awareness of their surroundings, and as she sits in the menagerie, she attempts to merge with the natural creatures around her in an effort to understand them better. As she says: "I took a garden chair, drew my hat pretty well over my face— birds are good observers, and we must manage with care or we shall alarm them—and watched their proceedings" (69).

This move is necessary in order to be a "good observer," in Treat's parlance, and to learn the intimate habits of these creatures. She understands the territorial nature of birds but also believes that they can be brought into her expanded household. In one instance, she notes: "Day after day I tried every means in my power to win these birds from their war-like attitude. . . . At last they came to the shrubbery to bathe, and were now fully domesticated" (36). Vera Norwood argues that Treat "domesticates" nature in order to show the cooperative harmony of objects in nature's household. She allies Treat's view of nature with the morally infused one of her "soul-mate" Susan Cooper and writes: "Nature 'red in tooth and claw' receives short shrift in [Treat's] work, whereas images of cooperative behavior predominate" (42).

Treat's view of the natural world, however, does put her work more closely in line with Darwin than Cooper, and her notion of "domesticating nature" means quite a bit more than simple accommodation. Her definitions of both home and nature indicate how deeply evolutionary ideas had influenced both the author and her culture. Struggle and violence are as much a part of the world that Treat describes as they were of the one found within the pages of *On the Origin of Species*: wasps kill spiders that do not build sufficiently protective nests, red ants subdue and enslave black ants, humans abuse all creatures equally. Yet even though Darwin portrayed life in the natural world as a series of struggles, models of cooperation are a hallmark of his later works on interspecies relationships (i.e., his descriptions of domestic animals like dogs and cats). Darwin talks about communities of beings with equal status, if different abilities. In her studies, Treat extends the notion of home until it is quite expansive—bird homes equal human homes not because a divine creator has given them to humans but because they are fundamentally the same. Human homes, instead of remaining apart from "nature's homes," become one part of a web of communities. Nature in this scheme has an order that is quite distinct from the moral one that keeps Cooper's world together; natural selection, adaptation, and chance, the apparatus of evolution—not special creation, stasis, and divine order, the mechanisms of natural theology—are the tools by which nature is maintained.

The difference in these two worldviews is significant. A moral scheme rooted in natural theology makes the natural world understandable only in terms of a relational model: nature exists as a model for human behavior, and it reveals to humans their moral obligations respective to their position at the top of creation. Human action—even if deemed wicked—is justified because nonhumans are "lower" in the natural order than humans, and they have been given to humans for them to dominate as part of God's plan.

In Treat's world, humans possess no such rights. A moral scheme rooted in evolutionary terms as envisioned by Darwin not only levels the playing field by placing all organisms on equal footing in the mechanisms of the natural world, but it also places an increased emphasis on humans and nonhumans as parts of and participants in distinct yet interrelated communities.[4] In *The Descent Of Man*, Darwin argues that evolutionary principles replace a morality based on " 'Selfishness' " and the instinct for self-preservation with one that "comes into existence only with the social instincts" (Rachels 158). Darwin explains this concept further when he writes of the "moral sense" and the "social instincts": "They have . . . certainly been developed for the general good of the community. . . . *As the social instincts both of man and the lower animals have no doubt been developed by the same steps, it would be advisable . . . to use the same definition in both cases,* and to take as the test of morality, the general good or welfare of the community." (97–98, emphasis added). Darwinian morality, then, is a shared characteristic since it originates from the social instinct, which is something that is also shared. Nor is morality necessarily a singular characteristic of humans, according to Darwin, who says "any animal whatever, endowed with well-marked social instincts [as birds are], would inevitably acquire a moral sense or conscience, as soon as its intellectual powers had become as well developed . . . as in man" (71–72). It is just a matter of time, then, not of biology.

Evolution was not antithetical to moral principles precisely because it stressed community, as Asa Gray argued in his influential review of *On the Origin of Species*. The birds that share Treat's grounds become her community, her society, and she must acknowledge the responsibilities attendant upon this reciprocal relationship. Humans cannot separate themselves from the "general good" of a larger community, of a "society" that was becoming defined in the late nineteenth century as "a rule-bound entity that was greater than the sum of its parts" (Borus 13). The idea of the home functions in Treat's book both as that which makes it possible to extend the bounds of "society" to include the nonhuman (as Darwin demands) and as the thing that is " 'common to all,' " or that which makes it possible to forge bonds across social distances (Glazener 40).

Treat tackles these difficult questions of responsibility, extended community, and hierarchy in nature in a striking passage on the repeated effects of violence on nesting robins. Here, Treat unsuccessfully tries to study a pair of robins that were "new-comers" to her yard. She notes that robins, unless disturbed, always build a nest for the season close to their nest of the previous season; since this is not the case with the newcomers, she concludes: "So these strangers had undoubtedly been badly used by some member of the genus *homo*, who had broken up and destroyed their home, making them hate and distrust all mankind" (33). Since human communities operate according to laws, so must the extended community, and Treat argues that there "ought to be a rigid law enforced to protect our songsters against such vandals" (34). While it is true that many other women writers demand legal protection for birds (Cooper, Mabel Osgood Wright, Florence Merriam, and Olive Thorne Miller, among others), Treat argues for such protection based on a bird's equal standing as a rational creature. As Norwood notes, "the explosion of theory attendant upon the publication of Darwin's *On the Origins of Species*" enables Treat to argue "against human supremacy in a hierarchical natural world created in one stroke by God" (38).[5]

Treat uses this example of the nesting robins "to show man his proper place," and she happily agrees with her cited sources, who argue that humans "are not in all respects the head of animal creation" (35). The hierarchy of nature is not fixed but fluid, and supremacy is not a matter of absolute and immutable fact but one of circumstance and perspective. Indeed, if birds "were to discuss their own zoological position," Treat says, "they might show abundant reason why they were at the head of creation" (34). Birds are perfectly adapted for their tasks; in terms of the ability to fly, bird structure supersedes that of humans. Treat appeals to Darwin and his sources to show that "the difference in mind between" human and nonhuman, "great as it is, is certainly one of degree and not of kind" (*Descent* 105). All animals have special abilities, all animals adapt to their special conditions, and the most successful animals turn circumstances to their advantage.

Darwin's theory emphasized a dynamic interaction between an organism and its environment; successful individuals developed mechanisms to deal with life in an uncertain, chance-driven world. Animals in Treat's fluid world adapt to their environments—they do not have fixed habits or responses; rather they conform to changing environments. Morality, in this case, takes on a remarkably different meaning, and Treat uses her discussions of reason and adaptation to challenge inherited ideas of morality based on the notion of the fixity and infallible design of the natural world. Treat embeds these complex discussions of chance and adaptation into a seemingly conventional essay on the nesting patterns of common birds in the opening chapter of *Home Studies in Nature*. She writes: "Let me ask those who deny to animals any faculty except instinct what it is that induces birds to vary from their usual mode of procedure. They sometimes leave their habitat in the woods for our lawns and gardens, and, as opportunity offers, choose new materials and new methods for the construction of their nests" (74). In one instance, Treat gives "chance" a hand and supplies her New Jersey birds with some Florida moss—good building material from her perspective. Her view of the moss was accurate: "Several pairs of orioles soon . . . used it in the construction of their nests" (18–19).[6]

Alone, this description of bird habits is not particularly striking—some birds found the material useful and employed it in their nest building, while others were "determined to preserve the established customs of their ancestors" and "seemed to look with distrust upon all the feathered builders who were so quick to take up with anything new" (20). Nevertheless, the passage takes on new meaning when placed in context with Treat's investigations into instinct, adaptation, and the role of reason in an animal's life. Again, Treat borrows Darwin's language from *The Descent of Man* as she confronts directly the contested question of whether animals possess reason. In *Descent*, Darwin imagines an "anthropomorphous ape" taking a "dispassionate view" of his standing in the natural world (104). Treat imagines a similar conversation with the birds. In her essay "Do Birds Improve as Architects?" she argues: "If birds were allowed to discuss their own merits as architects, they might bring forward abundant proof to show that they do improve in building." Moreover, she continues, "they also might lay fair claim to the possession of reason" (68). Treat reiterates this point later in the chapter and adds that mere "instinct" cannot account for all animal behavior: "A *close observer* of birds cannot fail to see that they exercise reason and forethought, *not only in the management of their young*, but in many other things" (74, emphasis added).

This notion that animals and insects are thinking, reasoning beings has significant consequences in how Treat views her world and in the picture of that world that she presents to her readers. Why argue that animals have reason? Again we see that the "home" in *Home Studies in Nature* is more than it initially appears. Treat always couches her discussions of reason in the context of nonhuman animals building homes—this holds true in all her discussions of nonhuman communities (birds, ants, spiders, wasps, and bees). Consider, for instance, the following passages from the chapter titled "Ground Spiders." Treat begins the chapter by asking the question, "Do insects possess mind? If not, what is it that often impels them to behave precisely as reasoning beings?" According to Treat, the noticeable behavior that signals the similarity between "reasoning beings" and insects is that of home building: "Many spiders build for themselves homes—not merely

nests to rear the young . . . but homes to which they become strongly attached" (103). This statement does not *seem* particularly striking; after all,
the home in nature has long been seen as the proper object of study for
women. Treat appears merely to continue the tradition, except that in her
model, humans have responsibilities toward the natural world not because
of supremacy but because of *communality*.

But what is truly remarkable about Treat's discussion of the home is
precisely the prominence of reason—not morality—as the thing that holds
the home together. Treat reverses the model she inherits from her prede-
cessors: Humans exhibit reason by their ability to construct homes. Similarly birds, insects, and other creatures create homes that resemble human
homes. Therefore, creatures other than humans must possess reason. Treat
argues that the best homes (whether human or nonhuman) are the simple
ones that best protect the inhabitants from enemies and other dangers. In
her depictions of the construction of nonhuman homes, Treat questions the
supposed substantive difference between human and nonhuman, and she
uses nest construction to show kinship through reason.

By using the home, Treat does engage, although indirectly, with discussions of the status of the woman in the home as observer of the natural world. And although Treat never once mentions her own training nor
seems concerned with making a statement about women's education in the
sciences, she does imply that women possess the necessary characteristics
to become "good observers"—access to a limited field of study (i.e., the
yard) and the ability to reason. If reason—not sentiment or even morality—
governs the construction and composition of the home, women, who as
natural beings share this notion of home, are necessarily rational. And even
if one reads Treat's descriptions of female birds and insects as adhering to
traditional gender codes, she still grants to women an observer position
based solely on their ability to reason, not on their heightened affinity as
moral beings. Accordingly, Treat's new model profoundly reenvisions the
domestic woman-as-nature-observer.

The limited range of the home becomes a boon in Treat's model. Like
the birds that adapt to new materials, women should adapt to changing
social conditions and turn their homes into laboratories. Any woman with
a yard, the absence of other distractions, and of course the means, can build
an insect menagerie. All such a woman has to do to disprove the claims of
"naturalists" is look carefully at the ground under her feet. After all, good
observing means close observing, a thing that is not possible when one takes
a "wide range" as professional (male) naturalists do. At the same time, Treat

understands that in order for her individual observations to make sense, they need to be inserted into a larger sphere of inquiry. Just as Treat sent her own discoveries out into the public space, so she encouraged women to observe and participate in conversations about those observations. She repeatedly notes that several of the women in her neighborhood were "good observers" who often shared with her what they saw—in this, Treat prefigures a woman scientist like Rachel Carson, who relied upon the reports of amateur bird-watchers (mostly housewives) to support her claims on the dangers of DDT.

Mary Treat's careful, ordered investigations into nature teach her that the natural world is not a moral space held together by divine order. Spiders, wasps, and even birds engage in fierce territorial battles. The world is a dangerous place and is not always kind to the individual. Chance lures an insect to a carnivorous plant: some lucky species slowly develop mechanisms to avoid the trap of the plant, while those without such luck are turned into a "putrid," "filthy mass" that the observer can always only partly understand (202). But the continual warfare present in the natural world does not hinder these same creatures from living their lives, pairing with their mates, and raising their families. Nature is still, in the end, a collection of interrelated communities.

NOTES

1. A complete bibliography of Treat's publications will be published in *American Nature Writers before 1900: Prose*, ed. Daniel Patterson (forthcoming).

2. See Norwood and Rossiter.

3. The bulk of Treat's correspondence is housed at the Vineland Historical Society in Vineland, New Jersey. Treat's research on butterfly larvae, specifically on the relationship effect of larval nutrition on the resulting sex of the butterfly was among Treat's most controversial work. When she published her article "Controlling Sex in Butterflies" in 1873, she met with both criticism and ridicule from her esteemed colleagues (excepting Darwin), who chastised her for publishing results that had not been confirmed by experts. It took thirty years for Treat's findings to be validated.

4. Many critics convincingly argue that the traditional notions of morality are forever changed by Darwin's explanation of evolutionary principles. See Rachels and Ruse (qtd. in Olding xvii).

5. Mabel Osgood Wright argued that birds had rights as citizens; see *Citizen Bird: Scenes from Bird-life in Plain English for Beginners* (1897).

6. This statement seems to share more affinity with Lamarckianism, a slightly older, popular evolutionary theory, which claims that animals adapt in a single generation, as opposed to Darwinian adaptation, which posits that animals unwittingly

adapt over generations. Treat clearly draws on Darwin, not the more outdated views of Lamarck, in her nature observations. In this example, she does not argue that the adaptation will be *immediately* replicated in the succeeding generation, which is what follows from Lamarck's argument.

WORKS CITED

Borus, Daniel. *Writing Realism: Howells, James, and Norris in the Mass Market*. Chapel Hill: University of North Carolina Press, 1989.

Creese, Mary. *Ladies in the Laboratory? American and British Women in Science, 1800–1900*. Lanham, Md.: Scarecrow Press, 1998.

Darwin, Charles. *The Descent of Man and Selection in Relation to Sex*. Princeton: Princeton University Press, 1981.

———. *Insectivorous Plants*. New York: D. Appleton, 1896.

Glazener, Nancy. *Reading for Realism: The History of a U.S. Literary Institution, 1850–1910*. Durham: Duke University Press, 1997.

Gray, Asa. *Dawiniana: Essays and Reviews Pertaining to Darwinism*. Ed. A. Hunter Dupree. Cambridge: Belknap Press, 1963.

Harshberger, John W. *The Botanists of Philadelphia and Their Work*. Philadelphia: T. C. Davis and Sons, 1899.

Norwood, Vera. *Made from This Earth: American Women and Nature*. Chapel Hill: University of North Carolina Press, 1993.

Olding, Alan. *Modern Biology and Natural Theology*. New York: Routledge, 1991.

Rachels, James. *Created from Animals: The Moral Implications of Darwinism*. New York: Oxford University Press, 1990.

Rossiter, Margaret W. *Women Scientists in America: Struggles and Strategies to 1940*. Baltimore: Johns Hopkins University Press, 1982.

Treat, Mary. *Home Studies in Nature*. New York: American Book Company, 1885.

———. *Two Chapters on Ants*. New York: Harpers, 1879.

Wright, Mabel Osgood. *Citizen Bird: Scenes from Bird-life in Plain English for Beginners*. New York: Macmillan, 1897.

The Great, Shaggy Barbaric Earth

Geological Writings of John Burroughs

THROUGHOUT HIS CAREER John Burroughs insisted that nature, and ultimately the earth, should be the basis for all observations, all interpretations,
and for beauty itself.[1] As far as Burroughs was concerned, observations
could be embellished, as an artist might emphasize certain aspects of a view
to enhance its beauty. Observations could also be described with emotion,
and indeed it made for poor writing if the author wrote without some degree of passion. In the end, however, Burroughs felt that observations and
their interpretations must be true to the nature of that which was being described. In "Before Beauty" he put it this way: "the great, shaggy barbaric
earth,—yet the summing up, the plenum, of all we know or can know of
beauty! So the orbic poems of the world have a foundation as of the earth
itself, and are beautiful because they are something else first" (172). That
phrase, "shaggy barbaric earth," appeals to the geologist in me.

Burroughs's fascination with the earth, and with geology, began in his
youth when, as he says in the preface to *Time and Change*, "I delighted in
lingering about and beneath the ledges of my native hills" (v). This delight
sprang partly from a thirst for adventure and partly from his curiosity about
the stories the rocks might tell. Burroughs's early nature writings concentrated on flowers and birds, but as he matured, his focus shifted from organic nature toward inorganic nature or, in other words, from biology to
geology. This is not to say that he wrote less about plants and animals and
more about rocks: *Under the Maples*, published in the year of his death, 1921,
is filled with essays on topics such as birds, seals, weasels, mosquitoes, and
fleas. But as Burroughs's understanding of the world developed, he came to
appreciate more fully the fact that the natural world of plants and animals
depended on the soil as the basis of life and that the soil, in turn, depended
on the underlying rocks for its fertility.

This essay explores ways in which John Burroughs's interest in geology
influenced his writings; the effects of this interest can be divided into four

broad categories. The first category includes writings that specifically explore a particular geological concept, as illustrated in his essay "The Old Ice Flood." The second category includes essays that use geology to help set the scene, as illustrated by "A River View." The third includes moments when Burroughs contemplates scientific mysteries and asks prescient questions, as seen in an example from "The Divine Abyss." The final category includes writings for which geology is but a backdrop for speculations on the dependence of humans upon the natural world, as illustrated by "The Grist of the Gods." In all these examples we see Burroughs's fascination with geologic processes and with the immensity of geologic time as well as his ability to distill scientific concepts into plain language that his general audience could understand.

The Old Ice Flood

"The Old Ice Flood" is an essay on the effects of the continental-scale glaciers that covered the northern half of North America approximately 15,000 years ago. The essay calls to mind Burroughs's journal entry in which he describes a visit by John Muir in June 1896: "Ask him to tell you his famous dog story . . . and you get the whole theory of glaciation thrown in" (qtd. in Barrus 1:360). By contrast, "The Old Ice Flood" is the whole theory of glaciation with stories from Burroughs's Hudson Valley home thrown in. In fact, these inclusions are what make so interesting the explanation of such phenomena as glacial erratics, glacial polish and striations, and the geographical limits of the most recent continental ice sheet.

For instance, instead of simply telling us that a glacial erratic is "a large boulder carried by glacial ice to an area removed from its point of origin" (Hamblin 503), Burroughs makes the following comment about a rock on a neighbor's property: "Had I seen the old farmer I am sure I could have added to his interest and pride in his monument by telling him that it was Adirondack gneiss, and had been brought from that region on the back, or in the maw, of a glacier, many tens of thousands of years ago" (164). The scientific explanation is that gneiss is a high-pressure metamorphic rock formed deep within the earth's crust (20–30 kilometers deep). Further, the Adirondack Mountains from whence this boulder came are located about a hundred miles north of the mid–Hudson River Valley where Burroughs lived, and the boulder either fell onto the top of the glacier ("on the back") or was scraped from the earth's surface and carried within the glacial ice ("in the maw"). Once incorporated in the ice, the rock was transported south by the slow-moving glacier until melting caused it to be deposited in the farmer's streambed almost 10,000 years ago. How much more poetic, compact, and interesting is Burroughs's description!

Similarly, Burroughs describes a hike to Julian's Rock, a promontory near his cabin retreat, "Slabsides." The top of the rock had been smoothed and scratched by the glacier, but weathering over the millennia since the ice retreated has made the surface rough. Nearby, however, is a rock that was turned upside down so that the glaciated surface was protected from weathering. By describing this rock, and the reaction of a group of Vassar College students to the place, Burroughs makes lively the topic of glacial polish (smoothing by the abrasion of sand grains in the base of the glacier, somewhat like the action of sandpaper) and striations (scratches made by larger rocks frozen in the glacier) (Bloom 387–88):

> The surface is ten or twelve feet long, and four or five feet wide, and it is as straight and smooth, and the scratches and grooves are as sharp and distinct as if made yesterday. I often take the college girls there who come to visit me, to show them, as I tell them, where the old ice gods left their signatures. The girls take turns in stooping down and looking along the under surface of the rock, and feeling it with their hands, and marveling. They have read or heard about these things, but the reading or hearing made little impression upon their minds. When they see a concrete example, and feel it with their hands, they are impressed. (162)

In addition to Burroughs's use of the remarkable image of ice gods leaving their signature on the land to describe the geological feature, this passage illustrates his lifelong conviction that nature is best observed first-hand in the out-of-doors, whereas book learning, albeit useful, pales in its ability to make a lasting impression.

John Burroughs was a farmer for most of his life, and the perspective he adopts in his writings is often that of a farmer. In "The Old Ice Flood" he couches his observations about the difference between glaciated and unglaciated soils in terms of how conducive they are to farming: glacial soils are commonly thin and very rocky; unglaciated soils are thick and without stones. In the following passage Burroughs deftly combines a farmer's viewpoint with a catalog of the major erosional and depositional features of glaciated landscapes, some of which are only vaguely related to soils and farming:

South of the line that runs irregularly through the middle of New Jersey, Pennsylvania, Ohio, Indiana, Illinois, Iowa, and so on to the Rockies, he [a farmer] will find few loose stones scattered over the soil, no detached boulders sitting upon the surface, no hills or mounds of gravel and sand, no clay banks packed full of rounded stones, little and big, no rocky floors under the soil which look as if they had been dressed down with a huge but dulled and nicked jackplane. The reason is that the line I have indicated marks the limit of the old ice sheet which more than one hundred thousand years ago covered all the northern part of the continent to a depth of from two to four thousand feet and was the chief instrument in rounding off the mountaintops, scattering rock-fragments, little and big, over our landscape, grinding down and breaking off the protruding rock strata, building up our banks of mingled clay and stone, changing the courses of streams and rivers, deepening and widening our valleys, transplanting boulders of one formation for hundreds of miles, and dropping them upon the surface of another formation. (158–59)

This passage accurately describes many features of continental-scale glaciation as it is understood today. Although 100,000 years is somewhat old for the age of the most recent glacial maximum, which established the line to which Burroughs refers (15,000 to 18,000 years is more like it; Bloom 438), it is remarkably close when one considers that in 1912, the dating of geological features by quantitative methods such as carbon 14 was still in its infancy.

In other respects, the information given in the passage is accurate. The most recent glacier is thought to have been up to a mile thick, so "two to four thousand feet" is a reasonable range. More important, Burroughs makes a point of saying that glaciers are responsible for "deepening and widening our valleys." This comment refers to a feature of glacial landscapes that is often misunderstood, and which led to a famous controversy between John Burroughs and John Muir. Glaciers are powerful agents of erosion, but they are not able to carve brand new topography—they can only modify what is already there. In other words, glaciers can widen and/or deepen valleys, but streams and rivers must cut those valleys in the first place. John Muir believed that Yosemite Valley was entirely the result of glacial erosion. On the other hand, based on his reading of geological literature, John Burroughs felt that the valley was produced by both stream erosion and glacial activity. Geological investigations in the valley since the time of Burroughs and Muir find evidence for at least two different episodes of stream erosion, one that created a broad shallow valley and a second that cut a steep narrow gorge, before the valley was eroded to its present shape by a glacier (Hunt 587).

This episode is one of many in which Burroughs demonstrates his ability to read and digest scientific literature and then form his own opinion. What makes Burroughs unique is that he takes that knowledge one step further by turning it into an interesting and informative story that appeals to a general audience.

A River View

"A River View" is like a detailed painting of the Hudson River Valley in the late nineteenth century. The essay presents the landscape, but included in that landscape are vignettes of human activity on the river, such as ice harvesting or the work of steamboats, along with descriptions of its natural history, such as the comings and goings of eagles. Behind it all, however, is the physical setting of the river as an arm of the sea (an "estuary," according to scientists), and Burroughs's conviction that the river owes much of its untamed character to a wildness inherited from the sea: "This great metropolitan river, as it were, with its floating palaces, and shores lined with villas, is thus an inlet and a highway of the wild and savage" (209).

Although "A River View" is more geographical than geological, Burroughs evidently feels that the geological history of the river's development is at least as important as its cultural history. Because the former is not as recognizable as the latter, he chooses to end the essay by describing the river's geological setting. He begins by noting features typical of any estuary that are readily apparent to those living on the shores of the Hudson, such as the movement of tides and the mixing of fresh and salt water. Burroughs then discusses how the river established its course. The ideas in this discussion are attributed to "Professor Newberry," probably John Strong Newberry, a geologist for the United States Geological Survey. Newberry's piece "The Geological History of the New York Island and Harbor" appeared in 1878 in *Popular Science Monthly*, to which Burroughs was a long-time subscriber.

The question of how the Hudson River established its course is an important and not altogether simple one, because whereas most erosion takes place above sea level, the bed of the Hudson River was known to be several hundred feet below sea level, and the bedrock channel hundreds of feet below that. Burroughs describes several theories that would have produced conditions right for erosion below the current sea level. The first assumes that sea level was lower in the past, allowing for more downcutting by the river. The second holds that during the time that the St. Lawrence River was dammed by still-melting ice, the Hudson was a drainage outlet for the Great Lakes, thereby providing more water and sediment to the river and increasing its erosive power. Recent investigations on the geological history of New York find ample evidence that lowered sea levels allowed the Hudson River to cut its bedrock channel well below sea level. Also, evidence from the melting of the last continental ice sheet supports the notion that the Hudson River was a major drainage outlet for both the Great Lakes and the Lake Champlain Basin up until about 11,000 years ago (New York State Geological Survey 179).

Burroughs concedes, however, that no matter how powerful the river, erosion of a major valley takes time. Writing as he often does when he is talking about time and changes, Burroughs finds that geologic time is long enough for plenty of transformations: "for a million years are but as one tick of the timepiece of the Lord . . . one only has to allow time enough, and the most stupendous changes in the topography of the country are as easy and natural as the going out or the coming in of spring or summer" (212–13).

The Divine Abyss

John Burroughs was not always content simply to describe a geologic process or to use geology to understand the physical setting of a region. At times he asked questions of the discipline, some of which were very insightful. A striking example is found in the essay "The Divine Abyss." Near the end of the essay we find this comment:

> It is an interesting fact, the full geologic significance of which I suppose I do not appreciate, that the different formations are usually marked off from one another in [a] sharp way, as if each one was, indeed, the work of a separate day of creation. . . . The transition from one geologic age to another appears to be abrupt: new colors, new constituents, new qualities appear in the rocks with a suddenness hard to reconcile with Lyell's doctrine of uniformitarianism, just as new species appear in the life of the globe with an abruptness hard to reconcile with Darwin's slow process of natural selection. Is sudden mutation, after all, the key to all these phenomena? (68)

What is so startling about this passage is that both Charles Lyell and Charles Darwin were heroes to Burroughs, for their writings helped him to understand the natural world as he saw it.

The doctrine of uniformitarianism was first proposed by the Scottish geologist James Hutton in the mid–eighteenth century. It formed the core of Charles Lyell's famous *Principles of Geology*, which is widely regarded as the first modern textbook of geology. The theory states that the processes shaping the earth today, such as the tectonic forces that uplift the land and create mountain ranges, or the erosional forces that wear those mountains back down to sea level, have been at work throughout the earth's history at roughly the same rates. The almost imperceptible slowness of uplift and erosion leads naturally to the conclusion that the world is the product of slow, steady change over millions of years. Charles Darwin read Lyell's book on the voyage of the *Beagle* and based his theory of evolution through natural selection in part on the assumption that the principles of uniformitarianism applied to the biological world as well as to the geological. Burroughs alludes to uniformitarianism often when he discusses the magnitude of geologic time and the slowness of geologic change.

It is all the more amazing, therefore, that Burroughs, gazing down into the Grand Canyon, which to geologists at first glance represents the record of several hundred million years of quiet, almost unbroken sedimentation in a shallow inland sea (Hamblin 94), would recognize that the changes between the different formations of sandstone, limestone, and shale are not gradual at all. Each rock type represents a significantly different water depth and energy of depositional environment. For instance, sandstone forms in a shallow, high-energy environment, such as a beach or a swift-moving stream, whereas limestone forms in a shallow, relatively quiet marine environment at a low latitude, where warm, clear water is conducive to the growth of reef-building organisms, and shale forms in quiet, relatively deep water (Hamblin 98–99). The sudden transitions between different rock types represent periods when the earth's surface was raised above sea level and rocks were eroded away. The geologic history of the Grand Canyon, therefore, is indeed one of many relatively abrupt changes.

That Burroughs could extend this reasoning to the work of Darwin, whose theories he worked so hard to explicate to the general public, is all the more noteworthy. In fact, the controversy between gradual and sudden change dogged evolutionary biologists until the latter part of the twentieth century, when the late Stephen J. Gould and his colleague Niles Eldridge reconciled the two ideas in the theory of "punctuated equilibrium," which holds that the history of life is characterized by periods of stability "punctuated" by periods of sudden mutation that produced variations to be acted upon by natural selection (Gould 54).

The Grist of the Gods

Finally, in "The Grist of the Gods," Burroughs puts it all together, blending geological information with speculations on human relationships to the earth and the cosmos. This essay treats a geological subject, the soil, yet it is not about soil in a strictly geologic sense. Although it does describe how soils form and how they maintain fertility, it also discusses the spiritual dimensions of soil and asks what the future will be like for humans if they continue to treat the soil, and the world, as a limitless resource.

The workings of the soil are characterized by endless recycling processes inherent in its role as an intermediary between living organisms and the inorganic world of rocks and nutrients. Atoms incorporated into the rocks of the Earth during the formation of the solar system are continually released to the soil by organisms that extract those atoms as nutrients to build tissues or to provide energy. When an organism dies, decay releases the atoms back into the soil to be used again. The transformation of rock to soil is accomplished by what Burroughs refers to as "gentle forces," and which geologists lump together under the general term *weathering*: "The rain's gentle fall, the air's velvet touch, the sun's noiseless rays, the frost's exquisite crystals, these combined are the agents that crush the rocks and pulverize the mountains, and transform continents of sterile granite into a world of fertile soil" (202).

In "The Grist of the Gods," Burroughs returns several times to the biblical tenet that humans were made from dust and will return to dust when they die. The notion describes well the intimate physical relationship between people and the soil already discussed. It also gives many good reasons for humans to respect the soil, for it is a gift from the creator, it supports our life, and it is the source of our spirit: "I do not wonder that the Creator found the dust of the earth the right stuff to make Adam of. It was half man already. I can easily believe that his spirit was evoked from the same stuff, that it was latent there, and in due time, under the brooding warmth of the creative energy, awoke to life" (208).

Despite this intimate relationship between humans and the earth, Burroughs worries because the demands of civilization, especially over the past two hundred years, have been hard on soil and on the earth itself. The consequences of these pressures could be disastrous for living things, as Burroughs predicts in this bleak vision:

One cannot but reflect what a sucked orange the earth will be in the course of a few more centuries. Our civilization is terribly expensive to all its natural

resources; one hundred years of modern life doubtless exhausts its stores more
than a millennium of the life of antiquity. Its coal and oil will be about used up,
all its mineral wealth greatly depleted, the fertility of its soil will have been
washed into the sea through the drainage of its cities, its wild game will be
nearly extinct, its primitive forests gone, and soon how nearly bankrupt the
planet will be! (204)

Burroughs's vision has two striking elements about it. The first is that, writing as he did in the early part of the Industrial Revolution, he could so accurately predict the time frame for the end of an industrial economy because
of pollution and scarcity of resources ("the course of a few more centuries").
Barely one hundred years after he wrote those words, we find civilization
racing to fulfill his prophesy. At current levels of consumption, petroleum
resources are not expected to last more than thirty years, while coal will not
last more than one hundred years (Hamblin 454–55). These projections do
not take into account the fact that demand increases each year, and so the
actual limits may be much shorter. Mining for metal ores is becoming less
and less common as older deposits are exhausted, and environmental and
social costs make it difficult to open new mines. Despite the fact that wild
game such as turkey and white-tail deer have returned to Burroughs's native New York–New England region, and much of the forest clear-cut in the
late nineteenth century has regenerated, ecosystems elsewhere in the world
are continually under pressure from overhunting, overfishing, and habitat
loss due to deforestation. Even the most optimistic person must find it hard
to believe that the biosphere as we know it will survive another century.

The second striking element in this passage is a subtle understanding
of the processes of soil depletion. Because much of the fertility of a soil is
removed with the crop when it is harvested, and because most of that crop
goes to feed people in cities who do not grow their own food, that fertility
drains from the sewers of the cities into the sea. In essence, the cities suck
the fertility from the land and, instead of returning it, pass it, irrevocably
on a human time scale, to the sea.

Conclusion

In the preface to *Time and Change*, a self-effacing John Burroughs writes that
his interest in geology "far outruns" his knowledge, for he has loved the
rocks more than he has studied them. Fortunately for his readers, he did not
let a lack of schooling deter his insatiable thirst for knowledge or his belief

that simple interest in a phenomenon can lead to careful observation that will, in turn, lead to understanding. The examples discussed demonstrate that Burroughs was, in fact, able to describe geologic concepts in cogent and interesting ways and to use geology and geologic history to create a sense of place in an essay. The "uneducated" Burroughs was able to do much more, however, for he asked probing questions of the discipline and ultimately used the backdrop of geology to examine the place of humans on the earth and in the cosmos itself. In so doing, he left a rich body of geological writings.

NOTE

1. I thank Frank Bergon for introducing me to John Burroughs and for calling the title quotation to my attention. Stephen Mercier, Kirsten Menking, and Kathy Walker read the manuscript and offered many valuable suggestions.

WORKS CITED

Barrus, C. *The Life and Letters of John Burroughs*. 2 vols. New York: Russell and Russell, 1925.

Bloom, A. L. *Geomorphology*. 2nd ed. Englewood Cliffs, N.J.: Prentice Hall, 1978.

Burroughs, J. "Before Beauty." In *Birds and Poets*. New York: Houghton Mifflin, 1877. 167–77.

———. "The Divine Abyss." In *Time and Change*. New York: Houghton Mifflin, 1912. 39–70.

———. "The Grist of the Gods." In *Leaf and Tendril*. New York: Houghton Mifflin, 1908. 199–214.

———. "The Old Ice Flood." In *Time and Change*. New York: Houghton Mifflin, 1912. 157–66.

———. "A River View." In *Signs and Seasons*. New York: Houghton Mifflin, 1886. 195–213.

Gould, S. J. "Punctuated Equilibrium in Fact and Theory." In *The Dynamics of Evolution: The Punctuated Equilibrium Debate in the Natural and Social Sciences*, ed. Albert Somit and Steven Peterson. Ithaca: Cornell University Press, 1992. 54–84.

Hamblin, W. K. *Earth's Dynamic Systems*. 4th ed. Minneapolis: Burgess, 1985.

Hunt, C. B. *Natural Regions of the United States and Canada*. San Francisco: W. H. Freeman, 1974.

Lyell, Charles. *Principles of Geology*. London: J. Murray, 1830.

Newberry, J. S. "The Geological History of the New York Island and Harbor." *Popular Science Monthly* 13 (1878): 641–60.

New York State Geological Survey. *Geology of New York: A Simplified Account*. Educational leaflet no. 28. Albany: New York State Museum, 1987.

Contributors

The Editors

ANNIE MERRILL INGRAM is associate professor of English at Davidson College in Davidson, North Carolina. She specializes in nineteenth-century American literature and has published on women writers, environmental justice literature, and service learning in ecocomposition.

IAN MARSHALL is professor of English and co-coordinator of the Environmental Studies program at Penn State Altoona. He is the author of *Story Line: Exploring the Literature of the Appalachian Trail* (1998) and *Peak Experiences: Walking Meditations on Literature, Nature, and Need* (2003). He has hiked the Appalachian Trail and is now spending portions of each summer walking sections of the International Appalachian Trail, which runs from Mount Katahdin in Maine to the tip of the Gaspé Peninsula in Quebec.

DANIEL J. PHILIPPON is associate professor of rhetoric at the University of Minnesota, Twin Cities, where he teaches courses in environmental rhetoric, history, and ethics. He is the author of *Conserving Words: How American Nature Writers Shaped the Environmental Movement* (2004), the editor of *The Friendship of Nature* (1999), and the co-editor of *The Height of Our Mountains* (1998).

ADAM W. SWEETING is associate professor of humanities at Boston University, College of General Studies. He is the author of *Reading Houses and Building Books: Andrew Jackson Downing and the Architecture of Popular Antebellum Literature* (1996) and *Beneath the Second Sun: A Cultural History of Indian Summer* (2003).

The Authors

BRUCE ALLEN is assistant professor of English at Juntendo University in Japan and is the author of *Voices of the Earth: Stories of People, Place and Nature*. His recent work focuses on problems of urban nature and the writings of Ishimure Michiko and Ando Shoeki. He has recently completed a translation of Ishimure Michiko's novel *Tenko* (*Lake of Heaven*).

JAMES BARILLA is assistant professor of English at Lake Forest College. While a graduate student at the University of California, Davis, he helped manage a sixty-five-acre tract of the university campus called the Experimental Ecosystem. His research focuses on the intersections between ecological restoration and literature. He has published essays in *Terra Nova* (2005), *You Are Here: The Journal of Creative Geography* (2002), and *Eco Man: Essays on Nature and Masculinity* (2004). His study of Aldo Leopold appeared in Scribner's *American Writers* Series (2004).

MICHAEL P. COHEN is the author of *A Garden of Bristlecones: Tales of Change in the Great Basin* (1998), *The History of the Sierra Club: 1892 to 1970* (1988), and *The Pathless Way: John Muir and American Wilderness* (1984) as well as of numerous articles about environmental literature and history. He lives in Reno, Nevada.

TINA GIANQUITTO received her Ph.D. in American literature from Columbia University and is an assistant professor of literature at the Colorado School of Mines, where she teaches courses on literature and the environment. She specializes in the intersections of nature and science in American literature and in representations of the natural world by nineteenth-century women. She has published articles on Susan Fenimore Cooper, Jack London, and Mary Treat.

ROBERT T. HAYASHI is assistant professor of English at the University of Wisconsin, Oshkosh, where he teaches American ethnic literatures, autobiography, and environmental studies. His most recent publication is "Transfigured Patterns: Contesting Memories at the Manzanar National Historic Site," in *The Public Historian*.

TIM LINDGREN is an instructional designer at Boston College, where his dissertation research in composition and rhetoric examines how bloggers use new media to construct a sense of place. He is the author most recently of "Blogging Places: Locating Pedagogy in the Whereness of Weblogs" and the co-editor of *Writing Places* (2005), a composition reader.

ANTHONY LIOI is assistant professor of writing and humanities in the Program of Writing and Humanistic Studies at the Massachusetts Institute of Technology. He is at work on a book about the concept of enchantment as it relates to contemporary American environmental nonfiction. He has published essays about the anthropologist Loren Eiseley, Composition Studies, and religious cosmology in *Angels in America*.

DANIEL J. MARTIN is associate professor of English at Rockhurst University in Kansas City, Missouri. His recent work includes "Arm-Chair Cyber Travelers" (with Safia El Wakil) in *Kairos*, an online journal for computers and writing, and "The Landscape of Childhood," a personal essay that appeared in *North Dakota Quarterly*.

DAVID MAZEL is associate professor of English at Adams State College in Alamosa, Colorado. His recent publications include *American Literary Environmentalism, A Century of Early Ecocriticism*, and the "Regionalism and Ecology" entry in the *Blackwell Companion to the Regional Literatures of America*.

ONNO OERLEMANS is associate professor of English at Hamilton College in Clinton, New York. He recently published *Romanticism and the Materiality of Nature* (2002), a book of ecocriticism.

AMY M. PATRICK is assistant professor in the Department of English and Journalism at Western Illinois University. Her research interests include the rhetoric of sustainability, apocalypticism, and issues of environmental and human health. Her dissertation examines the tradition of apocalyptic and precautionary writing in environmental literature.

LEE SCHWENINGER is professor of English at the University of North Carolina at Wilmington, where he teaches American Indian literatures and coordinates the Native American studies minor. In addition to a book-length study of N. Scott Momaday, he has recently published essays on Native American novels set in Europe in the *American Indian Culture and Research Journal* and on Susan Power's *The Grass Dancer* in *SAIL: Studies in American Indian Literature*.

ANGELA WALDIE completed her M.A. at Utah State University, where she held a fellowship with the journal *Western American Literature*. Her Ph.D. research at the University of Calgary focuses on expressions of species extinction in Canadian and American literature.

JEFF WALKER is associate professor of geology in the Department of Geology and Geography at Vassar College in Poughkeepsie, New York. He has delivered several lectures on John Burroughs, including "Phases of Farm Life: Agricultural Writings of John Burroughs" and "The Insolence of Social Power: Bovine Nonchalance, Gentle Persuasion or What?" He is the editor for a reissue of Burroughs's anthology *Signs and Seasons* (2006).

LAURA DASSOW WALLS is the John H. Bennett, Jr. Professor of English at the University of South Carolina. She is the author of *Emerson's Life in Science: The Culture of Truth* (2003) and *Seeing New Worlds: Henry David Thoreau and Nineteenth-Century Natural Science* (1995).

JENNIFER C. WHEAT is associate professor of English at the University of Hawaii at Hilo. Her recent publications include "Preserved in Righteousness? Notes on Living and Teaching in Rural Hawaii" in *ISLE* and "Metamorphosis: Privilege or Punishment?" in *Common Ground*, the online journal of conservation biology.

Index

Horticulturist, 237
How the Leopard Changed Its Spots
    (Goodwin), 229–30
Hubbell, Sue, 33
Hudson River, 254, 255
Hudson River Valley, 251, 254
Hughes, Ted, 98
humanities, 200–202, 207. See also under
    science
Hurlbert, C. Mark, 122
Hutton, James, 256

Idylls (Theocritus), 94
immigration from China, 64–68
individualism, 107
Industrial Revolution, 111, 112, 122, 258
information model of life, 188
"In Search of Evanescence" (Ali), 58
In Search of Swampland (Tiner), 21
Insectivorous Plants (Darwin), 236, 242
interconnectedness, 86, 88, 163
interdisciplinarity, 12, 14, 61, 226
International Code of Zoological
    Nomenclature, 210
Internet, 124
internment camps, 39–41, 45, 47, 49,
    51–52, 67
Interstate Neighborhood Project, 122
"In the Longhouse, Oneida Museum"
    (Whiteman), 85–86
Iroquois, 78–79, 81, 83
Iroquois Confederacy, 81, 90n5
ISLE: Interdisciplinary Studies in
    Literature and Environment, 4
ISLE Reader (Branch and Slovic), 18, 19
Issa, Kobayashi, 42, 44
Issei, 40, 45
I Tell You Now (Kenny), 79

Jackson, Wes, 136, 139n6
James, Henry, 100
Japanese Haiku, The (Yasuda), 42

Japanese literature, 156, 162. See also
    haiku
Japan Ministry of Science and
    Education, 165
Jehlen, Myra, 24
jeremiad, 34n1
Jerome Detention Center, AR, 47–48, 51
Jersey Devil, 21, 35n9
Jerusalem (Blake), 181
Jihad, 139n4
Jim Crow laws, 59, 96, 98, 101, 103–4
Job, 9, 10–11, 22, 194n1. See also Book of
    Job
Johnson Foundation, 152n2
Jones, Leroi, 215
Jordan, William, III, 128
Josephson, Barney, 97

kaiko style (haiku), 56n5
Kanow, Soichi, 47
Kansas City, MO, 93
Kansas City Star, 93
Katahdin, Mt., 1, 2
Katrack, Ketu, 63
Keller, Catherine, 22
Keller, Evelyn Fox, 222, 230
Kellert, Stephen, 144
Kenny, Maurice, 78–82, 89, 90n3
kigo, 42, 45, 51, 55n2
Killingsworth, M. Jimmie, 141–43
Kincaid, Jamaica, 215, 216
King, Rodney, 103
King, Ross, 172–73
Kingston, Maxine Hong, 7, 65–67, 69–71
Kitcher, Philip, 222, 231
Kittatinny Range, 18, 34n2
Kolodny, Annette, 125
Komuro, Kyotaro, 53
kotodama, 155, 162–63
Kress, Gunther, 112, 116, 118
"Ktaadn" (Thoreau), 1–3, 8
Kunimori, Honjyoshi, 47